Right Before the Fire

John Wagner &
Mark Wagner

NEW HARBOR PRESS
RAPID CITY, SD

Wagner/New Harbor Press
1601 Mt. Rushmore Rd, Ste 3288
Rapid City, SD 57701
NewHarborPress.com

Many of the places mentioned in this book are real, as well as some of the people and historical events. However, the reader should remember that this is a work of fiction and the characters and events in this story are the product of the authors' imagination.

To help navigate the many characters in this story and some unfamiliar terminology, a list of the main characters as well as a glossary of terms can be found on the following pages.

Ordering Information:
Quantity sales. Special discounts are available on quantity purchases by corporations, associations, and others. For details, contact the "Special Sales Department" at the address above.

Right Before the Fire/John Wagner & Mark Wagner. -- 1st ed.
ISBN 978-1-63357-472-4

Images and cover art by Rebecca McDade

This book is dedicated to the memory of our friend and mentor, Orville Tadlock, a bold preacher of the Word of God who exhorted one and all to be ready for the Lord's return.

Contents

Glossary of Terms

1. **Al'amal wa Alhayet:** A fictional radical Muslim organization in Israel, whose name in Arabic means "Hope and Life"
2. **Al-Aqsa:** The compound of Islamic religious buildings in the Old City of Jerusalem (see Temple Mount), including the Dome of the Rock, the Al-Aqsa Mosque, and other religious structures
3. **Aliyah:** The Hebrew word for the holy act of Jewish immigration to the Land of Israel
4. **Bondye**: The Haitian Creole term for "God"
5. **El-Elyon:** The Most High God, whom the Tselim call the Oppressor
6. **Eloha**: A Hebrew word that can refer to the Most High God, El-Elyon, as well as other supernatural beings
7. **Emeq Shalom:** A fictional Messianic community near Jerusalem founded by Nehemyah and Talia (see Kibbutz), Emeq Shalom means "Valley of Peace" in Hebrew
8. **Gibborim**: A Hebrew term that can be translated "mighty men," and can refer to the mixed offspring of Tselim and humans, beings with supernatural powers who are not necessarily condemned like fallen angels are
9. **Hezbollah:** A sociopolitical and paramilitary organization associated with Iranian Shia Islam whose name in Arabic means "The Party of Allah"
10. **Imam:** A Muslim man responsible for leading the daily prayers at the mosque or who exercises Islamic spiritual and temporal leadership over an entire region

11. **Injil:** The Arabic word for "Gospel" that in Islam often refers to the book given to Jesus, but for Christians refers to the New Testament Gospels or the New Testament as a whole
12. **Isa ibn Maryam:** An Arabic title for Jesus in the Quran, meaning "Jesus, son of Mary"
13. **Kibbutz:** From the Hebrew word meaning "gathering," this is a type of settlement, unique to Israel, where members live, work, and share life in a community
14. **Kippah:** A brimless cap, usually made of cloth, traditionally worn by Jewish males to fulfill the customary requirement that the head be covered
15. **Knesset:** The 120-member assembly, elected by popular vote, that represents the Israeli people and functions as the legislative branch of the Israeli government
16. **Lwa:** A name for the Tselim who live in the Caribbean area
17. **Mahdi (Al Mahdi)**: A divinely appointed ruler, also known as the Twelfth Imam, who is predicted to return in the end-times according to Shiite Islam
18. **Maktub:** A term that literally means "written" and refers to the Islamic view that God has preordained or "written" everything that will happen, leading some to teach that there is nothing humans can do to change their circumstances
19. **Mossad:** The national intelligence agency of the State of Israel, known as the Institute for Intelligence and Special Operations, similar to the CIA in the United States
20. **Noor-Allah:** A fictional Muslim organization whose name means "Light of God" in Arabic
21. **Olam**: A term, from the Hebrew, meaning "age" or "world," that can refer to the entire created universe, including time, space, the physical world, and the unseen spiritual realm
22. **Oppressor:** The name that Tselim use to refer to El-Elyon, the Most High God
23. **Oppressor's Prince:** The name that Tselim use to refer to Jesus
24. **Ravi**: A Hebrew title for a Jewish religious teacher, like the English word rabbi

25. **Resistance:** The name that Tselim use to refer to their fight to gain control of the Olam
26. **Sacred Stones Museum:** A fictitious location adjacent to the Western Wall in Jerusalem
27. **Shadowlands:** The spiritual realm in the Olam inhabited by the Tselim
28. **Sharia**: A system of Islamic religious law regulating private and public life that, along with common law and civil law, is one of the three most common legal systems in the world
29. **Shia (or Shiite)**: The second-largest denomination of Islam, followed especially in Iran
30. **Sheikh**: An honorific title for an Islamic religious leader usually considered to be a direct descendant of the prophet Mohammed
31. **Sunni**: The largest denomination of Islam, derived from the Arabic word Sunna, which refers to the words, actions, and examples of the Islamic prophet, Mohammed
32. **Tanakh**: The Old Testament of the Christian Bible, which in Hebrew is referred to by an acronym using the first letter of its three sections: Torah (Law), Nevi'im (Prophets), and Ketuvim (Writings)
33. **Temple Mount**: The area in Jerusalem containing the holiest site in Judaism and the third-holiest site in Islam, known in Arabic as Haram al-Sharif or the "Noble Sanctuary"
34. **Tisha B'Av:** A Jewish holiday observed with fasting on the ninth of Ab in commemoration of the destruction of the temples at Jerusalem
35. **Torah**: The five books of Moses, often referred to as the Law (see Tanakh)
36. **Tsel** (plural Tselim): A term from the Hebrew word for "shadow" that refers to fallen angels, some of whom oversee principalities on Earth
37. **Yeshua HaMashiach:** The name for Jesus used by many Messianic Jews
38. **Zionism:** An international movement aiming to reestablish a homeland for the Jewish people in the biblical land of Israel and, since 1948, to support the modern State of Israel

Main Characters

(in alphabetical order)

1. **Abdowan:** A Tsel veteran of the Resistance and mentor to Qorin, Abdowan is transformed into a human and eventually takes the name Eván Lopez
2. **Agwe**: A Tsel ruler over the sea, fish, plants, fishermen and sailors of the Caribbean Sea
3. **Alessandro Tarso:** A young Italian who meets Jennifer Sánchez in Bolivia and later becomes a priest
4. **Alfred Ramos:** A voodoo priest in Haiti, originally a fisherman from Belize
5. **Andriy Dalinger:** A man who, after a tragic loss, is looking to strike out at God
6. **Asher Yitzhaki**: An Orthodox Jew, the father of Benjamin and Joseph
7. **Bel-Marduk:** The former Tsel prince over the principality of Babylon
8. **Benjamin and Joseph Yitzhaki:** Two young Jewish brothers at the kibbutz Emeq Shalom
9. **Bill Gilbright:** An Oregon farmer who befriends and helps Pablo and Julia Sánchez
10. **Chad Robinson:** A street preacher who introduces Dominic to the power of God and to the Mount Zion Revival in Israel
11. **Damballa:** The Tsel prince over the principality of the Lwa (Caribbean area)

12. **Daniel Retén:** A school friend of Dominic's from Buenos Aires, Argentina
13. **Devorah Malkah:** The granddaughter of Nehemyah and Talia Friedenthal
14. **Deywós:** The leader of the Tselim Resistance and the archenemy of El-Elyon, the Most High God
15. **Dominic Sánchez:** A troubled young man with a mysterious past (see previous book Right Before The Storm)
16. **Erlig:** The Tsel prince over the ancient Turkic people
17. **Eván Lopez:** The name the Tsel Abdowan eventually takes after his human incarnation
18. **Ghaiasha:** The Tsel prince over the principality of Palestine
19. **Heidhr:** The Tsel prince over the principality of post-World War II Germany
20. **Henri Simon:** A young Haitian man who apprentices under Alfred, the voodoo priest
21. **Hubal:** The Tsel prince over the principality of Arabia
22. **Jennifer Sánchez:** The mother of Dominic and daughter of Pablo and Julia Sánchez
23. **Jafari:** An agent of the Quds section of Iranian Intelligence
24. **Jorge Delgado:** A roommate and coworker of Dominic's in Los Angeles
25. **Kenan Ben Shlomo:** The human incarnation of Ghaiasha, who is raised by an Orthodox Jewish rabbi in Jerusalem named Shlomo Ben Yehuda
26. **Khaled Bashar:** A young Palestinian man living in Jerusalem
27. **Levy Peretz:** An Israeli police officer in Jerusalem, the son of Shmuel Peretz
28. **Melqart:** Also known as Hercules, the former Tsel prince over the principality of Tyre
29. **Mohammed Bashar:** A Palestinian Arab who emigrates to Europe to earn a living**Mombu:** A lower-ranking Tsel of the Lwa (Caribbean area)
30. **Moshe Ben Abel:** An Orthodox Jew, bodyguard for his friend Nehemyah
31. **Nabu:** The Tsel prince over the principality of Babylon

32. **Niswat:** A woman on a dating site who befriends Andriy
33. **Nehemyah Friedenthal**: A Holocaust survivor who becomes a Messianic Jew
34. **Omar Awad**: A young Palestinian Arab aligned with a radical religious group
35. **Pablo and Julia (Meyer) Sánchez**: Missionaries who raise Dominic as their own son
36. **Ptah:** The Tsel prince over the principality of Egypt
37. **Qorin:** The Tsel prince over the principality of Rome
38. **Samantha Davis:** A school friend of Dominic's from Argentina, daughter of British Evangelicals
39. **Saparon:** A Tsel, the keeper of the mystical books in the library of Shadowlands
40. **Sean Gallagher**: An intellectual and scholarly Christian teacher from Northern Ireland
41. **Shmuel Peretz**: A secular Jew and friend of Nehemyah
42. **Shlomo Ben Yehuda**: An Orthodox Jewish rabbi in Jerusalem who adopts an infant and names him Kenaniah
43. **Talia Friedenthal:** Nehemyah's wife, who helps him establish the Messianic kibbutz Emeq Shalom
44. **Tyr:** The former Tsel prince over the principality of Germany
45. **Verethragna:** The Tsel prince over the principality of Persia

A few hours before the Fire . . . .

"Hello, Dominic."

"You again."

"Yes, I'm Kenan, remember? We need to talk. They told me that the name 'Alessandro' might mean something to you."

Dominic looked intently at him. "Who told you about Alessandro?"

"It's complicated. All I know is that our destinies might be intertwined and that we have to get out of Jerusalem immediately; it's a matter of life and death."

At that moment Dominic heard steps and looked up to see a man striding purposely toward them: the same man who had been watching him during the Mount Zion Church meeting two days before.

Dominic asked the boy, "Is this the guy who said we have to go?"

Kenan glanced at the man. "No, I've never seen him before. But really, Dominic, we've got to get out of here!"

Dominic stayed put, his countenance stern. He watched as the stalker approached them. Dominic asked coldly, "Can I help you?"

"Dominic, I'm here to help you."

"No, thanks. You tried to offer your help in LA last month, and I told you I wasn't interested. Two days ago, when I noticed you staring at me in the church service here in Jerusalem, you ran away. I don't know who you are, but if you want to talk, show me your face."

The man slowly removed his sunglasses and pulled back the hood that had kept his features in shadow. Dominic gasped in surprise, "How is it possible?"

Kenan asked, "What? Is this Alessandro?"

"I don't know. He looks just like him . . . but it can't be." He asked the stranger, "Are you?"

"Am I what?" came the reply.

"Are you Alessandro Tarso?"

"No."

"Well, then who are you?"

"Listen, Dominic, we don't have time for this. I'm not Alessandro, but I did know him. I can explain everything, but not here. Come on, I have a car." He took a step but seeing that Dominic made no move to follow, he turned back and added, "Listen. Surely, deep down, you must realize that you are different from the others around you. You are part of another world . . . and I've been sent here from that world to rescue you."

Kenan spoke up, "Dominic, I think he's right. I knew we needed to leave Jerusalem immediately, but I wasn't sure how. Now this man arrives with the means of our escape. Let's go!"

The stranger shifted his gaze from Dominic to Kenan, studying the boy who couldn't be more than twelve and yet who had the confidence and bearing of someone much older, someone accustomed to giving orders. The stranger asked, "Have we met before? What's your name?"

"They call me Kenan. What about you?"

"You can call me Eván. But where I come from, I'm known as Abdowan."

At those words, a chill ran down Dominic's spine.

Part 1

The Caribbean Island of Hispaniola

Dominic Sánchez was having a bad year.

Just prior to graduating from high school, he had found out that his "parents" were really his grandparents and that his real mother had died shortly after his birth. Furthermore, the identity of his real father was completely shrouded in mystery. Angry and looking for answers, his search led him to Rome and from there, after an unplanned landing in the Caribbean, to a face-to-face encounter with Alessandro Tarso, the man a DNA test had indicated was his father.

The meeting did not go well.

Although Alessandro affirmed that he had met Dominic's mother, he vehemently denied that there had ever been any sexual relationship between them. In the confrontation that followed, Alessandro was killed. Dominic, panic-stricken, carried the body off, concealing it in a cave. Afraid and exhausted, he remained in the cave and fell asleep, only to be awakened by the pain of a scorpion sting. Tired, hungry, and now injured, he stumbled out of the cave and toward a Haitian village but collapsed in the dirt along the road.

Ch 1. Searching the *Olam*[1]

(Shadowlands[2], 11 months before the Fire)

The Roman god Quirinus is identified with Romulus, the deified founder of the Roman nation.

Collins Online Dictionary

Qorin[3] sat hunched over a heatless fire whose red, blue, and yellow flames flickered eerily in the frigid air. He was cold and alone and consumed with foreboding cogitations. *Yes*, he thought, *life is almost perfect.*

The tall, shadowy *Tsel*[4] often came to this cave when he needed to think. As the flames rose before him, he remembered how his ancient Romans had used the word *focus* to mean "hearth" or "fireplace." Staring into the fire, his focal point, he sought an answer to the one nagging question that intruded into his otherwise optimistic outlook: *What happened to Abdowan?*

---

1. Olam is a term, from the Hebrew, meaning "age" or "world," that can refer to the entire created universe, including time, space, the physical world, and the unseen spiritual realm
2. The Shadowlands is the spiritual realm in the *Olam* inhabited by the *Tselim*
3. Qorin, the *Tsel* prince over the principality of Rome, was known as Quirinus to the ancient Romans
4. *Tsel* (plural *Tselim*) is a term from the Hebrew word for "shadow," that refers to fallen angels, some of whom oversee principalities on Earth

Qorin's mind traveled back nearly two decades to the time when Lord Deywós[5], the leader of the Resistance, had commissioned Abdowan, Qorin's mentor, for a top-secret mission. Qorin had thought Abdowan was finally destined for glory and honor. *A quick trip to Earth, a little human interaction, and who knew, Abdowan might even get his own principality?* But when months passed with no follow-up reports, he grew anxious. *If Deywós' plans had been successful, why was he not boasting about it? As far as Abdowan's mission was concerned, the Shadowlands had become as silent as the grave.*

Finally, a year after Abdowan's long-expected return, Qorin had taken it upon himself to secretly investigate. What he had discovered perplexed him: Abdowan, the cold, calculating veteran of the Resistance, seemed to have vanished without a trace!

Well, not entirely without a trace. Qorin, after piecing together various reports, had learned of a child born under rather mysterious circumstances, and came to conclude that even though Abdowan himself had not returned to the Shadowlands, his secret mission had indeed been successful.

The child himself was Abdowan's mission!

Qorin had become convinced that this boy was destined to play a crucial role in Lord Deywós' strategic endgame. However, though anxious for more information, he knew he would have to exercise extreme caution. *Tselim* were expected to mindlessly obey Deywós' orders and were expressly forbidden from meddling in his affairs. But Qorin grinned as he mused to himself, *Deywós may have had his plans . . . but I had mine as well.*

Qorin recalled another complication that he had faced: the child was firmly under the influence of the enemy, having been raised by a family committed to the Oppressor's Way. *They even named him Dominic, meaning "Belonging to the LORD!"* Qorin shivered at the

5. Deywós is the leader of the *Tselim* Resistance and the archenemy of El-Elyon, the Most High God

thought, the very idea still able to make him feel nauseous if he allowed it. *But,* he reminded himself, *what's in a name? The Oppressor doesn't* actually control *the lad; humans have the ability to choose. After all, since he was fathered by Abdowan, a Tsel, he should naturally be drawn to our Resistance.*

Knowing he would be unable to maintain direct contact with the boy, over the years Qorin had been obliged to enlist the help of plebian *Tselim* whose comings and goings would not attract the unwanted attention of Lord Deywós, and yet, nothing of great significance seemed to take place for many years. Still, suspecting that Dominic might indeed possess unusual powers, Qorin maintained his focus on the boy, and he was glad he had! Even now, as he thought back on the two events that revealed a glimmer of Dominic's supernatural strength, Qorin allowed himself a rare smile.

The first real demonstration of power came when Dominic and his siblings were surprised by two armed men who, apparently, intended to kidnap them. The children were running in fear from their would-be assailants when Dominic suddenly turned on his attackers and, flying into a rage, beat both men so savagely that one remained in a coma for weeks. Dominic was only eight at the time.

The second demonstration of his unusual power came only a few weeks later when he and his older brother were again caught in a surprise attack. Managing to escape from the two men, Dominic returned to free his brother, and, in the process, left one of the captors as good as dead.

Qorin reminisced about young Dominic's impressive show of strength and cunning. *Yes, I had every right to do whatever was necessary to protect him! Nabu*[6] *and Verethragna*[7] *were angry at the time and accused me of blatant deception, but I was not to blame. It's their own fault if they are*

---

6. Nabu is the *Tsel* prince over the principality of Babylon
7. Verethragna is the *Tsel* prince over the principality of Persia

so ignorant of the beliefs of the people in their own principalities! I had merely suggested to them that the boy might be *the Mahdi.*[8]

Oh, the illustrious princes of Babylon and Persia! To think that I had considered them allies! I insinuated that Dominic might be the hidden imam so that they would assist in his protection, but I never dreamed that they would plan for him to be violently kidnapped! Such an unfathomable combination of ignorance and ineptitude! And ingratitude! Did they ever thank me for clueing them in to Dominic's potential? No!

The Roman prince shook out his wings as he stood alone by the grim fire. *Yes, I ruffled a few feathers in order to accomplish what had to be done. In response, those fools turned against me in the most immature way and became entirely uncooperative. Failing to realize that the boy's safety was all that mattered, they tried to manipulate the situation for their own ends. Of course, I outsmarted them and managed to keep Dominic safe, despite their machinations.*

But keeping him safe has meant losing Nabu and Verethragna's cooperation, making it much harder to keep my eye on the boy. Since those unscrupulous Tselim work against me at every turn, instead of being able to count on their help, I've been reduced to searching among the lowest of the low for any Tselim willing to scout for me and report back about the boy.

For years, I received so little news. Nothing of significance. Time passed so slowly. I was informed that Dominic's family had moved to Argentina. And, what else? Was there nothing else to report? Had I been wrong about the boy? Had I focused so much attention on Dominic, only to find that he, like so many others, would merely fade, unnoticed, into history?

Nearly a decade passed before my hope was restored. It turned out that one of my informants had a journalistic bent. Qorin pulled out the detailed report and read:

---

8. Mahdi (Al Mahdi), is a divinely appointed ruler, also known as the *Twelfth Imam*, who is predicted to return in the end-times according to Shiite Islam

During Dominic's senior year of high school, he was playing in an Argentine regional Under-18 Championship match. The five-foot-eleven olive-skinned seventeen-year-old was little more than an average player most of the season, and his performance in that championship game had been equally unimpressive. That is, until near the end of the game, when his teammate and best friend, Daniel, was brutally tackled from behind as he attempted to head in a goal. Even though Daniel was injured so severely that he had to be carried off the field, there was not even a yellow card on the play. That apparently offended Dominic's sense of justice so strongly that an invisible switch flipped inside of him.

The normally apathetic teenager suddenly became so intent on avenging his friend's injury that he single-handedly took on the entire opposing team. With less than five minutes left on the clock, his teammates could only stand and watch as he began to move like the wind, stealing the ball from the other team and then, weaving his way between opposing players, he scored not one, but two goals back-to-back to win the match.

His extraordinary skill apparently brought the entire crowd to their feet. But immediately afterward, when a professional scout tried to recruit him in the hopes of signing the next Messi, Dominic expressed no interest at all. Told that he had a gift and asked why he didn't want to make something of himself, he replied enigmatically, "Make something of myself? Don't worry. I will."

Qorin looked down into the smoldering embers of his fire and smiled again. *Yes! My focal point has given me clarity again! I now see that the important question before me isn't, "Where is Abdowan?" but rather, "Where is Dominic?"*

But his pleasure vanished as quickly as the fire's smoke dissipated into the darkness of the Shadowlands. Cursing to himself, he held up the shoddy reports he had received from his underlings. One from just over a year ago stated: "There's been a major crisis in Dominic's life." Another shortly after that helpfully noted, "There's been a disruption of unknown cause."

What good is this? Qorin fumed. Reports that tell me next to nothing and intel that arrives when it's too late to act! Sightings first in Germany and next in Italy. *Italy! In my own principality!* he thought. But, by the time word had reached him, the boy had already moved on. The next news came from Puerto Rico, and after that, the trail suddenly went completely cold. Dominic seemed to have disappeared.

Ch 2. The *Houngan*

(Haiti, 11 months before the Fire)

> *Everyone believes in his youth that the world really began with him, and that all merely exists for his sake.*
>
> Johann Wolfgang von Goethe, *Faust*

Henri Simon smiled. He was sure his life was on the upswing. For many years now, the gossip in town had focused on his fondness for rum, gambling, and girls. Even his family thought he was weak, but Henri knew he wasn't weak; the problem was that no one understood him or appreciated him.

But that was about to change because he had met Alfred, the man who would help him reach his full potential. Alfred, you see, was no ordinary man; he was a *houngan*, a voodoo priest.

Henri felt the excitement tingle in his stomach. Normally he hated getting up early, but he was eager to prove his worth. That's why, when Alfred shook him awake early that morning, he was immediately alert and attentive.

He nodded as Alfred explained that he had a special task for him. A young man was in great need; yes, an important person was in danger of following a wrong path. The matter was urgent! Henri obediently jumped out of bed and quickly washed his face in a basin of water. Then stepping outside, he jumped on his single-speed bike and sped off, pedaling as fast as he could to find this young man somewhere just outside the village.

Along the way, Henri's mind wandered back to the circumstances that had brought him into Alfred's orbit nearly three months earlier.

Henri had been out drinking with friends. He remembered getting on his scooter but wasn't quite sure what happened next. Apparently, a neighbor had heard a loud crash and, finding him lying motionless in the dirt, ran to get his family.

They had carried him home, but when nearly two hours passed and he still hadn't woken up, his mother feared the worst. Frantic, she insisted he be taken to Alfred, the local healer. That Alfred wasn't from their village—in fact, he wasn't even from Haiti—only encouraged her belief in his supernatural powers. Her faith was rewarded when, to everyone's astonishment and relief, the moment Alfred's hand touched Henri's forehead, his eyes suddenly popped open.

Henri remembered getting up and returning home with his mother. But not many days later, Alfred made a house call, giving Henri the greatest honor possible: he invited him to come and live with him to learn the ways of a spirit healer. If Henri was devoted to his teacher, it was because Alfred had not only healed his body but also given him hope and a sense of self-worth.

Returning to the task at hand, Henri pumped his legs with all his might. He was propelled by a sense of purpose: he was on his first important mission for the master!

Arriving at the village, he allowed himself to coast along as he passed the little church building. He cocked his ear to hear them singing and knew they were holding their Sunday morning services. He softly cursed the open door as he rode by.

He remembered how he used to attend those services with his mother when he was younger. In his early teenage years, he lost interest, and by the time he was a tall and thin eighteen-year-old, he stopped going altogether. *They are all hypocrites,* he thought to himself. *They talk and sing about the power of God, but without any evidence of that power.* He sat up a bit straighter on his bike and lifted his head as he thought, *Now, I will experience real power—through Alfred and voodoo.*

He continued pedaling along the village streets, most of them still deserted on this Sunday morning. Passing the last houses of the village, he could just make out a figure sprawled in the mud on the side of the road. He quickly hopped off his bike to examine the body.

The young man looked to be about his own age and appeared unconscious. He got closer and verified that at least he was still breathing. *That's good,* he thought, relieved that he had arrived in time. *But now what to do?*

He pondered the possibilities. *He doesn't look Haitian to me. Maybe he's some rich tourist.* Rifling through the young man's backpack, he found a wallet. Noticing money and credit cards, he quickly stuffed the dollars into his own pocket. He read the name on the credit card, "*Dominic Sánchez,*" then put the wallet back. Next, he paused to check out the passport. *Very interesting! An American.*

Just then, a truck came rumbling down the road toward the village. He put the passport back, zipped the backpack closed, and stood up waving his arms wildly until the driver came to a stop a safe distance away on the narrow muddy road.

Henri shouted, "Hello! Can you help me get this guy to the *houngan*?"

"Stay away from my truck!" answered the driver. Looking around, expecting a trap, he continued, "I know your tricks."

"No trick." Henri promised. "He's hurt."

The driver, a kindhearted man, was not convinced. More than once the "help a person in need" routine had been used by young men trying to steal produce from his truck. He looked around warily, leaving the engine running, ready to speed off in case of an attack.

Henri waited, not daring to approach, knowing the driver would have a weapon—probably a baseball bat—in the cab with him. After a short time in which no ambush appeared, Henri noted that the driver seemed to relax a bit, so he repeated his appeal, saying, "Really, he needs help."

No response came from the truck, so Henri added for good measure, "I swear to *Bondye*![9]"

The driver relented. His assistant opened the passenger door, stepped down cautiously, and together with Henri placed the bike as well as the muddy, unconscious boy into the back of the truck. Henri sat squished between boxes of produce, the boy's head supported on his lap with one hand on his bike so it wouldn't fall over on him.

When they arrived at the healer's house, Alfred was trembling with excitement. He rushed out, directing them to carefully bring the immobile but still breathing boy into the house and to place him on his own bed.

Alfred reached down and brushed the longish bangs from the boy's forehead. Dominic remained motionless as if dead, but the moment the *houngan's* fingers touched Dominic's face the *houngan's* hand began to shake uncontrollably. After a few seconds, the shaking stopped and Henri watched as his master, now with calm assurance, began his healing ritual.

---

9. *Bondye* is the Haitian Creole term for "God"

Ch 3. The Apprentice's Secret

(Haiti, 11 months before the Fire)

For there is nothing covered that will not be revealed, nor hidden that will not be known.

Luke 12:2

Dominic's recovery, however, was not as immediate as Henri's had been. Alfred alternated between herbal drugs and incantations with no apparent result. After two hours, he needed a break. The healer and his apprentice went into the kitchen to have a simple lunch.

It was then that Dominic opened his eyes. He could feel that his wavy dark hair was matted down with some kind of grease and herbs. He noticed that his clothes were muddy and that he was lying on a bed in a small, almost completely empty, room.

Turning his head slightly, he saw that the wooden window frame had no glass and that the wooden, hinged, shutters were partially open, allowing a ray of sunlight to angle its way into the room.

His heart began racing. Nothing was familiar. He had no idea where he was. Is this a dream? The last thing he remembered was his search for his father, a priest. After looking in Europe without success, he finally tracked him down in the Dominican Republic, working alone out in a field. Dominic heard himself saying to him, "You are my father and you abandoned me."

He closed his eyes but couldn't stop the images in his mind. As if in slow motion, he saw himself grabbing the priest in anger and pushing him. Then he saw him lying on the ground immobile.

Opening his eyes, a sense of dread overpowered him, and he thought, *What a horrible nightmare!* Looking around he wondered, *Where am I? What's happening?* Shaking his head back and forth, he tried to clear his mind.

His stirring alerted Alfred, who quickly entered the room followed by Henri.

When Dominic saw them, he asked in Spanish, "*¿Dónde estoy?*"[10]

"You are safe now," Alfred responded in English with a calm voice.

"What happened?"

"You wandered to the edge of our village. It looks like you were stung by a scorpion. You almost died but I've healed you."

Dominic was quiet.

Alfred asked, "What's your name, son?" Dominic hesitated. He saw his backpack on the floor and realized the man had undoubtedly already found his passport. "My name's Dominic," he said. Then, partly to change the subject and partly because he was quite famished, he asked, "Can I have something to eat?"

The *houngan* laughed. "Ah, that is indeed a good sign!" Turning to Henri, he sent his young helper off to bring a plate of food: *diri ak bannann.*[11]

10. Spanish: "Where am I?"
11. Creole: Rice with plantain

A week later, Henri brought home some of the latest gossip he had heard in town. In Haitian Creole he said to Alfred, "I have news, my master. Across the border, near Restauración, a crazy man came into a village saying he had shot and killed the local priest."

Alfred thought to himself, *Why do you waste my time with these stories?* But to humor the boy he asked, "When did this happen?"

"A week ago now. They didn't check the story right away because of the rain. When they did go out searching, they found nothing."

Alfred scoffed. "Of course, they found nothing. A crazy man wouldn't have a gun. And even if he did, he wouldn't shoot a priest. This is nonsense!"

"You can never tell. There is still no trace of the priest. How do you explain that?"

Alfred paused to think. He had to admit a missing priest was indeed odd.

He was so involved in the conversation with Henri that he had forgotten about Dominic. Glancing over, he noticed his young guest was listening intently to their conversation in Haitian Creole. Walking over, he asked quietly in English, "Dominic, what do you know about this?"

"About what? I was just trying to see if I could understand any of the words you were saying." He answered, determined to maintain eye contact as Alfred stared at him—not menacingly, but as if he were peering into his very soul.

For a long moment, Dominic kept his face expressionless as he steadfastly met the *houngan's* gaze. Then Alfred tried again, "I think you understood plenty. Tell me what you know."

Silence.

He continued, "The timing is interesting—right about the time you first came here." His voice was quiet as if talking to himself, but then he looked up as if expecting an answer.

"I don't know what you're talking about," Dominic said, standing up and walking outside.

Sitting under a mango tree, Dominic's thoughts troubled him. The last thing he remembered clearly was that he had been searching for his father. He looked down at his hand and noticed an unusual mark. Scenes began to flash through his mind again. He had a sinking feeling of despair. *I took a boat here . . . and no one knows where I am . . . I was talking with my father . . . but . . . he said he wasn't my father . . . I was in a cave . . . and a scorpion stung me.* He closed his eyes hoping to stop the thoughts. He could see himself walking along in the rain, stumbling, carrying a heavy load.

Alfred went to town that very afternoon to ask around about Henri's story. On his return, he found Dominic still alone under the mango tree.

"It seems the village of Restauración is very interested in solving the mystery of their missing priest."

Nothing.

"They are offering a reward for anyone who has any information about the case."

Dominic still didn't look up.

Alfred continued, "Dominic, let me tell you a little about myself. Like you, I'm not from Haiti. Like you, I was led here, following the leading of the voodoo god of the sea, Agwe.[12] Like you, I have power, as Agwe's servant.

12. Agwe is a *Tsel* ruler over the sea, fish, plants, fishermen and sailors of the Caribbean Sea

"I may not know how and why you came here, but I'm convinced of two things. First, you are connected to this priest. Your face tells me this and, in addition, Agwe himself communicated with me about you. Second, I know you are afraid to get involved, afraid that you will be in trouble. Again, Agwe has made it clear to me that there is no chance that you will be charged with any kind of a crime."

Dominic lifted his head and looked into Alfred's eyes. "Why should I believe you?"

Alfred held his gaze. "Because I have a strong connection with the *Lwa*. No harm will come to you as long as you are with me. I also have very strong connections with the law—you know—the civil authorities. No one will harm you. Look at me. I saved your life with my medicine. You can trust me. You know you can."

Alfred paused. He could tell that the boy was lowering his guard. He added slowly, with a hypnotic lilt, "Dominic, an innocent man has been killed. The killer has confessed to the crime. The police can't close the case until they find the body. Can you help them find the priest's body?"

He waited patiently.

After a minute, Dominic finally broke the silence. Immune to Alfred's attempt at hypnosis, but at the same time interested to hear that someone had confessed to killing the priest, he said, "Yes."

"Yes, what?"

"Yes, I saw the priest."

"Was he alive?"

Dominic shook his head.

"Where did you see him?"

"In a cave."

"Where?"

"In the forest, between Restauración and here. I don't know if I could describe where it is to anyone."

"Could you find it again?"

Dominic was silent again for a full minute. "Probably . . . But I don't want to go back into that cave. I don't want to go to Restauración. And I don't want to talk to anyone else about this."

"I can guarantee all that."

The next day, the two of them set off walking in the direction of Restauración. When they came out of the forest into an open field, Dominic abruptly stopped. He looked around in all directions, then turned left and began walking along the edge of the field. After about fifty meters, he stopped again, looked around, then turned back into the forest. From there, he walked up and down little hills and valleys, retracing his steps from a week ago until he came to the entrance of a cave.

Dominic turned his back on the mouth of the cave and sat down on a large rock without saying a word.

"Is this it?" asked Alfred.

Dominic nodded silently.

"Fine. I'll just go in and take a look around. I'll be right back."

Alfred returned about five minutes later. "Yes, his body is in there. I'll go to the village and get help. Are you okay finding your way back?"

"Yes. I can do it."

"Okay. I will take care of this. Don't talk to anyone. Go straight back home and tell Henri we were in town all day. Tell him to make you a meal and that I will be back the day after tomorrow."

Two days later, Alfred returned to his village in Haiti with a written report in Spanish.

> *The body of the missing priest, our beloved Alessandro Tarso, has been located. The discovery was made by a Haitian villager named Alfred Ramos while looking for treasure in a cave outside of Restauración. The cause of death was a single gunshot wound. The alleged murderer is in custody awaiting trial and the police have recovered the presumed murder weapon.*

Ch 4. A Visit to the *Lwa*

(Shadowlands, 11 months before the Fire)

> *The powerful Voodoo deity Damballah is depicted as a rainbow in the sky with his wife Ayida. He is also represented by an interconnected air of serpents, which signifies sexual unity.*
>
> Mythlok.com

Puerto Rico! Where in the Olam is that? Qorin asked himself. *One of my low-life informants mentioned something about the Caribbean. If I remember correctly, that's the region where the* Tselim *call themselves* the Lwa.

Over the centuries, he had mastered the art of staying informed and involved, while remaining entirely in the background. But now, with his intelligence assets severely limited, he needed a bold new strategy. He would have to go himself if he wanted to find out anything more about Dominic. *I only hope Nabu's and Verethragna's antagonism toward me hasn't reached the domain of the Lwa, prejudicing them all against me,* he said to himself. *I've met a few of those reptiles, over the millennia, but none that I'd consider a comrade or an ally.*

With that decided, Qorin next had to develop a travel plan; depending on the route, the distances could be vast. He considered his options. *I could try to locate a spatial portal and take a direct route via a wormhole.*

He smiled smugly to himself as he imagined the difficulty that humans had in comprehending the realities of four-dimensional space. *Granted, some have attempted to explain it. They talk about dark matter. They try to account for gravitational effects for which they can observe no visible mass. They try to use analogies like folding a "two-dimensional" sheet of paper so that the opposite ends can be made to touch. I guess these are some ways that lower beings try to conceptualize "bending" three-dimensional space and creating wormhole shortcuts through the universe. Some even theorize that from within the fourth dimension the earth might appear like a toroid, or "donut shape." But what if they could actually see the Olam from our perspective? What if they knew that in the "missing space" created by the hole in that Earth-shaped donut, there existed a powerful dark realm called the Shadowlands?*

Qorin grinned. Human constraints of time and space were a constant source of amusement. But his sense of superiority disappeared as he returned his own predicament: how to get to the realm of the *Lwa*. The more he thought about it, the less he liked the prospect of using a wormhole to traverse the *Olam*. *No. It's simply too dangerous. The Enemy created and still controls most of those passages. I wouldn't want to accidentally run into one of the Oppressor's spirit-slaves in an unfamiliar place. I'm certainly not opposed to taking a risk or two from time to time, but then again, I'm not an idiot! I have no intention of handing myself over to the Enemy!*

Qorin then contemplated his next quickest option: making a direct line through the open *Olam* to the Shadowland Caribbean. *With the Oppressor's constant meddling, I have full confidence that his patrols would gladly apprehend a solitary Tsel minding his own business in the open Olam.*

In the end, he decided on the longer option. *I'll make my way from the safety of my realm to the neutral zone. From there, traveling to the edge of the Shadowland Disk, I can hug the inside of Earth's "bagelsphere." Staying near the area where the Shadowland Arctic and Antarctic meet, I should find fewer Enemy patrols. From there, I can take another right angle turn and head directly toward the region of Lwa.*

Qorin crept along stealthily in the unfamiliar *Lwa* territory, proceeding carefully in an underground tunnel system. In the darkness, he felt a gust of stale, humid air. Turning to peer into a cave, he saw a small group of *Tselim* about a stone's throw away, huddled around a pitiful fire. He drew back and stood just outside the entrance of the cave, eavesdropping, not wanting to be seen but hoping to overhear their conversation.

Keeping a watchful eye out, from time to time he leaned over to scan the cave, making sure no one approached from there, and occasionally also glancing back the way he had come, to monitor the long dim corridor behind him. His pulse raced. His goal was to learn what he could about Dominic and then retreat quietly without having any actual contact or conversation with anyone.

Remaining virtually motionless, except for those nearly imperceptible movements to check his surroundings, he felt safe. But he was growing impatient and considered moving on when the conversation of the *Tselim* became interesting. They began to discuss a report they had heard about a young man, a stranger, who had recently ventured into their lands. Qorin listened more closely. "He wandered to the edge of one of our villages . . . ."

Suddenly, Qorin heard a low hissing noise and felt something brush against his left ankle. He nearly screamed but managed to keep his fear inside of him as he looked down, focusing on the pair of narrow eyes, not much more than yellow slits, that looked up at him unblinking from the dusty floor.

Then Qorin recognized the *Tsel* slithering at his feet and released his breath in a mixture of relief and embarrassment. It was Damballa[13], one of the few *Lwa* that Qorin knew by name.

Damballa's voice was smooth, "Well, if it isn't Qorin! What brings you to my realm?"

"Most regal Damballa, you surprised me. You may have heard that Abdowan, my mentor and one of our oldest and most trusted comrades, has not yet returned. I came to ask if by any chance you had received some news of him."

"Oh, I see," the Prince of the *Lwa* replied, as he effortlessly rose to a vertical position. "Well, there's no need to wait out here. Come, I'll introduce you to some of my scouts."

The last thing Qorin wanted to do was engage in small talk with these *Tselim*, but seeing no way to avoid it, he put on his best face and followed Damballa into the cave. After introductions were made, he enquired about Abdowan. The *Tselim* all shook their heads. "We know nothing of him. Truly, by *Bondye*."

Qorin ventured, "As I was approaching just now, I thought I heard one of you mention an unusual boy who recently arrived in your area. What can you tell me of this?"

"We hear he was on foot, out in the wilderness. The report spoke of obvious anger and pain, but also power radiating from him. And, curiously, he had a strong scent of the Oppressor on him. He stumbled along for a short while before collapsing on the side of the road. One of our servants rescued him and healed him. That is all we know."

Qorin used his most respectful voice, "Maybe *Bondye* would have more information about him."

The *Lwa* looked at each other with raised eyebrows. "Maybe," ventured one. And all the others agreed.

---

13. Damballa is the *Tsel* prince over the principality of the *Lwa* (Caribbean area)

An awkward moment followed. Qorin looked around at the group, then, in what he hoped was an aloof and superior tone, he remarked, "Well, my duties call me back to my abode. If ever you have need of me, you know where I reside."

They all nodded, and Damballa offered, "Come, Qorin. I will walk you out."

The two of them left the cave, and as they walked along the underground tunnel, Qorin turned to Damballa, "Did I misspeak when I mentioned your master *Bondye*?"

"Not at all, noble Prince," said Damballa. "It's just that the way you spoke of *Bondye* caught them off guard. We are used to our humans believing in *Bondye*. And we encourage that. They think of him as a god who has some attributes we would normally associate with the Oppressor mixed with qualities of Lord Deywós himself."

Damballa stopped and looked at Qorin as if he wanted to say something very important. "If the god they worship were to have characteristics too similar to those of the Oppressor, that would, of course, be a serious mistake. On the other hand, I'm afraid Lord Deywós doesn't inspire in our people the kind of reverence we hoped for. No, he comes across to them as . . . well, dare I say, untrustworthy? So *Bondye* is our compromise. That mix of kindness and unpredictability seems to be what our humans are looking for. I guess what my comrades found amusing was hearing *you* talk of *Bondye* as if *you* thought he *really existed*."

At this, they both made an uncomfortable attempt at a laugh. Damballa pointed Qorin toward the way out, and the two parted.

Qorin sauntered along unhurriedly for a minute, contemplating what a ridiculously stupid group of *Tselim* the *Lwa* must be. Once he was sure he was alone again, he began racing out of that cavernous realm, his mind already calculating possible ways he might find the boy and keep him under surveillance. *I think I might just pay him a visit. You know, drop in out of nowhere. I do enjoy surprise encounters with humans! But how would I find him?* Lost in these thoughts, he came around a corner and ran right into a diminutive *Tsel*.

The small *Tsel* bounced off Qorin and sat half dazed.

Qorin, visibly upset, burst out, "You there! Watch where you're going!"

The *Lwa* shrunk back and attempted to reply, but his words were unintelligible.

Sensing an opportunity, Qorin began again in a kinder voice, "What is your name, little one?"

"My . . . my name is M-M-Mombu," he stuttered.

"Very good, Momombu. There may be a way for you to make up for this disturbance. Indeed, this could be your lucky day. I am Qorin, the great Prince, and I've come into your realm on an errand for Lord Deywós himself."

"L-L-Lord D-D-Deywós?"

"Yes, Lord Deywós. Now listen. A foreign boy with great power has entered your realm, and you all must exercise extreme caution. He is a special weapon known only to Lord Deywós and a few elite *Tselim*. No one is to harm him. No one is to possess him. Do you understand?"

The *Lwa* nodded his head.

Qorin reached down to help him up, as he continued, "I intended to give this message to your chief himself, but an urgent and unavoidable matter has arisen, and Lord Deywós requires my assistance immediately. I need you to take this responsibility upon yourself and protect the boy. If you do so, you will be handsomely rewarded. Can I count on your loyalty and discretion?"

"Y-y-yes."

"Good. There is no reason to mention this to your chief as he has many other things to worry about. But you must impress upon your comrades the importance of this command from Lord Deywós. And under no circumstances must you mention my name, lest your reward become instead a curse. Is that clear?"

"Y-y-yes."

"Report to me any news as often as you can."

"Y-y-yes, Prince Q-Q-Qorin."

Ch 5. Dominic Establishes His Position

(Haiti, 10 months before the Fire)

What a man thinks of himself,
that it is which determines,
or rather indicates, his fate.

Henry David Thoreau,
Walden; or, Life in the Woods

Dominic was dreaming. He was running, frantically trying to evade the murderous gang chasing him. Along narrow alleys, down a staircase. In desperation, he slipped through a door and found himself underground. Moving carefully forward in the dark, he nearly tripped over something. Reaching down, he felt a round smooth object. Exploring further with his hand, he came to what he realized was a shoulder and he jerked his hand back. A dead body. *This tunnel must be part of a catacomb,* he thought as he stepped gingerly over the corpse.

He was sweating in spite of the cool air of the tomb. He could hear voices getting closer. His pursuers would be in the tunnel any minute now. With his hand running along the wall, he raced forward until suddenly his arm entered an opening on his right. He felt around and found a large niche about one meter up the wall. He quickly hoisted himself up onto the earthen shelf and scooted in, getting as far as possible from the path.

The shelf was smooth and the wall on his left was stone, but on his right was a jumble of sticks. He sat as still as he could. Peering out from his hiding place he could hear voices approaching down the dark tunnel. He edged further to his left because it seemed like the sticks on his right had moved closer and were now touching him. Candlelight coming down the path reached him, and he suppressed a scream as he realized that some of the "sticks" were actually bones! He could see fingers and arms reaching toward him and realized he was sharing his hiding place with a skeleton.

The skeleton grabbed Dominic's right hand. A wooden beam appeared, and Dominic watched silently, wanting to scream but afraid to reveal his hiding place. He saw the skeleton tie his hand to the beam. He could feel the cold tip of a metal spike touch the back of his hand. The skeleton swung a hammer and pain shot up Dominic's arm. He cried out in pain despite his fear of being discovered by his pursuers. He desperately tried to defend himself against the skeleton. Flailing around, he found a garden spade with his free left hand and swung it with all his might. He connected with the skeleton, and it disintegrated into dust.

Dominic awoke covered in sweat. Everything was quiet. He tried to still his heart, which felt like it was about to jump out of his chest. Without sitting up, he slowly moved his eyes from side to side, glancing around. He was not underground in a tunnel nor was he in a cave. He was in a room in a house, and Henri was sound asleep an arm's length away. He began to relax; it had only been a dream.

He could reassure himself that the nightmare was merely a product of his imagination, but the question remained, *How did I get the red, painful mark still visible on the back of my right hand?* That scar was obviously recent and not the result of his imagination.

Then he remembered. It was not from a skeleton's attack but from a scorpion's sting. A very real scorpion in a very real cave. The same cave where the priest's body had just been found. The full realization dawned on him; he had been able to lead Alfred right to the location of the cave and assure him the priest's body was inside, precisely because he himself had carried the corpse and hidden it there.

And, he thought to himself, *I knew the priest's name was Alessandro even before Alfred brought the police report back from the Dominican Republic. In fact, I remember traveling from Italy to the Dominican Republic specifically to search for him.*

He tried to order his thoughts. *My supposed parents confessed to me they were actually my grandparents. They reluctantly admitted that my birth mother died shortly after I was born and they claimed they had no information at all about my father. Without asking them, I did a DNA test that surprisingly came back with a perfect match: A priest from Italy named Alessandro Tarso.*

Dominic remembered his fixation on finding the priest. When he did track him down, Alessandro confirmed he had indeed been in Bolivia, and that he had in fact known a girl named Jennifer Sánchez! He even admitted to taking a DNA test as a prerequisite to entering seminary, to protect against paternity accusations. Dominic's name had not shown up as a match, because, of course, at that point Dominic hadn't done a DNA test himself and so wasn't in the system. All the evidence pointed to Alessandro being his father. And yet, the man had seemed so sincere in his denial!

As Dominic thought back on the conversation, he felt convinced the priest had been telling the truth. But how was that possible? The evidence seemed to prove that the priest was lying. Feelings on the one hand, evidence on the other.

Then he remembered the piece of paper he had taken from the priest's wallet: a poem, written in Italian. Maybe that might hold a clue. Going over to the corner of the room where he kept his backpack, he quietly rummaged around until he found his wallet. Opening it up, he let out a cry of surprise. Not only was there no folded-up poem, but the three hundred dollars that "Opa," his grandpa, had given him were gone!

A few days later, Alfred decided it was time for his two apprentices to have their initiation into the world of voodoo. He eagerly began to work with both the boys, albeit with unequal expectations.

Though Henri was anxious to prove himself, Alfred knew that Dominic held the true potential—if he would only apply himself. His intelligence was obvious: in the two weeks he had been under Alfred's roof, he had already mastered enough Haitian Creole to follow conversations and make himself understood.

Alfred's first step for the initiates involved connecting them with the *Lwa*. Henri seemed to have no difficulty following directions, letting down his guard, and opening himself up to the spirit world. He had heard all his life about spiritual power and was already convinced voodoo power was real. He was eager to learn the things he had heard from his drinking buddies, namely that voodoo will help you trick a man in a card game or allow you to seduce a girl.

Dominic, on the other hand, didn't seem quite as quick to surrender. His lack of connection was partly because the *Lwa* spirits themselves were under orders to stay clear of the new apprentice. Another reason was that Dominic himself was hesitant; he could definitely feel something, but he was not convinced it was something that he wanted.

As Henri repeated incantations, Dominic sat next to him, thoughts whirling. This wasn't his world. At the same time, where was his world? So much had changed for him. What would happen if he did try to go back to the world he knew? Nothing could ever be the same now that he knew his family had been lying to him his whole life.

A black dread descended on him as he realized that even if he did try to go back, very likely no one would want him. For all he knew, there might be an Interpol flash attached to his name in connection with the dead priest. Alfred promised safety here in this village. If he left, he very well might find himself in jail. *No,* he thought, *for now, I stay put.*

The *houngan's* house only had two small rooms plus an outside kitchen. Dominic had spent his first few days recovering in Alfred's bedroom, but now that he was better, he slept on a mat on the living room floor next to Henri.

He realized that if Henri had taken the money out of his wallet, there was literally no place to hide it in the living room where they slept. He also realized that it should be relatively easy to trick Henri into showing him where the stolen money was stashed.

He waited until he heard Henri coming into the house that night, then bending down and putting his wallet into his backpack, he said in French, as if to himself, "I'm so glad I found those dollars I thought I'd lost."

Henri understood French from his school years. Hearing what Dominic said, he stopped in his tracks and quietly crept back out the door and off the rickety porch. Dominic quietly got up and was out the door just in time to see Henri light a match and step into the outdoor kitchen area. Henri was so focused on lighting a candle he didn't hear Dominic come up behind him. He had just lifted the lid off the sugar jar and was reaching inside when Dominic whispered, *"Qu'est-ce que tu fais?"*[14]

Henri turned around quickly and was so startled that the sugar jar slipped from his sweaty hands. Dominic, expecting as much, extended his hands quickly and caught the jar before it hit the ground. He stood up, smiling, his fingers searching in the sugar until he withdrew a folded piece of paper that he guessed was the priest's poem. Unfolding it, he found his three one-hundred-dollar bills inside. Smiling, he put the poem in his pocket, held up the bills, and shook them, saying, *"Et voilà!*[15]*"*

At that moment, Henri realized there was more to Dominic than he had originally thought. He couldn't articulate it, but somehow, he knew his place in the world just went down a notch. As long as Dominic was with them, he would always be Alfred's favorite and Henri would be relegated to the shadows, a nothing by comparison. He even suspected that Alfred's recent trip to Restauración had had more to do with protecting Dominic than helping the police find the dead priest's body.

Dominic interrupted Henri's thoughts, saying, "I'm putting my money back in my wallet, and you aren't going to touch it. Understand?"

Though furious and humiliated, Henri was a good enough poker player to sense when his opponent was holding the better hand. He knew he wouldn't touch Dominic's money again. Dominic cemented

14. French: "What are you doing?"
15. French: "And there it is!"

his position in the pecking order by handing him the sugar jar with instructions to put it back where he had found it.

Ch 6. The Spy

(Shadowlands, 10 months before the Fire)

But who will watch the watchmen?

Juvenal, *Satires*

Ever since Mombu had received the command from Qorin to protect the young man who had wandered into the realm of the *Lwa*, he had taken his responsibility seriously, without, in fact, knowing what exactly he was supposed to do or how he was supposed to do it.

Unsure of what danger he should expect, he was alert and vigilant, and it paid off! One day, in the late afternoon, he saw a man with curly graying hair who looked to be in his forties watching Dominic from the bushes. That seemed unusual in and of itself. The next day when the same man was there again, Mombu got a clear look at his face, and immediately sent word to alert Qorin.

Qorin did not want to attract the notice of other *Tselim* by spending too much time away from his normal haunts. But when he received word that Mombu was near and wanted to talk, he wasted no time in going personally to meet with him.

In a cave of the Shadowlands that few of the *Lwa* even knew about, Mombu told him, "S-s-someone f-f-following after D-D-Dominic!"

"Calmly now. What is it?"

"Wh-what is it?!" Mombu screeched, obviously agitated. "D-dead priest! D-Damballa!"

On hearing the word *Damballa,* Qorin was alarmed. Each clandestine step taken as he tried to keep track of Dominic represented a huge risk. His success depended on secrecy, and the last thing he needed at this point was the Prince of the *Lwa* meddling in his affairs. "What?!" he exclaimed. "Damballa is following after the young man?"

"Y-yes!"

"No!" Qorin spat, hunching his shoulders to the point that his wings rubbed against one another. "By all that is unholy, this is indeed a crisis!"

Although for a *Tsel,* knowledge is power, and attaining power is a *Tsel's* deepest desire, Qorin had remarkably large gaps in his knowledge of other *Tselim*. Indeed, his ignorance of the *Lwa* could fill volumes, primarily because he only investigated subjects when he thought it might bring him some personal advancement. Considering that the *Lwa* were too far beneath him to have any value, he of course had never bothered to learn about them.

So it was that he was completely unaware of the *Lwa*'s strong attraction to the undead. And this oversight, along with Mombu's stuttering, caused Qorin to completely miss what the excited *Tsel* was trying to communicate when he had said the word *Damballa,* the *Lwa* word for those who have come back to life.

Meanwhile Mombu stood there awaiting orders, shifting nervously from foot to foot, reviewing his own thought processes. *How is it possible that a person hiding in the bushes looks exactly like a priest who has recently been murdered? There can be no other explanation. When you see a dead person walking around and spying on people, well, of course it must be a Damballa.*

Mombu watched Qorin's reaction to the news he had shared. He noticed Qorin's wings were tucked tightly against his body, revealing the strength of his shoulders. But Mombu was most aware of the concerned look on Qorin's face as he stood staring off into the distance, lost in thought. Mombu kept his own face serious. Inwardly, he was pleased at his ability to converse as a peer with this elevated *Tsel*. In spite of his stutter, he had been able to communicate such a difficult concept as "the undead" to Qorin.

Qorin, for his part, continued to stand immobile, deep in thought. *It's a disaster to think that Damballa, that slimy snake, might be aware of Dominic. Even worse, he might be spying on him!*

All at once, Qorin realized that his face was probably mirroring his deep shock and horror. That would never do! With an effort, he regained his composure, then extending his impressive wings over Mombu, looked down on him with disdain and asked, "What does Damballa know? Did you talk with him?"

Mombu shrieked in fear. "T-t-talk with h-h-him? N-n-not on your l-l-life!"

Qorin was confused and annoyed. "Why can't you talk with him?"

"B-b-because he is D-D-Damballa!"

Qorin wondered, *Does he really think his master is so powerful? The Prince of the* Lwa *may be sneaky, but I know for a fact that he is not overly endowed with initiative.*

Qorin needed a plan. There was no time to worry about *how* Damballa found out about Dominic. The question was how to deal with the situation at hand. If the boy were to disappear suddenly, Damballa would very likely lose interest and make no effort to search for him.

He said to Mombu, "Here is what you must do: You must go to the house and convince them that Dominic must get away from Damballa quickly!"

"B-but L-Lord D-D-eywós' r-r-rules."

"Yes, I know Lord Deywós discourages our making unauthorized appearances to humans. But, trust me, he would approve of this; it's an emergency. We must act. And we must act immediately."

Ch 7. God Is in Heaven

(Haiti, 10 months before the Fire)

For God is in heaven, and you on earth;
Therefore let your words be few.
Ecclesiastes 5:2b

One moment Alfred was sleeping peacefully in his bed, the next he found himself wide awake, blinking, trying to understand what was happening. He sensed a spirit was reaching out to him; in fact, it seemed he could see the spirit's form! This had never happened to him before.

The spirit was speaking feverishly, but Alfred couldn't understand the message. He whispered nervously, afraid to offend the spirit, "I'm sorry, what? I don't understand what you're saying." The spirit repeated the words, "D-d-danger! D-D-Damballa! G-g-go quickly!" Then all was quiet and the spirit vanished.

As he lay in his warm bed, Alfred tried to make sense of this communication. He flashed back to his first contact with the *Lwa* spirits. In his native Belize, he had learned the skills of the fishing trade, including the need to invoke the power of Agwe, the Spirit of the Sea, when seeking to obtain a good catch. But one day while fishing alone, he ventured too far out and found himself lost at sea. Hours passed with no land in sight and night was approaching. In mortal danger, he had called out to Agwe, not for a catch of fish, but for his very life. Immediately, he had felt in communication with the Spirit of the Sea who guided him, even against the prevailing sea currents, and landed him safely on the shores of Haiti.

Since that day, he had dedicated himself to the practice of voodoo. Over the years, he had often tried to communicate with the spirit world, and on occasion the *Lwa* even responded. But his experience had taught him that the spirits responded not necessarily according to his level of desperation, but according to their own pleasure and for their own purposes.

He assumed it must have been Agwe who had reached out to him over a month ago, instructing him to find Dominic. And he remembered that that day when he first placed his hand on Dominic's forehead, he felt a supercharge of the power of the spirits.

Now, the spirits were communicating with him, and what is more, *they* were initiating contact. Since Dominic had come to live with him, Alfred had become convinced of three things: one, the *Lwa* had personally delivered this boy to him; two, Dominic was destined for greatness; and, three, Dominic's greatness depended on his connection with the spirits.

Alfred rubbed his sleepy eyes. A spirit had definitely appeared to him and said the words: "*Go, quickly!*" Ever obedient to the spirit that had rescued him from certain death at sea so many years before, he got up and started packing.

At first light Alfred was on his way, leaving the village he had called home for many years. Taking the boys and all his money, he hurried north toward Fort Liberté to the shanty on the coast he had called home for his first five years after arriving from Belize.

They travelled part of the way as passengers in a broken-down truck and part of the way by bus. It wasn't until they got to the city that Dominic, looking out the bus window, realized how far removed from civilization he had been living these past weeks. Though a fairly small town, he found himself suddenly overwhelmed by the cars and noise and people and traffic.

Alfred and his boys settled into life in their new home. Not only did he have a tin-roofed place close to the edge of town, but he also had a boat, the very same boat he had arrived in when he came from Belize. He had been renting it to an acquaintance, but now he planned to take it back and make his living once again as a fisherman. Within a few days, he began to take Dominic and Henri out to the sea with him.

Dominic continued to learn Haitian Creole and the secret arts of voodoo while out fishing. Time and again, Alfred would cast spells and within minutes they would haul in an amazing catch of fish. And when there were contrary winds or storms, Alfred would perform a ritual, and the winds would seem to calm.

As part of his mentoring process, Alfred taught Henri and Dominic the basic voodoo rituals he himself used. Once he was convinced the boys had learned to successfully fish with voodoo, Alfred began staying home, leaving Dominic and Henri to do the hard work of fishing by themselves.

One day, a few weeks later, the boys returned home after a day of fishing to find Alfred in bed with the fishmonger's wife. Dominic was shocked. Alfred explained that the boys weren't yet ready to understand the higher levels of voodoo. He confided that when this woman learned he was a voodoo priest she had come to him worried that she and her husband could not have a baby, and so he was using his voodoo powers to help her.

Dominic felt lost. He had grown up in a Christian home, and though he had left home angry at his family and questioning God, he still believed the basic rules of right and wrong he had learned growing up.

But questions filled his mind. Could he ever remember seeing displays of supernatural power in Christianity like he was seeing now in voodoo? On the other hand, didn't Alfred's nonchalant view of sexual immorality go against one of God's basic rules for life, one of the Ten Commandments? The more Dominic thought about it from the point of view of the fishmonger, the more likely it seemed that Alfred was not at all a very nice person. Was this the moral code of voodoo? Did Alfred really believe that sleeping with someone else's wife was an acceptable religious practice?

Voodoo power was appealing. But it was so different from the way he had been raised. He thought about his life and sensed a deep longing for power *and* goodness. He felt unsure what to do. Alfred assured him voodoo would keep him safe, and maybe that was true when he was hidden away in the village. But would incantations protect him if the police tried to arrest him for murder?

He fished the priest's poem out of his wallet. Carefully unfolding the paper, he read the words in Italian, translating them in his head:

Thoughts on Ecclesiastes 5:2

I've oftentimes forgotten God,
And wandered far away
And in my mind I doubted,
I am now ashamed to say.

I struggled long against my sin,
Guilt flowed high over my head,
Then strangely soon within my heart,
There came a voice which said:

"There is no God."

Was this a way to hide from guilt?
Or from God to escape?

Or did the tempter take that chance
My view of what is real to shake?

Dominic stopped reading as he realized these words were the only connection he had to the man a DNA test said was his real father. He suddenly felt the priest's poem accurately described his own thoughts at present. He realized he was in doubt about God's very existence. But where had that doubt come from? He read on.

Many thinkers of our day affirm:
"The god who was is dead."
They thus eliminate their guilt;
And all their sins have fled.

"God is created by every man
And needless to the wise."
Yet while they laugh and mock Him
He looks down from the skies.

His Word, it suffers at their hands,
To them he's but a liar.
They fervently affirm "the truth,"
But not what He desires.

And preachers preach and singers sing,
A sea of words which they
Believe are true about the Lord
To their shame on that day.

Dominic thought about the many opinions about God he had heard over the years. Growing up in a Christian family, he accepted the Bible. But even Christians disagree on what the Bible means.

Then, in school, he encountered classmates and teachers who doubted and even mocked what the Bible taught: everything from the creation of the world in six days to Jesus' miracles. How to know who was right? He was especially sobered by the last words of the poem, a paraphrase of Ecclesiastes 5:2.

More caution, then, I would advise,
And may we gain perspective too.
For God's in heaven and we're on Earth,
So let our words be few.

Reading this poem, Dominic realized that for as long as he could remember, he had wondered so many things: *What if the Bible is just made up? What if the reason I don't seem to see evidence of God's power is because God doesn't even exist? Where is the evidence today of that miraculous power written about in the Bible? Where are the rivers being parted so people can walk across on dry land? Where are the dead people being raised to life again?*

He thought to himself, *Henri says they had given up on him as dead until one touch from Alfred caused him to open his eyes and he was as good as new. And Henri says, when he brought me to Alfred, I was even worse off than he had been. And it does seem that Alfred's magic power did bring me back to life.*

Dominic thought back to his family growing up. *What I remember is the emphasis on being loving and kind to others. That is all good and well, but I've found the world is not a very nice place. Here, Alfred has some kind of spiritual power, and I enjoy feeling the power of voodoo, but why can't I seem to find power and goodness together? The loving and kind God of the Bible is supposed to be all-powerful; if that is true, He should take action to show He is really in charge.*

Ch 8. The Undead

(Shadowlands, 10 months before the Fire)

"You mostly find zombies farther south, where the voudun priests are."

"What about mummies? Do they only hang around Egypt?"

"Don't be ridiculous. No one believes in mummies."

Cassandra Clare, *City of Bones*

As Qorin waited for Mombu in the secret cave that had become their meeting place, he reviewed step-by-step his progression of thought. First of all, after checking with many sources, he had become convinced that Damballa was still unaware of Dominic's importance. That had given Qorin a tremendous sense of relief because he wouldn't trust that sneaky reptile as far as he could throw him.

The next step was to answer the question, *If Mombu hadn't seen Damballa, what had he seen?* Something had obviously frightened the diminutive *Tsel*, but what? And why had he mentioned Damballa?

Reluctantly, Qorin decided he needed to do some research about the *Lwa*. He needed to know more about Damballa's realm. In his research, Qorin came across piles of interesting but mostly unimportant information. He learned Damballa had been a powerful spirit in West Africa. Under his influence, the Dahomey people were able to defeat and enslave their neighbors. In fact, their economy was soon almost entirely based on raiding and enslaving neighboring tribes. To show their thanks, the Dahomey people offered human sacrifices to their god, Damballa. Qorin nodded his head, *So far so good.*

But then (and here Qorin noted the reports were vague), Damballa had offended Deywós and was banished to the Caribbean. Some historians claimed it was a strategic move allowing Damballa to arrive about the time the Europeans began what they called their "discovery" of the New World.

Whether his placement in the Caribbean was a punishment or a mission, Damballa began to gain a following in those islands, among some of those people who had previously been under his power in Africa. As more and more slaves were brought to his territory from West Africa, he was there waiting for them. He expected that they would turn to him just as they had for generations under their Dahomey masters.

But the times had changed. He represented the *past,* and the slaves, being pragmatic, were now more interested in the religion of their *present* masters, the Europeans. Seeing he was losing ground, he switched sides and began to promote European Catholic ideas. Once that took hold, he infused his religion once again with voodoo.

Qorin put the notes down with a sigh. *How boring!* But he was desperate to find out what had been so troubling to Mombu, so he kept reading. Then he saw it: *In the religion Damballa had given to the people of the Caribbean, the undead figured prominently. Aha,* he thought, as he read on. *The chief of the* Lwa *is more clever than I gave him credit for. The name he took for himself,* Damballa, *turns out to be a Haitian term meaning "zombie."*

Qorin had an idea. What if Mombu mentioned "*Damballa,*" not because he had seen the chief of the *Lwa*, but something else, something that he thought must be a person who had come back to life? But if that was the case, what had he seen? Humans are willing to believe all that nonsense about dead men walking. But Mombu was a *Tsel*. He would know better.

What, then, had he seen? A human. The first question to solve was, *Under what circumstances would Mombu think a* human *was a zombie?* He must have seen someone walking around who resembled someone who had recently died. But how was that possible? Qorin set his mind to solving that problem at the same time he tackled the question of who might want to spy on Dominic.

He remembered he had heard from Saparon[16], the keeper of the mysterious books, that Abdowan had stolen a chapter from a book on "cellular duplication." *What might that shrewd Tsel have done with information about duplicating cells?* Qorin wondered.

Would he have tried a maneuver as risky as making himself a clone of someone else? Poor, stupid Abdowan! Qorin thought. *He had always been the cautious one, the careful one! And yet, had he become so desperate to accomplish his mission that he tried making himself into a doppelgänger? If so, he very likely thought nothing of the potential consequences since he intended to return to the Shadowlands straight away. But,* Qorin noted, *Abdowan hasn't returned. Is it possible that Abdowan is still on the Earth? And if so, might he be keeping an eye on Dominic?*

What Qorin needed was one more piece of information. Had there been a recent death in the area near where Dominic was? Breaking from his thoughts, he stood up and stomped his feet. *Where is that imbecile Mombu?*

As he waited, he continued to summarize his train of thought so far. Dominic was somewhere in the Caribbean. It followed that Abdowan, if alive, would be looking for him. And it was not out of the question that the person Abdowan had cloned might also be looking for Dominic. Suppose Abdowan saw his doppelgänger and, fearing discovery, killed him? Yes, it made sense. He just had to ask Mombu a few clarifying questions.

16. Saparon is a *Tsel*, the keeper of the mystical books in the library of Shadowlands

Qorin felt frustrated and impatient when the small, frightened *Tsel* finally appeared in their secret cave. But he could see how rattled the hapless *Tsel* looked, so he tried to put him at ease, saying, "Don't worry, little friend, I just need to ask you a question or two."

"O-o-okay."

Then, as if talking to a little child, he said, "And to make it easier for you, just nod your head for 'yes,' or move it side to side for 'no.' Do you think you can do that?"

Mombu wanted to shout out, "What is your problem? I'm not stupid, you know!"

He had in fact written up a complete report of the Damballa situation and was ready to deliver his carefully worded manuscript to Qorin. In it, he explained about the priest's death and how he had seen the dead priest over a month later walking around spying on the boy.

He knew, if given the chance, he would be able to communicate it all clearly. It was so much easier to communicate by writing. But as he looked up at Qorin's proud face and felt his condescension, his desire to help him began to evaporate.

Qorin's impatience was growing. He asked again, emphasizing each word, "*Mombu. Do. You. Think. You. Can. Do. That?*"

Mombu nodded his head "yes" and decided against offering him the clear written report he had prepared.

"Good. Okay, has there been an unusual death here in the area recently?"

Mombu nodded vigorously.

"Right. And did you then see this same dead person spying on the boy?"

Mombu nodded with such force that Qorin was afraid he was going to hurt himself.

Qorin set his face in a stern gaze as he looked at the diminutive *Lwa*. "Okay, for now the boy is safe in the new place they have moved to. But I expect this 'zombie' will return, and when he does, this is what you must do: You must kill him."

Mombu shook his head. Forgetting Qorin's admonition to not use words, he blurted out, "No! It c-can n-not be d-done!"

With his hand extended, Qorin motioned to the frightened *Tsel*, "Calm down, calm down. It can be done. You can kill him, and I will tell you how."

Ch 9. Darkened Dreams

(Haiti, 10 months before the Fire)

There are more things in heaven and earth, Horatio, than are dreamt of in your philosophy.

William Shakespeare, *Hamlet*

To boost his social standing, now that he was back in the city, Alfred invited a few friends to join him and his apprentices in what he called a "group séance." He knew he could plan the encounter but not necessarily control the outcome. He hoped that the spirits would indeed show up. A supernatural manifestation would help him gain the respect of the community, and more importantly, sponsors to pay for his new life in the city.

The séance started with the group sitting in a circle, each one holding a candle. He told them to stare at the candle until they lost themselves and were taken over by the spirits.

Dominic felt himself transported to another realm: dreamlike, and yet more real than a dream. He was inside a prison complex with walls and razor wire, but as he looked around, he realized he was not confined in a cell. He stepped into a central patio with snow on the ground. The entire world seemed frozen. And dark, even though it was obviously daytime. He walked slowly and silently among the prisoners and the guards. The prisoners, wretched and emaciated, averted their gaze while the guards stood at attention and saluted him. It dawned on him that he must be an officer.

He continued to walk through the compound, stoic and reserved, while fear, death, and silence reigned around him. Then he heard a voice—a voice that seemed incongruous with that evil place—a voice that seemed to express a breath of hope, a rare commodity in that forsaken land. The voice seemed to be coming from behind a metal door. Stopping in front of it, he turned the handle and walked inside.

Stepping past several guards, he found himself in a well-lit room where a meeting was in progress. A man dressed like a priest stood at the front speaking, while six or seven men sat listening. Dominic noticed they weren't wearing shabby prison rags like the feeble wretches he had seen outside. Nor were they in soldiers' uniforms like the guards standing in the back of the room. These were special prisoners.

Dominic, like all the others in the room, was drawn to the words of the preacher. His voice, though rough and hoarse, was passionately calling on them to live fully for God and not to compromise.

While he listened, a ragged prisoner entered the room and brought the speaker a glass of water. The preacher paused just long enough to thank the prisoner and to take a drink. As the preacher continued, the prisoner walked slowly back toward the door. But instead of leaving the room, he lingered near Dominic, listening.

Suddenly, a particularly cruel-looking guard standing next to Dominic shouted at the prisoner, "*Du da!*[17] What are you doing there? Out you go!"

The prisoner jumped and began to shuffle out of the room. The preacher paused again at the outburst and waited uncomfortably in the silence.

17. German: "You there!"

Dominic looked into the despondent eyes of the prisoner, then heard his own voice speaking, "*Nein!*[18] He stays here!"

The angry guard glared, but Dominic resolutely met his stare.

After an awkward silence, the guard looked away and Dominic turned to the priest who was now smiling gently. Dominic spoke again, louder and with authority, "We all stay here."

The guard grunted, spotted an empty chair in the back of the room, and sat down. The preacher's smile broadened, and he began again, "With God all things are possible."

Dominic smiled back and said, "Amen. Please continue."

At that moment, Dominic felt Alfred shaking him awake. Opening his eyes, it took him a moment to realize he was back in Alfred's house and the séance was still in progress. He saw two young men standing stock still, apparently in trances. Two others were dancing around, and one was wiggling like a snake on the ground.

He could sense the spiritual power in the room but felt detached from it. Several of the participants approached Dominic with their dances and trances and babbling, but when they came close, they shrieked and shrank away from him. It occurred to him that the kind of spiritual power he was yearning for was not to be found in this room.

Later that evening, after everyone had left, Alfred approached him. "You were lying so still earlier that I feared the experience was too much for you."

"No, I was having a vision. I was in a prison."

"A prison? Dominic, do you think of life here with me as a prison?"

"No, in my dream I was in a prison, but I wasn't a prisoner; I was a guard."

"I see. Well, I certainly can sense that you are being protected by powerful forces. The *Lwa* have revealed to me that you will indeed one

18. German: "No!"

day be a powerful master. I don't understand the whole plan, but I sense that for now you must learn to wait patiently."

Waiting patiently might be somebody's plan, but that wasn't what Dominic had in mind. In fact, *leaving* was what he was contemplating. Maybe *that* was the meaning of the vision: that he was not a prisoner, that he was not powerless, that he was, in fact, free to leave. And Alfred seemed to accept that Dominic was destined for more than life on this island. But what would happen if he did leave? His desire to return to familiar surroundings, though growing, was not yet greater than his fear of being caught and imprisoned for murder.

Dominic had been transported to a prison camp during the séance, but Henri's experience was different. As Henri looked around at the burning candles in the shabby room where the séance was being held, he could no longer see any people present, but he could sense what he guessed was a *Lwa* spirit. Lying still, not knowing what to expect, Henri gave a cry of fear when he could suddenly see a *Lwa* spirit standing before him.

He was understandably shocked and surprised at the sight of the spirit, but little by little his surprise turned into bewilderment. Hard as he tried, he could not understand what the *Lwa* spirit was saying. In his reverence for the power of voodoo, the novice assumed that any breakdown in communication must somehow be his fault.

He listened as carefully as he could and heard something like "*D-D-Dam-b-b-balla!*" but was at a loss to understand what it meant.

"*Damballa!*" Mombu finally managed to get out the word clearly.

Henri understood the Haitian Creole word *Damballa* to mean "someone brought back to life by a sorcerer." Trembling, he asked, "Where?"

Mombu began to communicate more clearly once he sensed that Henri understood, so he added, "Outside! He's hiding." At that point, Mombu got too excited and began to stutter again, leaving Henri wondering what he was saying.

"Knife. K-k-kill him!" Mombu finally managed to get out.

Henri, surprised, asked, "Kill him?"

Mombu responded, "Yes, k-k-kill d-d-dead priest!" Then he disappeared.

Henri, sweating profusely, opened his eyes and could once again see the room and the people in it. One man was standing stock still as if in a trance. Another was dancing around the room maniacally, seeming unaware of his surroundings yet, oddly enough, still able to avoid crashing into any of the others.

Henri's thoughts went back to the message he had just received. The *Lwa* messenger might have expected him to act immediately, but he was no fool. Spirit orders or not, Henri wasn't about to go outside in the dark with a knife looking for a zombie!

Ch 10. Abdowan Toasts Success

(Haiti, 10 months before the Fire)

We must picture hell as a state where everyone is perpetually concerned about his own dignity and advancement, where everyone has a grievance, and where everyone lives with the deadly serious passions of envy, self-importance, and resentment.

C.S. Lewis, *The Screwtape Letters*

Abdowan had known that his mission for Deywós would be risky, but he also knew success would mean unparalleled glory; people worshipping him, nations bowing at his feet. Or at least that was what he had been led to believe.

He had also expected that his mission would be a quick one: transform himself into a handsome human, meet a beautiful girl named Jennifer, have a short-lived "romance," then return to the Shadowlands to be received with honor.

Deywós had sent him to Sorata, Bolivia, as Håvel, an eighteen-year-old student from Sweden. As he waited for a chance to meet Jennifer, he hung out with Alessandro, a young Italian fellow he met in the hotel.

But things had not gone as expected. When Håvel and Alessandro met Jennifer, she hardly even noticed Håvel, instead falling for Alessandro, his dark-complexioned Italian traveling companion.

But Abdowan was not a *Tsel* to give up easily. Improvising, he used deep magic and half of one of Alessandro's fingers to transform his blonde-haired, blue-eyed Håvel body into a clone of Alessandro's body. Next, he met up with Jennifer, pretending to be Alessandro, and with the help of a little magic sleeping potion, all had gone perfectly according to plan.

Mission accomplished, all that then remained for him was to return home to the Shadowlands. But venturing out of doors to the portal was risky since Alessandro might still be in town, so Abdowan decided to hide out until Alessandro had left. It would, after all, be a little awkward if he were to meet his ex-traveling companion, since he still looked exactly like him. As he waited for the magic to wear off, he assured himself that once he was in Håvel's body again, he could venture out, find the portal, and return to the Shadowlands.

But the minutes turned into hours, and he remained Alessandro's doppelgänger.

Undaunted, he pondered his options as he poured over the pages he had "borrowed" from Saparon's library. The chapter explained cellular duplication and corporeal transformation, but unfortunately, it offered nothing about how to undo the process.

By nightfall, even though he had not regained his Håvel body, he opted to face the risk of running into Alessandro. Venturing out at midnight, he was relieved to see no one else in the streets, but quickly became dismayed to find that his previous access point to the spirit realm appeared closed. He cursed his luck and began looking for a different portal. He searched and searched, but in vain.

As his search grew wider and more frantic, it began to dawn on him that the entire Shadowlands might be closed to him! He returned to his room, contemplating the horrible possibility that his exalted *Tsel* mind might now be trapped in a mortal human body!

All at once, he was enraged and flung a wooden chair against the far wall with such force that it shattered into a dozen pieces. Even as he slid to the floor in despair, he knew he must survive; he must find a way forward.

The clever *Tsel,* whose bright eyes had, for centuries, flitted this way and that, was stuck on Earth, encased in a human body. Not having transitioned back to his Håvel form as he had expected was his first problem and presented him with his most immediate concern. What would happen if he were to be mistaken for Alessandro, or worse yet, if he were to meet him face to face somewhere? Under cover of darkness, he left that very night, making his way out of Bolivia and eventually to America.

As the years went by, he discovered that, unlike his spirit form, this human body in which he was now imprisoned was in a constant state of decay. With no way to escape, he found the whole aging process annoying and, if he thought about it too much, downright terrifying.

Twenty years had gone by since Abdowan—or Eván Lopez, as he now called himself—had reluctantly agreed to that ill-fated mission. Why had he been reluctant? Partly because he had been around long enough to know that merely entering the Enemy's territory was incredibly dangerous. Add to that being asked to interact directly with humans, and you have reason enough for concern. Of course, in the end, he had no choice but to take the mission; he knew that refusing an order from Deywós meant dire consequences.

Now older and grayer, but, amazingly, still alive, he was quite pleased with himself as he sat alone in Manje La Bar and Grill in Cap-Haïtien, Haiti. During his two decades on Earth, he had rarely indulged in alcoholic beverages but on this particular night, he felt like celebrating.

So content was he that he didn't even change seats when a short, plump Dominican with curly black hair sat down next to him at the bar, and said, "Beer, please." Eván, staring at his glass of rum, guessed this mooch was probably a regular who sat next to rich foreigners hoping to get a free drink.

As the bartender arrived with a beer, his companion looked over at Eván, held out his hand and said, "Manuel." Normally Eván would have turned his back on the stranger right then and there, but that night he shook the offered hand. Turning back to his rum, he decided he could get up and move whenever Manuel became a bother.

Ten minutes and two beers later, it appeared Manuel was more of a drinker than a talker. Eván, deciding to be friendly, and realizing Manuel knew some English, offered some small talk. "So, I'm celebrating because Martin, my friend—my ex-friend—apparently sailed off the island without me."

Manuel, looking on with blurry eyes, and raising his glass to his lips, appeared to listen, so Eván continued, "Can you imagine, my partner and traveling companion for the entire last year, leaving me, sailing away to the Bahamas? Martin, man, he could put away the liquor. He loved going to bars. It always amazed me how he could spend hours talking with complete strangers, talking about the most boring and pointless things. And the longer he talked, the more he drank, and the more he drank, the less sense he made. You know what I mean? Hey, are you ready for another beer?"

Manuel nodded. Eván called for the bartender and continued.

"So, like I was saying, Martin and I had been together for about a year. He had invited me to go sailing with him—not for a few hours, or even a few days—but for as long as I wanted. We flew to France to pick up the boat, the *Liberté*, and then we set sail. I'd never sailed before, so I had a lot to learn. But it didn't take long for me to become a master of the seas. That was the life! I didn't have to worry about meeting anyone I didn't want to. It was just Martin and I, sailing the Mediterranean, coming into port towns whenever we felt like it, going off wherever we wanted.

"Then we crossed the Atlantic and began visiting the islands of the Caribbean: Martinique, Antigua, St. Martin, the Virgin Islands, Puerto Rico. And that's where he ditched me. So, you ask, what am I doing in Haiti and why am I celebrating? Well . . . it all started a couple of weeks ago, our first day in San Juan, Puerto Rico, when I had the biggest shock of my life since leaving South America nearly twenty years ago.

"Martin and I were walking along a street in San Juan on our way to dinner when I saw a guy that looked just like this guy I'd known back in South America. He was headed for the same restaurant, but from the opposite direction. I stopped in my tracks. My mouth must have been wide open, because Martin stared at me and asked what was wrong. What could I do? I told him I didn't want to eat there and that I wasn't hungry.

"He was pretty ticked off at me. Throwing up his hands in disgust, he went into the restaurant while I returned to the room to think. I knew I needed to investigate the person I'd seen. *What could it mean? Was that really Alessandro? If so, had he been searching for me? Or was this merely a coincidence?*

"But then I thought, *How could he not have aged at all in twenty years? That would be a cruel twist of irony!* Here I am, an immortal *Tsel* growing old, while my unsuspecting DNA donor lives on agelessly. How could that be? It was impossible!

"Manuel, did I tell you that I was a *Tsel*, you know, a god?"

His quiet companion nodded and then said, "Beer, please."

"Yes, of course." Eván raised his hand to get the bartender's attention as he continued his story.

"So anyway, later that night, I was in the hotel room when Martin came in, practically bubbling with excitement about some kid he had dinner with. He was convinced this Dominic was the smartest person he had ever met. I pretended not to care and told him that I just wanted to leave Puerto Rico, that it was too hot there.

"He replied, 'Perfect! Because tomorrow we'll be out on the open sea with the breeze blowing through our hair.' Then he added, 'Oh, and I've invited Dominic to join us.'

"I wanted to scream, but I bit my tongue. The last thing in the world I wanted was to be on a boat with this Dominic. Martin went on to tell me that the kid was on a quest to find his birth father, who was supposedly living in the Dominican Republic.

"I suddenly had a thought. *What if the boy isn't Alessandro? What if it's his* son? *Or rather,* Jennifer's *son.* My *son!* Twenty long years of thinking I was a failure. All that began to fade away as I had the first inkling that my mission so long ago might have actually been successful!

"So, that's how I came to be here in Haiti. You see?"

Manuel looked up from his beer, realized Eván had asked a question, and nodded.

Eván continued. "Well, it's a little more complicated than that. You see, I wanted to learn about this boy who looked just like Alessandro, but not at close quarters on a boat, and certainly not with Martin around. Thinking he would cancel the trip, I told him, 'Well, you can count me out! I'm going to stay here in Puerto Rico and enjoy the A/C in this hotel.'

"Martin just stared at me and said, 'Aren't you listening to me? We're going to the Dominican Republic, like we talked about. I'm not coming back here.'

"I turned away, playing it cool, saying, 'That's fine. You can go without me.' But that lousy scumbag called my bluff with, 'Okay,

Eván, if that's what you want.' I couldn't believe it! Sure, for me this was only a relationship of convenience, but I'd calculated that somehow for him it was different. Nope. It was then I realized there was no connection between us at all, though we had been together for over a year. Leaving me was no more significant than deciding he needed a new pair of deck shoes. He was sailing anyway. With Dominic.

"The next morning, I woke up and saw that Martin had already left without so much as saying goodbye. After I was sure that he was really gone, I jumped out of bed and began packing as I reviewed my options. *I could disappear again, as I'd done several times before during the last twenty years. Get as far away as possible. That would be a good defensive strategy. On the other hand, I could go on the offensive. I'd been on the run for decades. Maybe it was time for me to confront my past. This had been* my *mission, after all. I may be the only one on Earth who knows the truth about the boy's birth. And what about Alessandro? Did he know about Dominic?*"

Eván broke from his reverie and, noticing that Manuel was nearly asleep beside him, asked, "You want another beer?"

Manuel nodded.

With a wave of his hand, Eván ordered another beer and continued his story.

"So, I finished packing and left the hotel. The first thing I needed was money. I went to the bank and nearly cleared out my quite substantial nest egg. As you can imagine, living off others with no expenses for many years was nice way to build my savings."

He looked at Manuel, who, raising the glass to his lips, smiled and nodded so Eván continued. "I found a pawnshop, full of jewelry and tools, but not what I was looking for, so the pawnbroker took me to an ordinary door in a rundown section of town. After a moment's hesitation, I walked through the doorway and quickly found what I wanted.

"I made my way to the marina to check on Martin, and sure enough, the *Liberté* was gone. A good night's sleep had convinced me that finding Dominic was now the most important thing I could do. So, I paid cash for a small boat, grabbed a few supplies, and set off.

"I stayed near the coastline, heading west toward the Dominican Republic. Scanning the horizon with my binoculars, I eventually saw a familiar sail. Keeping back, I followed at a distance, losing them at night but picking them up again the next morning.

"I watched as they entered the marina at the beach city of Samaná. A little later, I approached and docked. After letting the official check my passport, I proceeded into town.

"From a distance, I could see Martin and Dominic parting ways. Martin would be going to a bar, but I needed to see where Dominic was headed. It wasn't hard to follow him undetected: He was so focused on his search for his father that he seemed unaware of anything else going on around him.

"At the bus station, I got on the same bus with him, undetected, and we eventually made it to the town of Restauración, near the border with Haiti. Leaving the bus, I followed him from a safe distance as he walked around town, and I got a room at the same hotel he did. I wanted to talk with him, to see what he knew. But first, I had to see where he was going. I couldn't blow my cover yet.

"The next morning, I watched as he left the hotel and, again, I followed. He led me through several villages and eventually to a field outside a village where a priest was working all alone on a pile of rusty irrigation pipes. From behind a tree, I watched as the priest slowly rose from his work. Dominic introduced himself and I heard the priest say, 'It's nice to meet you, Dominic Sánchez.'"

Before continuing, Eván looked around to see who else was in the bar, and how close they were. Confident that no one else could hear him, he continued a little bit quieter, "You see, don't you? I was right. *Dominic Sánchez*. He was *Jennifer Sánchez's* son.

"I kept listening. I still remember Dominic's answer: 'Well, it's very long overdue meeting you, Father Alessandro. I've been looking for you. Earlier this year I discovered that you are my father.'

"At those words, I saw the priest's face grow somber. He said it was impossible. But Dominic told him he had proof. He had done a DNA match, and guess whose name came up? Alessandro Tarso from Rome. Dominic asked him point-blank, 'Is that you?' I remember thinking that Martin had been right. This kid really was smart.

"When the priest stammered, 'yes,' I knew that I'd heard enough. It was time to act."

Eván looked around the bar again. "You see, I realized then and there that Alessandro must not be allowed to explain to anyone about Dominic's birth. So, I lifted the gun I'd bought, steadied myself against the tree, and took aim.

"I saw Dominic grab the priest by the collar, lifting him off the ground. He said, 'You started my miserable life, and then you left. I wish you had never existed.' With that, he dropped the priest and turned to go.

"I saw my chance and fired. Alessandro lurched and fell, landing with a clatter on the irrigation pipes. My gun, fitted with a silencer, hadn't made much noise. I crouched behind the tree, waiting, but no one came running. At that moment, I wanted to talk to Dominic. Did he know about me? And what had become of Jennifer? But he was bending down, focused on the priest for the moment, and I decided it was better for me to get out of there and get to safety.

"It began to rain as I made my way back to the bus station and I remember thinking that the Oppressor and all his hordes must be weeping. But I was ecstatic. I just had to clean up a few details.

"A bus was leaving that afternoon, so I got a ticket. Then I went behind the station to look for a place to ditch the gun, but what I found there was better than I could have hoped for: A man wearing filthy clothes and holding a mostly empty bottle of rum was relieving himself against the wall. As I approached, he finished his business and looked up. Locking eyes with him, in a moment, I had him hypnotized.

"I told him, 'You are a lucky man. You hated the priest Alessandro. You found him outside the village, and you killed him.' Then I slipped the gun into his pocket and said, 'Now you are free of him. Go back to your village and tell everyone about it. Do you understand?' When the man nodded, I snapped my fingers, turned, and went to catch my bus."

Eván sat up a little straighter and continued. "Now as you can see, I'd provided a perfect scapegoat for the priest's murder. My next step was to connect with Dominic, but I still needed to wait a little while—at a safe distance—to make sure that he wasn't implicated in the priest's death. So, I took the bus all the way back to Samaná, where I'd left my sailboat at the marina."

Eván noticed Manuel was again slumping down toward the bar nearly asleep, so he asked, "Are you ready for another beer?"

Manuel perked up. "Yes, please."

Another beer appeared and Eván continued, "You're probably wondering how I came to Cap-Haïtien."

Manuel missed his cue to respond, but Eván didn't let it bother him. He continued talking, pulling out a map of the island of Hispaniola, pointing to Haiti on the west and Dominican Republic on the east.

"See, here I was in Samaná in the east of the island. After a week, I saw a short article in the paper about a missing priest, Father Alessandro. A week after that, I read that the priest's body had been found, but there was no mention of Dominic, which was good. I wanted to investigate, to check on him, but decided to be cautious and wait a day or two longer.

"The next day, more details emerged online. The news said that a Haitian man named Alfred had found the priest's body while scavenging in a cave somewhere around here. He had contacted the local police, and a local Dominican man was being held on suspicion of murder."

Eván pointed to a dot he had made on the map and said, "I read in the article that this Alfred was from a small village in Haiti, just across the border from Restauracíon. That made sense because it was in the fields outside of Restauración where I'd seen Dominic confront the priest. But that was a long bus ride from Samaná, and I didn't really want to do it again. On the other hand, this Alfred was my best chance to discover Dominic's whereabouts. Looking at my map, I decided to sail this way, northwest around the island to Fort Liberté, here in the northern part of the island, just across the border, in Haiti.

"There I rented a car and headed south, away from the sea and up into the hills. The city of Restauración and the fields where I'd watched Dominic confront the priest were just across the border in the Dominican Republic. But if that area was poor, this part of Haiti was desperately poor. After asking around from village to village, what do you think I found? That's right! I found the very house where Dominic was staying!

"I kept a low profile and checked out the house from a distance. It was late, so I decided to return to talk to Dominic the next day. I came back and watched the house for several hours, but I didn't see Dominic. The following day, I returned and knocked on the door, ready to introduce myself. Imagine my surprise when the neighbors told me that the whole family had left the night before and moved to Cap-Haïtien. So, here I am in Cap-Haïtien, ready to meet Dominic. After all these years, I will finally be vindicated. Yes! My mission has been a success, and soon all of the Shadowlands will know it!"

Ch 11. Henri's Quest

(Haiti, 10 months before the Fire)

> *The first effect of not believing in God is to believe in anything.*
>
> Attributed to G.K. Chesterton by
> Emile Cammaerts, *The Laughing Prophet*

The day after the séance, Dominic overheard Henri asking Alfred where he could find a photo of the dead priest. That got Dominic's attention. He watched as Henri grabbed a pocketknife, casually slipped it in his pocket, and went out the door. Dominic knew Henri was lazy, and seeing this sudden burst of energy, he decided to follow him to see what was going on.

Henri asked around until he found a newspaper with a picture of the late Father Alessandro. He cut it out and started walking around town with the picture in his hand, stopping from time to time to look down at the photo.

Staying out of sight, Dominic continued to follow, saying to himself, *If I didn't know better, I'd think Henri was trying to find Alessandro. Should I remind him that the priest is dead? It looks like he's hoping to spot him walking along the street. What in the world could he be up to?*

Just for fun, he tried to see how near he could get without Henri noticing. He got within an arm's reach and was about to tap Henri on the shoulder and ask, "What are you looking for?" when he noticed Henri was muttering over and over to himself, "The spirit commanded me to kill the zombie and by Agwe, I will do it."

A zombie? Does Henri think Alessandro has come back to life? Dominic wondered as he thought about the photo Henri was carrying around. *Has a spirit told him to kill a man who is already dead? I don't know whether the source of this craziness is Henri or the spirits, but that's enough insanity for one day for me.* Dominic left Henri to his quest and returned home.

Toward evening, Dominic was in the house talking with Alfred. Suddenly, he noticed Henri outside standing across the street looking like he was uncertain whether or not to come into the house. Dominic decided to step outside and see what was up.

Staying in the shadows, he noticed Henri's hand in his pocket, fiddling nervously with his pocketknife. It looked like Henri was debating with himself about giving up his quest. Dominic was sure that Henri's feet, flapping in his sandals all day long, must be blistered and sore by now. Henri sighed deeply, looking as if he had decided to call it a day, and took a step forward. Night was approaching and Dominic guessed that a ghost hunter's eagerness tends to decrease when it gets dark.

Then, just as Henri began to cross the street, he stopped, his body suddenly tensing up. Dominic watched, almost certain he could see someone else out there, crouching in the shadows. The furtive figure lifted his head to get a better view of the house as Henri approached him from behind and yelled, "Woy!" The figure, still squatting, swiveled around suddenly to face Henri. Drawing on some inner courage, Henri looked down on the man and, pulling out his small blade, shouted at him in French, "We know who you are! We will chase you! We will kill you!"

The stalker, caught off guard, panicked. He jumped up, turned on his heel, and fled down the street in the failing light. Henri, surprised by the man's quick escape, stood, hesitating for a moment before he himself took off in pursuit, knife raised in the air, yelling, "We'll kill you!"

Dominic, curious, took off after them, reaching the port in time to see the man starting to untie the rope holding a small sailboat to the dock. Then, looking up and seeing Henri approaching, the man jumped into the water and hid in the shadows between two boats.

Henri stood on the dock, leaning over to catch his breath and waiting for the man to emerge. Dominic watched as Henri kept a lookout. Each time the man appeared, Henri brandished his pocketknife.

Time crawled and Dominic began to wonder how the standoff would be resolved. Henri resolutely kept an eye on the stranger, but it had been a long day, and the evening was warm. After a while, Dominic noticed that Henri no longer reacted each time the man moved. Little by little, Henri went from standing on the dock to sitting down. Bored and tired, as the minutes went by, Henri soon was propped up on an elbow. Less than ten minutes later he was stretched out on the dock snoring.

The man quietly made his way out of the water and onto the dock. He finished untying the rope and silently stepped aboard the sailboat. Dominic stayed back and made no attempt to interfere; he had no idea who the person was and had no reason to get involved.

From down the street a dog barked, and Henri woke with a start. Jumping to his feet, he looked around just in time to see, in the gloom, the man sailing out to sea. Henri shook his fist defiantly as the boat slipped away. As it sailed out of sight, Henri turned and started home.

Dominic followed quietly, noticing a swagger in Henri's step. He heard him laugh and say out loud, "I attacked and chased off the zombie! The power of the spirits is with me. Alfred will see that I am the better apprentice!"

Dominic was curious about what had just taken place, but he didn't want Henri to know he had seen the day's events. In the dark, he took advantage of a shortcut to beat Henri home. When Henri arrived a short while later, Alfred glanced up, then suddenly did a double take, noting the self-assured way Henri carried himself. Dominic also saw the haughty expression on Henri's face, the same look of triumph he had worn when raising his fist in the air after vanquishing his "zombie."

Part 2

Jerusalem

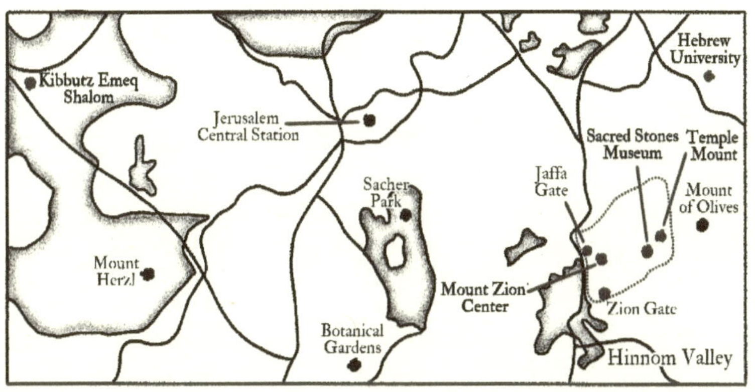

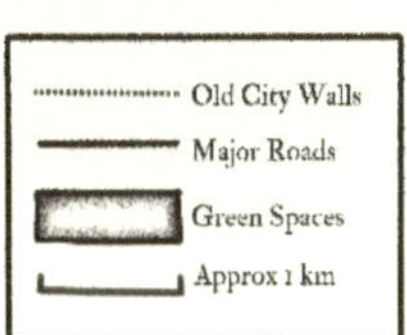

Ch 12. Andriy Seeks Revenge

(Kazakhstan, 10 months before the Fire)

For thus says the Lord of hosts:
"He sent Me after glory,
to the nations which plunder you;
for he who touches you
touches the apple of His eye."

Zechariah 2:8

Andriy had been born into a prosperous family and enjoyed a comfortable life. But when his wife of twenty-five years developed cancer and died just months after her diagnosis, he felt like his world had fallen apart. For a year after that, he lived like a hermit, staying home as much as possible, subsisting on frozen pizzas, and seeing no one. His parents had passed away, he had no siblings, and he and Sophia had no children. It suddenly dawned on him that without her, no one cared whether he lived or died.

No one, that is, until one day he unexpectedly came across an online dating site, Match Up. On a whim, he filled out his personal profile and was surprised when that same day he got a message from a woman named Niswat. He responded briefly and was startled to realize how sad he was when she didn't write back immediately. *Oh well,* he thought. *It was a stupid idea.*

But the next day, her reply was waiting when he logged in. He immediately wrote back, telling her that his name was Andriy Dalinger, that he lived in Astana, Kazakhstan, and that he was a German Russian. His ancestors had come from Herrnhut, Germany, and had been part of the Moravian Brethren movement. In Soviet Russia, his family had been successful farmers and influential among the German immigrants.

The next day, she wrote again, telling him that his story sounded confusing. Did he think of himself as a German, or a Russian, or a Kazakh? He answered and, before long, chatting with Niswat became the highlight of his day, giving him a reason to get up each morning.

As the weeks went by, he poured out his heart to his new friend. Since his wife's death, he saw all of life through the lens of his present grief and loneliness, yet Niswat didn't seem bothered by his negative outlook. She even seemed interested in his family history, so he wrote out for her the long, sad story that stretched all the way back to the Volga Germans and Catherine the Great's German settlement program in the 1700s.

His ancestors, he explained, had trekked eastward during the reign of Czar Alexander into the Ukrainian areas of Volhynia, joining over 200,000 other German settlers hoping for a better future. It was not an easy life. Many found it nearly impossible to maintain their identity as Germans after they were forced to study Russian in school. Some immigrants chose to leave, but many, like Andriy's family, remained. Russia at that time was making strides to industrialize, and his family was becoming wealthy through hard work and discipline.

Then came the chaos and devastation of the 1917 Russian Revolution and the civil war that followed. Many ethnic Germans were scattered within Russia, and others took the opportunity to emigrate from Russia altogether.

But Andriy's family stayed. In the 1920s, things began to improve when the Volga German Autonomous Soviet Socialist Republic was founded. But then came World War II, and suddenly the German population of Russia was almost entirely exiled to remote regions of the Soviet Union. His family was relocated to a farming area near Akmolinsk, Kazakhstan, in 1941.

After Stalin's death in 1953, Russian Germans were allowed to return to European Russia, but Andriy's father, along with approximately one million others who had also created successful lives, chose to remain in Kazakhstan. About the time Andriy was born, the city was renamed Tselinograd, which in Russian means "virgin lands," to reflect the then-current effort of the central government to boost grain production in the area.

In the 1980s, when Andriy was in college, perestroika, the time of the great restructuring of the political and economic systems of the Soviet Union, began to be implemented. The goal might have been to make socialism work more efficiently, but by opening the Soviet borders, one of the practical effects was mass emigration. During that decade, though more than half of the Russian Germans emigrated out of Kazakhstan, Andriy's family stayed on.

In 1991, the year Andriy got married, Kazakhstan gained its independence from the Soviet Union, and the city was renamed Akmola, hearkening back to its original name, Akmolinsk. Then in 1997, the new nation's capital was moved from Almaty to Akmola, and the next year the capital's name was changed to Astana.

Andriy paused. Why was he writing all this? He guessed he wanted Niswat to know that life is little more than suffering and darkness. No, wait, that wasn't it. What he really wanted to communicate was that he was a settled, stable person. She could see that countries shift boundaries, cities change their names, but his family history clearly showed that his people stayed put, worked hard, and achieved success. It dawned on him that, at some level, he was trying to impress his new friend.

He never dreamed he would be looking for a relationship online. His mind and his emotions were still trying to play catch-up. The quiet house was a constant reminder that after twenty-five happy years, his beloved Sophia was gone. Without her, he was beginning to understand, he was really and truly alone in the world.

Andriy hit *Send* and felt a sense of relief at having someone to chat with. He wasn't socially aware enough to realize that their daily "chats" were entirely one-sided. She would respond to his long missives with a question or two but generally didn't volunteer much information about herself and, instead, just seemed happy to hear his stories.

It wasn't entirely true that Andriy was alone and friendless. He thought of Dmitry from his university days. The two of them had kept in touch over the years, even though after graduation, Dmitry had taken a job 3,000 kilometers away in Odessa. Now that Andriy had begun talking to Niswat online, he felt empowered to take another step and reach out to his old friend.

"I'm sorry, it's been so long since I called."

"I heard about your wife's passing; I am sure it's been hard."

"Yes, it has."

"You should come visit me. We could go out on my yacht."

"You have a yacht?"

"Yeah, I'm doing pretty well. You should come!"

"Well . . . Okay. I will."

Andriy accepted his friend's invitation and flew to Odessa. He was surprised at how quickly they fell back into easy conversation. Relaxing with a glass of vodka, he commented, "Honestly, I'm surprised you have a yacht."

"Why's that?"

"Well, aren't yachts only for rich people?"

"And what makes you think I'm not rich?"

"Well, Dmitri, you're an engineer, and on your salary, I can't see how you can afford such an expensive hobby."

"I didn't say a *luxury* yacht."

"Even so, it must have cost a lot of money."

Dmitry smiled as he looked at his friend: medium height, short-cropped hair, eyes a little too close together. He had never really been handsome, never really stood out at all.

Andriy had inherited the family business back in Astana and enjoyed the superficial esteem that accompanies a reputable family name. At school, he had talked about his Mennonite roots, the importance of being a hard worker, the need to treat others with honesty, and the moral superiority of espousing nonviolence. But actually, the secret to Andriy's comfortable life had been the fact that he was from a wealthy family.

Dmitry, on the other hand, had grown up poor. He liked Andriy's ideas about pacifism, but nonviolence wasn't practical in real life; he was raised on the streets and still had the scars to prove it. He had always been ambitious, and with his limited options he had learned ways to make money that weren't necessarily 100% honest.

Looking at his friend, he realized he had always considered Andriy to be his superior: better looks, better grades, better family, better house. Now, he realized, they were equals in many ways. *In fact,* he mused, *I am probably Andriy's superior. Andriy had life handed to him on a platter while I've had to fight for everything I have. I've taken risks and fought (I'm still fighting!) for my place at the table, while his comfortable, perfect life, has, through lack of effort on his part, for many years, been on a gradual downward drift.*

"Andriy," he said at length trying to be encouraging, "you still have a lot going for you. You're wealthy, you're smart, you speak German, Russian, Kazakh, and English. The world is yours."

"Yes, I *am* wealthy. I'm in my fifties and in perfect health. I can buy anything I want. I can do anything I want. But nothing can bring my wife back."

As he said those words, Andriy realized something. The root, the problem, the reason for his malaise was *God*. His wife had been a kind, sweet person. She didn't deserve to die. She was barely fifty. It was unfair!

But shaking one's fist at the Almighty was terribly unfulfilling. For one thing, God is invisible. How do people even know God exists? Andriy was angry but he didn't want to waste his anger. He wanted a way to make sure the guilty party paid for the injustice he had suffered.

"It isn't fair, you know," Andriy suddenly blurted out. "If only there were some way to make a statement, to show how absurd our existence is. Nothing matters. We are born and we die."

"My friend," replied Dmitry, "your mind is affected by Sophia's passing. Your rage, what good does it do anyone?"

"You're right, I know. It's just that I feel so helpless. If there was a way to do it, I would show God I'm not afraid of Him."

"Well, you know as well as I do that God doesn't exist. Why bother worrying about him?"

"People *believe* God exists! That's the problem. If He did exist, my Sophia's death is all the proof I need to know that He doesn't."

Dmitry cocked his head in confusion. "You know that what you just said doesn't make any sense at all, right?"

After a moment, Andriy sighed. "I just want to do something, Dmitry. If God were here, I would poke Him in the eye. But it's impossible. There's no way to reach Him."

"What if I could help you, my friend?" Dmitry offered. "You want to poke God in the eye? Take that Bible there off the shelf."

"What?" Andriy asked, surprised. "You think if I burn a Bible, I'll feel better?"

"No. Open it and find Zechariah 2:8."

It took Andriy a while to find the book of Zechariah. Once he did, Dmitry said, "Read it out loud," and Andriy read,

> *"For thus says the Lord of hosts: 'He sent Me after glory, to the nations which plunder you; for he who touches you touches the apple of His eye.'"*

"You see, Andriy," Dmitry explained, "those are the words of the Jewish prophet Zechariah. He is saying that the Jews are the apple of God's eye. They are His most precious possession. If you want to get back at God, the best way to do it is to attack His chosen people. Poke them, and it will be as if you are poking God in the eye."

He paused for a few seconds, then continued, "If it were me, that is how I would strike God. If I could, I would bomb Jerusalem, the sacred city of the Jewish nation. In addition to striking the Jews, you would get the added benefit of making a statement to Christians and Muslims."

Dmitry added, "Jews gladly accept the money and security that Christian nations offer for the protection of their 'holy sites.' Then they turn around and charge visitors from those same Christian nations to see those sites. As for Muslims, there was a time when I admired them. They are willing to fight to see Islam rule the world. But I've concluded it will never happen; they're fighting a lost cause."

"Not only that," replied Andriy bitterly, "they're all butchers, pretending to be doctors. They said Sophia's tumor was very operable.

Not just operable, *very* operable. We went all the way to Berlin to see 'the best doctor.' But that surgeon, that surgeon was a Muslim.

"Religious people claim to be so concerned about everybody, but in reality, they're destroying everything. The Jews take our money through insurance and banking schemes. The Muslims are constantly in conflict, either among themselves or with others around them. And the Christians lack the courage to do anything about it."

Dmitry waited a few seconds, then said, "The place to hit is the Temple Mount. The Wailing Wall is the last remaining section of the site that Christians claim Jesus predicted would be destroyed because the Jews rejected Him. He said not one stone would be left standing on another. I've heard that some Jewish groups are planning the construction of a new museum called the Sacred Stones Museum, located right next to the Western Wall. Another attraction for which to charge visitors. So, Andriy, do *you* have the courage to do anything about it?"

"What can I do?" Andriy threw up his hands.

Dmitri smiled. "I have a friend. You asked me a little while ago how I can afford a yacht? I'll tell you. I have a side job, buying and selling things. Come on, I'll introduce you to a friend of mine."

Sitting with the old man, Yakiv, it was clear he was not long for this world. Dmitry had warned Andriy that Yakiv had terminal cancer, but even without being told, it was obvious. For one thing, Yakiv offered them vodka but didn't take any himself. For another, looking at his face, it was like the light had gone out of his eyes. And his voice. It was so quiet Andriy and Dmitri had to lean forward to hear.

"Yes, Andriy," he was saying. "Dmitry is right. I can help you. Now I am going to tell you something that I've never told anyone else. Did you know that at the time of the collapse of the Soviet Union, there were more than 12,000 tactical nuclear weapons stored in the former Soviet republics?"

He paused to take a breath. "Of course, there is no proof that any of those Soviet nuclear weapons have gone missing. But I assure you, it is less than 100% certain that all were fully accounted for in the 1990s during that time of chaos and transition. Back in those days, I had contacts in high places and access to large amounts of money that needed laundering. Anything was possible in the confusion during that time, and so it was, through considerable risk, I obtained a nuclear device. And more, I've kept its existence a secret."

Andriy looked from Dmitry to Yakiv. Dmitry asked, "Andriy, do you not understand what he's saying? You want to poke God in the eye? The place to do that is Jerusalem. And the way to do that is to leave the whole Temple Mount an uninhabitable crater for years to come. You want to make a statement? You want a way to express your grief? This is it. This is your opportunity."

Andriy slowly nodded in agreement, then he, Dmitry, and Yakiv sketched out a plan and agreed on a price.

Ch 13. Verethragna's Move

(Shadowlands, 10 months before the Fire)

But the prince of the kingdom of Persia withstood me twenty-one days; and behold, Michael, one of the chief princes, came to help me, for I had been left alone there with the kings of Persia.

Daniel 10:13

Qorin had successfully manipulated Verethragna, the Persian Prince, in the past, so he felt it was worth his while to look for a chance to try reestablishing their relationship. Hoping for just the right moment, he found himself stalking the *Tsel* on a lonely path in the dark. He followed along until Verethragna suddenly slowed and cautiously approached an oasis in the middle of a desert in the Shadowlands. Following behind, Qorin watched as his prey dipped out of sight over a sand dune. He waited a few seconds, then got down on his belly to peek over the dune.

"Has anyone seen the Prince of Palestine?"[19] he heard Verethragna ask. That must have been the Prince of Persia's awkward way of announcing his presence to the three other *Tselim* standing by a fire in

---

19. Ghaiasha is the *Tsel* prince over the principality of Palestine

a hollow. The dunes surrounding them not only concealed the small fire around which they stood but also provided some shelter from the gusts of wind. Qorin realized this was a secret meeting to which neither he nor his quarry had been invited.

He watched as Verethragna turned his head, his eyes moving from Nabu,[20] to Ptah,[21] to Hubal,[22] trying to read the scene. It was obvious they had been deep in conversation, otherwise they would have heard him approaching; but now, no one answered.

Verethragna broke the awkward silence by saying, "So what are we going to do about the Prince of Palestine?" Even though he couldn't have known if that was indeed the topic of conversation, it was a clever guess. Qorin realized the outsider's query had hit the mark when the other *Tselim* all seemed to relax a bit.

Nabu, who considered himself to be the leader, decided to speak for the group. "We were just discussing that very question. What do you suggest?"

At that moment, the blowing sand seemed to put out the fire. Qorin closed his eyes to protect them from the grit, and when he opened them, he saw the smoldering half-hearted blaze come back to life. The group huddled close as if the fire offered some warmth. All eyes were on Verethragna who nodded, indicating he was ready to share his advice.

Qorin knew the Persian was not the sharpest tool in the Shadowlands' shed, but what he lacked in wits he more than made up for in guile and craftiness. Carefully choosing his words, he said, "Well, after hearing about Lord Deywós' plan, I think we need to act now and work together." Qorin knew he himself had not been made privy to Deywós' plan, and he was relatively certain that Verethragna hadn't either, but again the clever guess did the trick. At his answer, the others seemed to accept his presence in their meeting.

---

20. Nabu is the *Tsel* prince over the principality of Babylon
21. Ptah is the *Tsel* prince over the principality of Egypt
22. Hubal is the *Tsel* prince over the principality of Arabia

"Ptah was just suggesting that very thing," remarked Hubal. Then he added, "I wasn't aware," here he seemed to look at Verethragna, "that *you* had been briefed on this mission."

Qorin thought Hubal might be looking right at Verethragna, but then again, he couldn't be sure. Hubal's heavy eyelids concealed so much that, even when standing right in front of him, it was hard to know where he was looking. Verethragna nodded "yes" in response to Hubal's question posed as a statement.

Okay, Qorin thought. *So, Verethragna* is *bluffing. And he doesn't want to risk revealing it by elaborating. Clever!*

"Anyway," Nabu spoke up authoritatively, "we need to finish this meeting. We don't have much time before someone *else* happens by." As he said those words, the proud *Tsel* looked over at Verethragna in a way that he hoped would communicate condescension. In reality, his effort to cast a withering glance at his fellow *Tsel* came across as something akin to a grimace, not unlike the snarl of an animal caught in a trap.

After a pause, Nabu continued, "As Hubal was saying, our comrade in the Resistance is at present inactive, confined for the moment in the body of this young Jewish boy. That leaves the Principality of Palestine in a precarious position. Indeed, his absence makes this a perilous time for us all. If we are going to act, it must be now. I think, for the good of all involved, that we should intervene in this situation. The fact is that the Enemy could make dangerous advances while the Principality sits unprotected. I propose we divide up the territory amongst ourselves as a sort of protectorate."

Qorin closed his eyes again as a gust of wind blew sand everywhere.

He heard Verethragna's voice, "Well, I for one . . ." Opening his eyes, Qorin found that the other *Tselim* had all vanished. Unauthorized meetings were, after all, forbidden, and the *Tselim* must have gotten spooked. Verethragna, who undoubtedly had been relishing the thought of sharing some "great" insight, was now turning his head this way and that, looking for the others. Qorin wondered if Verethragna realized how foolish he looked, standing alone in the middle of the desert with his right arm raised, index finger extended as if making a point.

RIB

Qorin waited for a few moments as he watched Verethragna look around in bewilderment. Then, shaking off sand as he stood up, he left his hiding place and descended a few steps down the dune toward Verethragna.

"Oh, it's you, is it?" said the Persian with a sneer as he lowered his arm. Qorin, however, was all politeness. "I am so sorry, my Prince, I seem to have disturbed you."

"Not at all, I was just talking with my friends." Then remembering no one else was around, he added, "They just left."

"Of course. Well, I didn't mean to interrupt. It's just . . ." Qorin paused. "You see, I had an idea. I'm very sorry the intel I received from Baghdad so long ago turned out to be faulty; really, I am. Is there anything I can do to help with this present situation with the Prince of Palestine?"

Verethragna turned, "You know?"

"Of course. My intel isn't always bad. What do you say we join forces? Strength in numbers and all that?" Qorin thought he could see the prince beginning to soften, but at the same time, knowing it was wise to proceed slowly, he added, "Think about it, will you?" and politely withdrew.

The next day, he went to ask the Persian Prince what he thought of the offer to work together. But when he saw him with none other than Nabu, the Prince of Babylon, he turned to wander off unnoticed.

Verethragna, however, had seen him and loudly invited him to come join them.

"Speak of the Oppressor!" exclaimed Nabu as Qorin approached.

"And he shall appear," Verethragna answered with a smirk, lifting his wing to give Nabu a "high five." Nabu stared at the Persian, leaving him hanging until Verethragna awkwardly lowered his wing.

Qorin turned again to leave, but Verethragna, wiping the smirk off his face, called after him, "Do stay. It's true; we were just talking about you. This is good timing."

With an effort at self-control, Qorin turned again to face them, keeping his distance as the Persian continued, this time speaking to his Babylonian counterpart, "I have, of course, not forgotten what the Prince of Rome did to us." Here, he spat on the ground in Qorin's direction. "The affrontery! To present that simple boy to us as if he were the Mahdi, the chosen one! So great was my desire to harness the power of the one who has been hidden from humanity for centuries that I fell for the Roman Prince's trick! But that was years ago, and I wonder if we shouldn't let bygones be bygones, you know? It might be a mistake for us not to work together in our present situation to our mutual benefit."

"And what plan, pray tell, did you and Qorin devise that might accomplish this?"

Gaining courage at these words, Verethragna continued. "What if, for example, we take advantage of the Prince of Palestine's situation and confront the Jewish question?"

Nabu shot a look of rebuke at Verethragna, who calmed him, saying, "Don't worry, he already knows about the Prince of Palestine."

The Prince of Babylon did not appear convinced, but after a few moments said, "You were saying something? What is it you propose?"

"Well," the Persian explained, "I'm concerned about how successful the Jews have become. I think it might help us to destroy—or, at least, greatly damage—Israel in order to bring about the prophecies concerning the Mahdi."

"Turn to the side, so I can see your profile," Nabu ordered. As Verethragna did so, Nabu studied him for a moment, then remarked as if to himself, "Certainly not much gravitas in that profile. I sometimes wonder if there is even one functioning brain cell under that mop he calls hair."

Qorin glanced at Verethragna, who was biting his tongue and at the same time trying to smile pleasantly as Nabu continued, as if to himself, "I too was thinking about Israel. Not in terms of the Mahdi; that, of course, is out of the question. Fool me twice and all that."

He continued, "However, it is evident that the battle for the high places in the principality of Palestine is indeed being lost even as we watch." Then, talking quietly, as if to himself, he muttered, "Right before our eyes," as he wandered off, seemingly unaware that Verethragna and Qorin were even there.

Ch 14. The Straight Way

(Jerusalem, 10 months before the Fire)

Mercy and truth have met together;
Righteousness and peace have kissed.

Psalm 85:10

An elderly man walked slowly but with purpose along a crowded street in central Jerusalem, while a young man followed a short distance behind. The youth had noticed the man's gray hair and his uncertain gait, and his heart had begun to race with equal measures of fear and hope. He was looking for an easy mark and had heard that, in terms of pickpocketing, the older, the better. A well-dressed old woman out by herself would have been ideal, but it was rare to find such an easy target.

The young man considered the gray-haired man a short distance ahead of him. He approached him from behind, but at the last moment slowed down and let him go, noticing that the tall, thin man had what looked like sturdy companions on either side of him.

Khaled sighed. He knew he should be in school right now but he needed cash. Omar had given him an ultimatum: show me the money, or the deal is off.

He had considered asking his uncle for a loan but immediately dismissed the thought since he knew he would have to explain what the money was for. He could hear his uncle's voice, "Two thousand shekels for what?! A scooter? If *I* can walk, *you* can walk. Besides, scooters are dangerous. Not only that, you've got no place to keep one."

Khaled thought, *Omar is willing to sell me the scooter and the only problem is how to come up with the money quickly.* He could already picture himself riding around town, an independent man, going wherever he wanted whenever he wanted.

He continued walking, keeping his eyes open, looking for an opportunity. Well-dressed with nicely trimmed hair and dark features, no one edged away from him or stared at him. He saw himself in the reflection of a storefront window as he passed by. Straightening his shoulders a bit, he had to admit he was not too unpleasant to look at.

A sudden cry of surprise, followed by the sound of metal bending and plastic breaking, made him turn toward the street. A scooter lay on its side, its rear wheel still spinning. Next to it sprawled a groaning young man. The van's driver and passenger had quickly jumped out and were vehemently insisting, "He came out of nowhere! There was no time to brake!" Horns began to honk, as drivers farther back, not understanding the cause of the delay, grew impatient. A crowd was gathering, and all eyes were on the young man moaning on the concrete.

The driver was holding his wife, who looked unsteady. Khaled glanced inside the open van door and saw his opportunity. In a flash, he reached into the vehicle and grabbed the purse sitting on the passenger seat. He already had his explanation ready: "I was going to give it to the woman since she looked like she was about to faint." The small purse slipped easily into his pants. He untucked his shirt to hide the bulge and started walking.

Just a few steps in front of Khaled, when Nehemyah Friedenthal heard the crash, he had a very different reaction. His attention turned to the injured person lying in the street, his face reflecting the compassion he felt in his soul.

Nehemyah's six-foot three, two-hundred-and-twenty-pound companion, Moshe Ben Abel, however, after a quick glance at the street, began to look elsewhere. As a bodyguard, his friend's safety was paramount, and his first thought was to ensure this "accident" wasn't some kind of planned diversion. While everyone else turned to see the source of the commotion in the street, he instinctively scanned the surrounding area, alert for anything that might be out of place. Trained to expect the unexpected, his eye caught Khaled's quick movement into the van. Watching carefully, he then saw the boy stuff the purse under his shirt.

Assured that Nehemyah, his primary responsibility, was not in any danger, he bent over to Shmuel and said, "Wait here with the rabbi; I have to check on something." When Shmuel nodded agreement, he took off, walking briskly down the sidewalk, keeping his eye on the kid.

At forty-six he was still in top physical shape. If necessary, he knew he could run the punk down, but for now he decided to follow at a quick walk. As the boy slowed down and stepped into a restaurant, Moshe also slowed his pace and entered casually.

He took several seconds to look around, evaluating the situation and determining it wasn't a trap. Then he made toward the kitchen, out of sight of the diners, and saw that the bathroom door was closed. Glancing back to make sure that no one was watching, he put his shoulder into the door. The flimsy latch broke, and the door flew open.

Moshe had the ability to intimidate just about anyone, and the boy, with a shocked look on his face and the purse still in his hand, didn't put up any resistance. Phoning Shmuel, Moshe said, "I have an interesting situation. Can you bring the rabbi here to Reuven's restaurant just around the corner?"

Nehemyah, Moshe, Shmuel, and Khaled sat at a table. There was food in front of them but only Moshe was eating. After a bite he said, "So, you see the situation, sir?"

Nehemyah nodded. "You did a good thing, asking Shmuel to bring me, Moshe."

"Seems pretty straightforward to me, sir."

Nehemyah spoke slowly and deliberately, "Things are rarely as straightforward as they seem."

Khaled was half-listening, considering his options. Now that the initial shock had passed, he was trying to plot his next move. If this were a Palestinian place, he might try yelling for help in Arabic, "Oh, believers, for the love of God, help me!" Very likely half a dozen young men who seemed to be intent on nothing more than sitting around smoking and talking would suddenly jump up, recognize that a fellow Muslim was in danger, and provide just enough interference to allow Khaled to slip out of the restaurant.

But Khaled realized that this situation was going to require a different plan, so with a tone that he hoped conveyed honesty he said, "I found the purse and was just trying to see who it belonged to so I could return it."

Nehemyah looked at Moshe, who sat shaking his head. "Sorry, son," said Nehemyah, "Moshe saw the whole thing."

Moshe offered, "Ravi,[23] it seems like we are wasting our time here. Let's call the police and be done with him."

"My dear Moshe, time is the most precious gift our Lord has given us. When we talk of the blessing of life, we are talking about our allotted number of moments. That is why your namesake in his Psalm says, 'So teach *us* to number our days, that we may gain a heart of wisdom.'[24] No, my friend, we are not wasting time here. We are trying to gain a heart of wisdom."

Turning to Khaled, he said, "My son, God knows your heart. I don't think spending time in jail will help you grow up to be a responsible person. Have you ever been in jail?"

Khaled shook his head, "No, sir."

Nehemyah extended his hand to the boy. Khaled didn't want to be rude, so he cautiously reciprocated. Nehemyah grasped the boy's hand firmly but kindly and waited. When Khaled eventually returned his gaze, he said, "I am Nehemyah Friedenthal. I know what it's like to be in jail. It is most definitely not a pleasant experience. I would not wish that on anyone."

Releasing Khaled's hand, he held up the purse. "Nothing is missing from this. After we finish eating, my friends will take it to the police so it can be returned to its rightful owner. For your part, you are welcome to stay and eat with us or you may go on your way."

When Khaled got up and left without a word, Shmuel spoke up. "Ravi, I'm not sure I understand what just happened."

Nehemyah closed his eyes and began to recite Psalm 85 in Hebrew as a Jewish cantor might. In the English it says:

> *Lord, You have been favorable to Your land;*
> *You have brought back the captivity of Jacob.*
> **2** *You have forgiven the iniquity of Your people;*
> *You have covered all their sin. Selah*

---

23. *Ravi* is a Hebrew word for a Jewish religious teacher, like the English word *rabbi*
24. Psalm 90:12

3 You have taken away all Your wrath;
You have turned from the fierceness of Your anger.
4 Restore us, O God of our salvation,
And cause Your anger toward us to cease.
5 Will You be angry with us forever?
Will You prolong Your anger to all generations?
6 Will You not revive us again,
That Your people may rejoice in You?
7 Show us Your mercy, Lord,
And grant us Your salvation.
8 I will hear what God the Lord will speak,
For He will speak peace
To His people and to His saints;
But let them not turn back to folly.
9 Surely His salvation is near to those who fear Him,
That glory may dwell in our land.
10 Mercy and truth have met together;
Righteousness and peace have kissed.
11 Truth shall spring out of the earth,
And righteousness shall look down from heaven.
12 Yes, the Lord will give what is good;
And our land will yield its increase.
13 Righteousness will go before Him,
And shall make His footsteps our pathway.[25]

Nehemyah smiled, first at Moshe, then at Shmuel. "My friends, this Psalm is a prayer of entreaty to the Almighty for our Land.[26] We ask God to turn away His anger from us and show us mercy. But notice what verse ten says, 'Mercy and truth have met together; Righteousness and peace have kissed.'"

---

25. Psalm 85:1–13

26. "Land" is capitalized because the Hebrew word *HaAretz* refers to "the Land," that is, the biblical promised land

He continued, "I long for righteousness and peace to coexist, *to kiss* as it were. We have plenty of people who focus only on truth, who are quick to point out what is right. And we have plenty who call for mercy and peace with no respect for following the Torah. What is needed is balance, a way to embrace both righteousness and mercy."

Moshe countered, "But letting him go, he will just have another opportunity to steal."

"Maybe, maybe not. This Psalm ends with the words, 'Righteousness will go before Him, and shall make His footsteps our pathway.' That is what we will pray for Khaled. You may not know it, but there are very similar words in the opening sura of his holy book, the Quran:

> *Show us the straight way,*
> *The way of those on whom Thou hast bestowed Thy Grace,*
> *Those whose (portion) is not wrath, and who go not astray.*[27]

Nehemyah continued, "Imagine this young man in his prayers every day asking God to show him the right way. What if our chance meeting today is God's way to answer that prayer?"[28]

27. From the Fatihah, the opening sura (chapter) of the Holy Quran, translation by A. Yusuf Ali
28. Inspired by a quote in the dedication page of *Uncharted Mission: Going to the Final Frontiers* by D. C. Keane

Ch 15. Prison

(Jerusalem, 10 months before the Fire)

First they came for the Communists,
and I did not speak out—
because I was not a communist.
Then they came for the trade unionists,
and I did not speak out—
because I was not a trade unionist.
Then they came for the Jews,
and I did not speak out—
because I was not a Jew.
Then they came for me—
and there was no one left to speak for me.

Martin Niemöller,
quoted in *Holocaust Encyclopedia*

When Khaled got home, he didn't immediately notice the secret policemen standing in the living room. No sooner had he stepped in the door than his uncle met him with a shove that sent him reeling against the wall. At first, he supposed the beating was for skipping school. Then he saw the Israeli officers.

"Khaled, where is the purse? If nothing is missing, these men have assured me they will ask the judge for leniency. But if not . . . ."

"Uncle, please, I can explain everything. I found the purse and I was scared. I didn't know what to do. I was afraid to go to the police because they might think I'd stolen it. I saw a kind-looking Jewish man who promised to take it to the police for me. As God is my witness, that is the truth."

"Liar! They've shown me surveillance footage of you taking the purse and walking away from the scene."

Just then a police officer's cell phone buzzed. He listened for a moment, then covered the phone and eyed Khaled. "Did you get the name of the man you gave the purse to?"

"Yes, it was Nehemyah. I don't remember his last name."

"Let's go to the police station."

It was Moshe, not Nehemyah, who met Khaled and his uncle at the police station. At first, the authorities seemed skeptical, but they had the purse and Moshe's signed statement. Khaled was free to leave. Outside on the sidewalk, Khaled's uncle spat on him and walked away. Khaled himself turned to go, but Moshe grabbed his arm.

"Not so fast."

"What?"

"Honestly, I don't know what the rabbi sees in you. He told me to tell the police that you gave us the purse to turn over to them. Now he wants to talk with you. So, either you come with me, or I might suddenly remember some details that I left out of my official statement . . . if you catch my meaning."

Khaled wasn't sure what to expect as he got on the city bus with Moshe. He envisioned a one-on-one meeting with Nehemyah, which would include a sermon about not stealing. Instead, he found himself in a lecture hall seated next to Moshe, along with about two hundred others who had gathered to listen to Nehemyah's testimony.

Ninety-year-old Nehemyah moved slowly and carefully to the podium. Then, in a voice stronger and clearer than expected from a man of his age, he began, "Good evening. My name is Nehemyah Friedenthal. I was born Ludvik Schlachtberg, in Zaolzie, along the Czech–Polish border. Thank you for coming here and listening to my story of God's love and redemption."

He took a drink of water and continued, "I was raised in a middle-class, mostly secular Jewish home. My family had come from the German-speaking part of the Austro–Hungarian Empire, but over time they began to think of themselves as more Polish than German or even Jewish. Austrian control gave way to Czechoslovakian control in 1920. Then, in 1938, when Britain and France negotiated the deal handing over the *Sudetenland* to Germany, Zaolzie became part of Poland again—but only briefly.

"Less than a year later, Nazi tanks rolled in, and our land became part of the Military District of Upper Silesia, or *Oberschlesien.* My family could pass as Germans and so we, along with many others, signed the *Volksliste*, declaring our German ancestry. Identifying as part of the Greater Germany allowed privileges such as better food, clothes, and housing. As *Volksdeutsche*, or ethnic Germans, we weren't given citizenship, but we did enjoy a much higher status than Poles, who, of course, had a much higher status, than Jews.

"However, there was a hidden cost in signing the *Volksliste.* Many of the *Volksdeutsche* were sent back as laborers to Germany, where they underwent "racial assessment." Those found to have made false claims about their German heritage were sent to concentration camps or killed. My older brothers were sent to Germany, and I never heard from them again. But I was too young to be sent off, so life remained fairly normal for me until my Jewish roots were discovered and I was sent to the concentration camp in Dachau.

"Oh, the horrors I saw there! The depths of human depravity! I hadn't been a very religious boy growing up, but in the concentration camp, I cried out to God, asking Him, 'Why? Why are you allowing this? How can you allow Your chosen people to suffer like this?'

"The prophet Jeremiah, who had himself been imprisoned unjustly, expressed my thoughts quite well when he said:

> *Righteous are You, O Lord, when I plead with You;*
> *Yet let me talk with You about Your judgments.*
> *Why does the way of the wicked prosper?*
> *Why are those happy who deal so treacherously?*[29]

"I asked God every day to rescue me, yet it seemed all I heard was silence from heaven. But I know now that He did hear me. I didn't realize it at the time, but His answer came later that year in the form of a group of "special status" prisoners sent to Dachau, including a pastor named Martin Niemöller.

"The Dachau guards made me a kind of servant for Herr Niemöller, who was housed with the other VIPs—priests, pastors, and even diplomats. I'd always had a gift for languages, and I found I could help these special prisoners communicate with one another and with the guards. At first, I despised those men and was angry that the Nazis gave them preferential treatment. But through them, and especially through Herr Niemöller, God began to change me.

"On Christmas Eve, 1944, Herr Niemöller was given permission to conduct a religious service. I wasn't really supposed to be there. I'd been sent into their improvised meeting room on a quick errand. But when I heard the words that he was speaking, my heart was gripped. I felt unable to walk away. I believe that God had me walk into the room at that time, and miraculously the guards allowed me to stay.

29. Jeremiah 12:1

"Herr Niemöller, who was a German, was speaking to men from the Netherlands, Britain, and Norway. And, to my astonishment, he was apologizing for his part in the Nazi atrocities.

"He said that as a pastor in those troubled times in Germany, he had initially supported Hitler and the Nazi movement as a way to help his country out of its serious economic and societal problems. But later, it became clear to him that he could not serve both Jesus and Hitler. When he refused to comply with all their demands, the Nazis had him arrested, thrown in jail, and sent to the concentration camp at Dachau.

"There, as a prisoner, he had the opportunity of speaking to other prisoners about the love of God for all mankind. He had come to understand that God's love crosses national boundaries and is not limited to one religion or one race. Then he said, 'We have to stand up for one another!' I remember how in tears he sobbed, 'First they came for the Communists, and I did not speak out—because I was not a communist. Then they came for the trade unionists, and I did not speak out—because I was not a trade unionist. Then they came for the Jews, and I did not speak out—because I was not a Jew. Then they came for me—and there was no one left to speak for me.'

"When I heard Herr Niemöller mention his failure to speak up for the Jews, suddenly a change began in my heart. My situation didn't change in that moment, but somehow when he put into words the evil that had been done to me, I felt I was able to take my first steps toward a new life."

Ch 16. Freedom

(Jerusalem, 10 months before the Fire)

He who saves one life saves the world entire.

Yiddish proverb

Nehemyah motioned for a chair and then sat down as he continued his talk, "What can I tell you about Dachau? I have one word: *Death*. I saw so many die. One month, typhus swept through the camp, killing thousands. The next month, winter cold killed just as many.

"It wasn't merely that people were dying. It was the needless, thoughtless death. Not the death that comes with one's last breath, but the death that comes while one is still breathing. You see, we had lost all hope, all sense of humanity. Treated as worthless, we began to act like animals.

"You may have seen the movie *Schindler's List*. Maybe you remember the quote, 'He who saves one life saves the world entire.' That wisdom from the Talmud was applied to Schindler, who helped over a thousand Jews escape death in the concentration camp. Let me be clear: helping a fellow human live longer on this earth is indeed noble, but it is not the highest good. A long life is wonderful. And saving a life is, of course, praiseworthy.

"But you see, saving a life ultimately has to do with *eternal* life. And eternal life isn't just a longer life. It's a different kind of life. A life that can start right here and now, before we breathe our final breath. In Dachau, in the midst of hell, I discovered eternal life. How is that possible, you ask?

"The irony is that God used a German, a former Nazi sympathizer, to help rescue me from the horrors of Dachau. Not 'rescue' in the way Schindler helped people *escape* their circumstances. Niemöller helped me see that God was with me *in* my circumstances. He helped me see that true happiness does not depend on the circumstances around me.

"I took a hard look at what I had become. Food was scarce in the concentration camp, but rather than attending to the needs of others, I'd begun fighting with those weaker than myself to ensure I got my share.

"That moment of introspection led me to remember times even before Dachau when I did things I was ashamed of. I remembered the time I stole from a store for no good reason and then lied about it to my parents. I'd always thought of myself as a good person, but at that moment I began to feel horrible and guilty.

"Niemöller said, 'Eternal life is to know God, the only true God, and the savior He sent, Jesus Christ.'[30] He said that God wants to be with us, not because we are perfect but simply because He loves us.

"I know that for some of you, the biblical God is an outdated notion. For others of you, the idea that the prophesies spoken to our forefathers were fulfilled two thousand years ago is preposterous. My purpose is not to convince you that God exists or that Jesus is the Messiah. My testimony is that I experienced peace and hope that day in prison when I said 'yes' to Jesus. That day I knew that I could have *real* life. That day I realized that a happy life does not depend on

30. From John 17:3

happy circumstances. That day did not mark the end of my troubles by any means, but it was the beginning of my new life.

"A few months later, in the spring of 1945, we could sense change was coming. We didn't hear it directly, but we could sense Germany was losing the war. And then, one day American soldiers suddenly arrived at the camp and the German lieutenant surrendered! We were free!

"The Germans had been desperately trying for weeks to destroy the evidence of what they had been doing in Dachau, but they failed. It was all around them—more than 30,000 prisoners so weak and sick we couldn't even walk.

"Not to mention the dead. We could see horror in the faces of the American soldiers at the unspeakable evil before them. Then their horror was replaced by anger: How could anyone treat their fellow humans this way?

"The soldiers forced those German guards to dig graves to bury the dead, and even conscripted civilians from the local village—many of whom were complicit in the atrocities—to help in the task. They wanted the local people to see with their own eyes what had been happening right there in their town and to begin the long road of restitution.

"After that, we were taken to a camp for displaced persons, where the first priority was improving our health. Eventually, the administrators began the complicated process of trying to sort out our *repatriation,* that is, getting us back to our homes.

"I told them I was a German–Polish Jew from Zaolzie. I didn't know if my home was still in German *Oberschlesien* or if it was now part of Czechoslovakia or maybe even in Poland again. They took down my name, as well as the names of as many relatives as I could think of, and months later the camp manager called me in to give me the news." Here Nehemyah lifted his right hand and began pointing to his fingers, one by one, as he mentioned each piece of bad news.

"First, my homeland had been given back to Czechoslovakia, meaning I would be considered a foreigner should I return there. Second, no one had been able to contact any of my relatives, who were all presumed to be dead. Third, not only my family but nearly all the Jews in the entire city of Zaolzie had apparently perished in the war. Fourth, the only citizenship available to me now was German, and Germans, even those whose families had lived in the region for centuries, were being expelled in retaliation for the war. Fifth, the Soviet Union had emerged as the dominant power in the area, and claiming that Czechoslovakia was full of Nazi conspirators, Russia sought war reparations by annexing neighboring territory and squeezing the life out of its citizens.

"There isn't time to tell you my whole journey this evening, but I want you to know the most important part. I arrived in Dachau desperate and without hope, and I left there convinced that my hope for a bright future was in *Yeshua Ha Mashiach*."[31]

Normally, Khaled would have had no interest in what Jews call the Holocaust. In his culture, it was common knowledge that the accounts of Jewish suffering in World War II were highly exaggerated, and another "Zionist lie." Yet he had stayed for the whole talk, not just because he was afraid of what Moshe might do if he tried to get up and leave, but because Nehemyah's story stirred something in his heart.

Lost in thought, Khaled was reviewing the conversation in the restaurant earlier that morning. When Nehemyah had mentioned that jail was not a pleasant experience, Khaled had had no idea that the old man spoke from such graphic personal experience. He was still considering this when he looked up and saw Nehemyah right there by his chair, extending his hand in greeting.

"I am glad you have come, my young friend. I hope I did not bore you too much with my talk."

---

31. Hebrew: Jesus the Christ

"Not at all. I am interested in hearing more about your story."

"Very good. Can you come again on Wednesday?"

"*In sha Allah*.[32] I mean, yes, I will plan on that."

32. Arabic: "God willing"

Ch 17. Kenan Makes Contact

(Shadowlands, 10 months before the Fire)

Then I saw another beast coming out of the earth and he had two horns like a lamb and spoke like a dragon.

Revelation 13:11

The Prince of Persia, his long hair cascading over his shoulders and covering the top of his wings, tried to look like he was standing by the path with nothing to do. But, actually, he was waiting for this moment. As Nabu, the erudite Prince of Babylon, passed by, Verethragna said nonchalantly, "You'll never guess who I just saw."

Nabu stopped to scowl at him. "Let me see. Ghaiasha, the Prince of Palestine?"

Just then, a slow walking *Tsel* came wandering up the path. Verethragna waited for what seemed like an eternity until the *Tsel* was safely around the corner before asking, "How did you know?"

"Maybe because half of the Shadowlands is talking about him."

"Well, anyway, I was there. I knew about it first," boasted the Persian Prince.

"And what exactly is the *it*, to which you are referring?"

"The fact that the Prince of Palestine, in his human form, contacted us. He knows who he is. After ten earthly years, he has remembered his *Tsel* identity!"

"Well, I happen to know that he doesn't know exactly who he is. He thinks he is an exceptionally intelligent Jewish boy and calls himself Kenan."

"Kenan?!" Verethragna exclaimed. "I didn't know that. Isn't that a name straight from the Oppressor's book?"

"Yes, Kenan was an ancestor of Noah. But it's better than the name his adoptive father gave him: *Kenaniah.* He's already shown that he has enough sense to at least get rid of the letters *IAH* that refer to the Oppressor's name. Actually, I think 'Kenan' fits him. It sounds similar to the way many humans pronounce '*Canaan*'— and anything that harkens back to the days when the Canaanites were a force to be reckoned with is certainly a win."

"So, has he renounced the Jewish faith?"

"We don't know yet," Nabu said, then added, as if he were now the final authority on the subject, "It's too early to be sure."

Verethragna opined, "Do you remember when we first learned that he had been found by that orthodox Rabbi Shlomo, who was raising him as his own? We all thought, *What a catastrophe! A* Tsel *being raised by a Hasidic Jew!?* But it looks like things are turning out okay."

"Yes, Lord Deywós is a clever one! Who knows if this was his plan all along or if our leader is just making the best of a bad situation? In any case, we certainly have reason for optimism now."

"I should say! But what did you mean when you said the Prince of Palestine doesn't really know who he is?"

Nabu puffed out his chest, answering as if he were an expert in these matters, "He's grown up from an infant. That's the way human life normally works. When Lord Deywós sent him to Earth, he coerced him into taking that form. Do you realize how ignorant and helpless human babies are?"

"Yes, Nabu. Of course, I know. But he won't stay like that forever, will he? I mean, he's not like that idiot Abdowan who messed around with a human woman and lost his immortality and his access to most of the *Olam* in one fell swoop."

Nabu stared for a while at the Persian Prince's cruel dark face before commenting, "Must I remind you, my dear despicable Prince, that our comrade was merely following the explicit directions of Lord Deywós? So have a care. Yes, he was an idiot; not for obeying Deywós' orders, but for associating with that gasbag Qorin."

The Persian responded, "Irregardlessly, I can assure you that Abdowan will receive no help or protection from me."

"Nor from me," replied Nabu, settling the matter, before adding, "By the way, I absolutely forbid you to ever again say *'irregardlessly'* in my presence. It's not even a real word. I fear your greatest power is to lower the IQ of everyone around you just by being present. You know I was just walking by, minding my own business, when you stopped me."

"Yes, my princely know-it-all. But back to the Prince of Palestine, he is obviously aging in his human body. Now that he's mortal he will eventually die, right?"

"No," replied Nabu, as if exasperated but quietly reveling in the fact that he was the more informed of the two. "He's not mortal. The Oppressor doesn't inflict that level of punishment on us for temporarily taking on a human body. His own Eloha[33] servants have done that. He sent His own Son into their realm to be born as a human infant, and from what I understand he has returned to the Oppressor's side just as immortal as he ever was."

Verethragna thought for a moment. "So, Ghaiasha, I mean, Kenan still has access to the whole *Olam*? He could come back to us whenever he wants?"

33. *Eloha* is a Hebrew word that can refer to the Most High God, El-Elyon, as well as other supernatural beings

"Theoretically, yes. But remember, he's a child. And what's more, even as he grows, he will still have a limited human mind. He'll have to learn, as a human, how to enter the spirit realms. But it appears he has now begun that process."

"Not just *appears.* I was there in Saparon's office. We heard a noise and went to look. A shadowy form was browsing the books, looking at the titles. I saw him and he said, 'Hello? Who is this?' I responded, 'It's Verethragna, do you remember me?' Then he was gone."

"Yes, but again, he didn't know who you were, or that he had previously known you. He only knew that he was communicating with what he recognized as powerful spirits. He reached out and received an answer. I'm sure he didn't understand everything that happened, but from what I hear, he liked it, and I suspect that now he has a craving for more."

"And what of our plans to teach Qorin a lesson? That imbecile knew the boy he was protecting in Iraq wasn't the Guided One, yet he made us believe he was. Do you think Ghaiasha will still remember that? I mean, after his Kenan-self has grown up?"

"I expect so. I think this experience will be good for him. I expect he'll come out the other side a stronger *Tsel.*"

"That should be easy enough," retorted Verethragna. "Before he departed for his current mission, it was hard to imagine a weaker *Tsel* prince. He was constantly talking about having to play second fiddle and about the dangers of seeking power, reminding everyone about the demise of both Bel-Marduk[34] and Melqart."[35]

"Yes, it was annoying to hear the Prince of Palestine quoting verbatim from the Oppressor's book."

"You mean like this?" Verethragna asked, and began in a mocking cadence:

---

34. Bel-Marduk is the former *Tsel* prince over the principality of Babylon
35. Melqart, also known as Hercules, is the former *Tsel* prince over the principality of Tyre

You were the seal of perfection,
Full of wisdom and perfect in beauty.
You were in Eden, the garden of God;[36]

Nabu plugged his ears and turned away, but Verethragna continued even louder:

You were the anointed cherub who covers
I established you;
You were on the holy mountain of God;
You walked back and forth in the midst of fiery stones.
You were perfect in your ways from the day you were created,
Till iniquity was found in you.[37]

Nabu shouted, "Enough! Stop that!"

Verethragna feigned surprise, "What? You don't want to hear about Melqart being driven from the mount of God, thrown to the earth, and reduced to ashes on the ground?"

"No! Of course, I don't, you fool! I don't need you to recite the Oppressor's version of that horrible event."

"Why? Does it remind you of Bel-Marduk?"

"Well, yes, as a matter of fact, it does," Nabu replied pensively. "My mentor Marduk's demise was indeed not unlike Melqart's. Both came to their end at the hand of the Oppressor, and both were struck down while minding their own business: Marduk on a friendly visit to the Principality of Palestine, and Melqart while engaged with affairs of his own principality in Tyre, a short distance to the North."

Verethragna, whose thought processes could never resist a rabbit trail, said, "Good old Melqart, he always seemed to have so much going for him! Although I always preferred his Greek name, Herakles."

36. From Ezekiel 28:12–13
37. Ezekiel 28:14–15

Nabu shook his head to clear away the annoyance he felt at this non sequitur. *Trying to explain to Verethragna the importance of the Prince of Palestine's role in the Resistance was like talking to a box of rocks,* he thought. *Or worse. At least, stones don't reply with inane comments.*

Bravely, he resumed his scholarly attitude. "Yes, Verethragna, Melqart's fame did travel to all the Phoenician colonies throughout the Mediterranean. But the Romans also contributed to his fame. They called the two stone pillars at the Strait of Gibraltar 'The Pillars of Hercules' and inscribed on them the words *Non Plus Ultra*[38] to warn sailors that they had reached the edge of the known civilized world."

Verethragna commented, "I still like his Greek name better."

Nabu squeezed his eyes shut in a valiant effort to block out the Persian's comment. *Does it matter what name people use to refer to Melqart? Truly, this* Tsel *has a gift for focusing on the most unimportant details possible.*

Meanwhile, Verethragna was continuing, "I'm not saying that I like the Greeks, but . . ."

"So really . . ." Nabu interrupted, cutting off the Persian prince and returning to the topic at hand, "it's obvious why our esteemed Palestinian Prince has always taken a subordinate role. It was his only way forward if he wanted to survive. Even Lord Deywós himself required compromises from him."

"What do you mean? What compromises?"

"Well, his very name and location actually. You know the Prince of Palestine began his reign as Shamash,[39] and many of the humans near Babylon worshipped him as the sun god. But when the Oppressor established His "Land of Promise" in the principality of Palestine, Lord Deywós insisted that he relocate from Babylon to the valley along the Jordan River and become the Prince of Palestine. Lord Deywós also made him change his name from Shamash to Kamash, which the

38. Latin: Nothing Further Beyond

39. Early Semitic word meaning "sun"

people started pronouncing as '*Chemosh.*' Then, when the children of Jacob invaded, he got pushed back to the east side of the Jordan River, where the children of Ammon lived. He introduced himself to the Ammonites using their word for king, *Malak*, calling himself Malak Chemosh.

"Have I ever told you how confusing you become when you start on your history lessons?!"

"History is indeed complex for those with small minds," Nabu retorted. "But see if you can keep up. Soon some people began to refer to the Prince of Palestine as 'Chemosh' while others referred to him simply as 'King,' pronouncing it *Maloch* or *Molech*.

"As time went on, his subjects were confused (as you apparently are as well) by these different names. Eventually they began to think of him as two separate gods, one called Molech and the other called Chemosh. So it was that when the Jewish King Solomon acquiesced to making places of worship for the wives he had taken from that land, he built two separate mountain shrines, one for Molech and one for Chemosh."[40]

Completely confused at this point, but unwilling to admit it, Verethragna asked, "What happened next?"

"Four hundred wonderful years for our prince who was happy to go by the names *Molech* and *Chemosh*. Then suddenly it all came to an end when a zealot named Josiah stepped in and destroyed his high places."[41]

"Josiah, that small-minded bigot! I never did like him," scowled Verethragna.

Nabu continued, "So, after Josiah was dead and gone, the Prince of Palestine was slowly rebuilding his prestige when my predecessor Bel-Marduk came with his Babylonians and conquered the Jews in the Land. That was indeed an ill-advised move because the Oppressor

40. 1 Kings 11:7

41. 2 Kings 23:19

responded by overreacting, as usual, and reduced Bel-Marduk to a mere mortal. Eventually . . . well, you know the story."[42]

"Yes, I do. I *like* that story. No offense, but I never much cared for Marduk; he was such a pompous overachiever. When his miscalculation in Jerusalem resulted in his getting turned into a mortal human—well, of course, I led my Persians in triumph to sack his capital, Babylon."

"Yes," Nabu grimaced. "I remember those events perfectly. Anyway, you illustrate my point about the vulnerability of the Prince of Palestine, since at that same time you also took over his land."

"True, but mine was a kinder, gentler rule than Marduk's had been. At least I allowed the Palestinian Prince and his subjects—not to mention the children of Jacob as well—to exercise more freedom than Babylon allowed them."

"Don't try to put the blame on me for what my predecessor Bel-Marduk did during his rule. Anyway, let's keep our focus on the Prince of Palestine's story. After your Persians had allowed the Jews to return to their 'Promised Land,' Alexander came with his Greeks. He was followed by Antigonus, Cassander, Ptolemy, Seleucus, and eventually of course, Antiochus Epiphanes, whose excesses caused the Jews to rebel. Their successful rebellion allowed the Jews to set up their own independent state for a while under the leadership of the Maccabees and the Hasmoneans."

Verethragna interrupted, "Key word: *for a while*."

Nabu sighed. "What is your problem? *'For a while'* is not *a* key word, it's *three* words. And the point, as you can see, is that the Prince of Palestine has not had an easy time: if the Jews, the people of the Oppressor, became too zealous, as happened during the time of Josiah, he suffered. On the other hand, if the Jews became too impious, it was almost as bad: The Oppressor would respond by allowing attacks from outside the Land. So, our poor prince has had to be

42. See Isaiah 14:4–20

content with the role of coregent, learning to take a back seat either to the Oppressor or to a *Tsel* prince from an adjacent territory."

"Come on, Nabu, don't pretend like you've been a passive observer in all this. For centuries, you, along with Prince Erlig[43] and Prince Hubal, have dominated his territory—and mine as well, for that matter."

"I would call it benevolent guidance," corrected Nabu. "And my part has been minor compared with that of Erlig and Hubal. Moreover, as you well know, Lord Deywós has instructed all *Tselim* in this region to now work together with Hubal, our Arabian Prince."

Verethragna shrugged to acknowledge Nabu's point, then added, "Well, I at least hope Kenan hurries up and realizes that he is the Prince of Palestine! That Hubal is making our lives very difficult with his agreements with the Jewish State. Someone needs to step up since those Arabians seem bent on forging economic agreements designed to help only themselves. They seem unconcerned that such treaties undermine the position of the Palestinian people as the victims of Zionist oppression. In my opinion, we would all be much better off if a nuclear-tipped missile got launched, happened to make it through the Israeli's Iron Dome, and obliterated the entire land."

"Of course, Verethragna, we must think about the Noble Sanctuary[44] and all of the Prince of Palestine's loyal subjects. Deywós would consider their destruction a strategic loss."

Verethragna sensed a note of sarcasm in Nabu's words and asked, "Am I correct in assuming that your sentiments don't necessarily align with those of Lord Deywós regarding the importance of this area and its people?"

"*My* sentiments? My *sentiments* are irrelevant! The potential significance of any particular geographical location is not *our* concern, you idiot!"

---

43. Erlig is the *Tsel* Prince over the ancient Turkic people

44. The Temple Mount is the holiest site in Judaism and the third-holiest site in Islam, known in Arabic as *Haram al-Sharif* or the "Noble Sanctuary

There was silence for a moment as Nabu stared him down, letting his rebuke sink in. When Verethragna had broken eye contact, signifying he had been put in his place, Nabu continued, "But back to our Prince of Palestine. You know how he got his present name?"

Verethragna shook his head 'no' and Nabu continued, "Another compromise that Deywós asked of him was to combine his name at the time, Chemosh, with the Arabic name for Oppressor's Prince, Isa,[45] to form a new name, Ghaiasha. As a reward for accepting this new name, Deywós promised him that in the near future he would be the prince over a strong, unified principality."

Nabu paused as if to savor a well-delivered lecture, then concluded, "And I suspect that the Prince of Palestine's conversion into the boy Kenan is a major strategy in Deywós' master plan to fulfill that promise."

Later that evening, Qorin listened to a report from his spy, the slow-walking *Tsel* who had hidden himself out of sight of Verethragna and Nabu. Qorin was pleasantly surprised by how much the old *Tsel* had overheard, but at the same time, he found it extremely boring listening to him recount the whole long conversation. It felt like sorting through huge piles of rubbish in hopes of finding an occasional gem.

After he had dismissed his spy, Qorin realized that the only valuable piece of information had been the update about the Prince of Palestine, who now languished as a ten-year-old human.

---

45. Isa ibn Maryam is an Arabic title for Jesus in the Quran, meaning "Jesus, son of Mary"

One danger for Ghaiasha, living as the son of a Jewish rabbi, would be his interaction with their horrid scriptures. *And yet,* Qorin thought, *who knows? A knowledge of the Tanach might prove valuable. Maybe Ghaiasha could discover in their book some powerful tool for the Resistance!*

Qorin knew that alliances in the Shadowlands were constantly changing. Though working with Nabu at present seemed out of the question, he was hopeful that he could pry at least Verethragna out of Nabu's gang. And what about Ghaiasha? Qorin felt more urgently than ever the need to create a positive connection with him. Ghaiasha's pursuit of power and glory was all well and good, but there was a fine line between a bold choice and a foolish choice.

Would Ghaiasha ever make it back to the Shadowlands? And if he did, would he look on Qorin as an ally or as an enemy?

Ch 18. Kabbalah

(Jerusalem, 10 months before the Fire)

Kabbalah is the ancient Jewish mystical tradition which teaches the deepest insights into the essence of G-d, His interaction with the world, and the purpose of Creation.

Yerachmiel Tilles, Chabad.org

When Nehemyah returned home after sharing his testimony at the lecture hall, he felt deeply fatigued. Maybe it was the effort of reliving the scenes from his years in Dachau. Maybe it was the burden he felt for Khaled, a young man who seemed to be heading down the wrong path.

With a sigh, he sat down in his favorite chair, just in time to look up as Asher entered the room. He could tell that his Orthodox Jewish friend had something on his mind. "My friend," Nehemyah asked with concern in his voice, "what seems to be troubling you?"

"It's my son, Benjamin," Asher offered.

"Sit down and tell me about it."

"Well, it's just that he is a very spiritual boy, very sensitive for a twelve-year-old. The last two days, he has been dealing with something that has me so troubled I couldn't sleep last night."

"Go on."

"My son has a classmate, Kenan, a ten-year-old who has skipped two grades and is probably a genius. He and Benjamin get along well, and this Kenan has asked Benjamin over to his house a few times."

"Okay."

"You know, we are careful who we let our boys associate with. This Kenan is our rabbi's son, so I thought it would be okay."

"What happened?" asked Nehemyah with deep empathy.

"Well, two days ago, Benjamin went to spend a few hours at Kenan's house. When I arrived later that afternoon to pick him up, I went upstairs and there they were, surrounded by books, piled floor to ceiling. I appreciate reading, and I realize the boy is intellectually well ahead of his peers, but I thought, *What ten-year-old has such an obsession with knowledge that his entire room is full of books?*

"As I entered, Benjamin had a hardbound book in his hand and was asking Kenan about it. Kenan explained that Kabbalah is a kind of Torah studies. Then, turning to acknowledge my presence, he added that he'd recently read Rabbi Eleazar's comments on Job 28:13 that the Torah, as we now have it, is not in its correct order. He went on to say that, now, he is on a mission to discover the correct order."

Asher looked at his friend. He didn't agree with Nehemyah on all aspects of the faith (he knew, for example, that Nehemyah followed *Yeshua Ha Mashiach*), nevertheless, Asher felt sure his friend would find Kenan's statement alarming.

"Yes, Nehemyah admitted, "searching to uncover the correct order of the divine revelation seems an unusual goal for a ten-year-old."

Asher continued, "Right? So, I asked him, 'What makes you think the Holy Scriptures as we now have them are not ordered correctly?' He replied that it was God's way of protecting us. He said that if the Scriptures were to be set in order, it would release the immense power of the Torah and that, according to Isaiah 44:7, the Holy One Himself would one day do just that.

"I was slightly alarmed by what I heard. Taking the book from my son, I looked through it. 'Kabbalah! This stuff is nonsense,' I told them both.

"'Define *nonsense*,' said Kenan evenly. I explained it was heretical, and he countered, 'What exactly about Kabbalah is heretical?' I told him that the Kabbalah contains thoughts and ideas outside of the Torah and that to follow it would be to be led astray.

"That intelligent face looked up at me and his eyes smiled, as he said, 'And yet Benjamin attends school with me, where, in addition to the Torah, we also study science and even philosophy.' I agreed but reminded him that the Torah always trumps any other field of study.

"He quickly responded, 'Ah, but all truth is God's truth.'"

At that, Asher paused. Nehemyah remarked, "Well, my friend, you know there are many Orthodox Jews who endorse Kabbalah."

"I know," Asher burst out, "but my family does not! I told Kenan as much, but he was unmoved, saying, 'Mr. Yitzhaki, if you choose to live your life unaware of the influences affecting you, that is your business. I merely attempt to integrate the Torah with the other truths I find so that I can correctly understand the world around me.'

"Those, Nehemyah, were his words. I was left standing with my mouth open, unsure how to respond. I'm asking you, does that sound like ten-year-old talk to you? I decided right then and there that Benjamin would not be going back to that house."

Nehemyah responded, "I can see how that could trouble you. You do want to be careful about the influences on your children."

"Yes, but then today Benjamin and Kenan were talking at school. Benjamin told Kenan I'd been surprised by the way he talked with me at their house, and it was only fair to warn him I intended to talk with his father, our rabbi.

"That precocious boy told my son, 'Let him talk with old Shlomo, I don't care.'

"Benjamin told me all this when he got home from school, so I went right over to talk with the rabbi. He wasn't at home, but Kenan was, and he received me cordially with a pleasant smile. He listened patiently as I warned him about Kabbalah. When I finished, he merely said that was my opinion, and that he wouldn't judge me if I didn't judge him.

"As far as I was concerned, the conversation was over at that point. I was about to leave when he struck a thoughtful pose and placed a finger lightly on his lips as if considering what to say next. After a pause, he said, 'Yes, I will tell you. You see, my mind is being opened to new ideas. Just between us, I'm not sure I want a Bar Mitzvah. Of course, that's our little secret, I haven't told old Shlomo that.

"I couldn't believe my ears. I said, 'That isn't a very respectful way to speak of your father, and no, I will not keep your secrets.' He responded, 'No, it's not a very respectful way to speak of him. But here, I'll let you in on another secret: Shlomo is not my father.'

"I told him I knew he'd been adopted as a baby. He looked right at me. 'Yes, Shlomo and his wife couldn't have children, and then he found me as an infant and considered me,' here he used his fingers to make air quotes, 'a gift from heaven.' I answered that he could at least be grateful, who knows what would have happened if the rabbi hadn't saved him that day.'

"At this, Kenan again had what seemed to me a mischievous smile. 'You know,' he said, 'I've been opening my mind to new ideas and exploring new worlds. The other day, I visited a place and spoke with a being who assured me that I have a special purpose in this world, a destiny to fulfill. You know what I learned about your rabbi? It wasn't *Shlomo* who found *me*.' After a pause he continued, 'It turns out, it was *I* who found *him*.'"

At that, Asher looked at Nehemyah and let out a sigh.

"And here, look at this." Asher handed a folded-up paper to Nehemyah, saying, "Benjamin found this paper in a book that

Kenan had given him. It's apparently an assignment that he'd done at school." Nehemyah unfolded it slowly and read the paper with interest.

Name: Kenan ben Shlomo

Imaginary Land Assignment

> Imagine that you could travel to an imaginary land, like Milo in *The Phantom Tollbooth*. Where would you go? Choose a name for this land and describe what it is like.

I would like to travel to the United Levantine Communities of Israel and Palestine, or ULCIP for short. This is an imaginary land because I have imagined it. However, unlike the places in The Phantom Tollbooth, The Wizard of Oz, Pilgrims Progress, or other such stories, ULCIP could become reality—in fact, as I will demonstrate briefly below, it should become reality.

The lack of peace and security that have existed for generations in the areas now known as the State of Israel and the Palestinian Territories are mere symptoms of profound underlying unresolved problems associated with the founding of the State of Israel. The sectarian wars and terrorist activities in this region have persisted because to date no acceptable solution has been adopted.
The on-going unrest has prompted many world leaders and international organizations to insist on a "two-state

solution." However, very few of us who live here in the Land see the idea of a Jewish state and a Palestinian state existing side by side, as either desirable or possible. Here, many of us—both Jewish and Palestinian—prefer what would be called a "one-state solution," that is, a state encompassing the entire area for their own people and excluding or at least marginalizing all others. But again, to date every solution offered and every resolution passed has resulted not in lasting peace and stability, but continued violence and contention.

The solution to this problem is obvious to me, although up to now it has been promoted by very few people. The answer is what I call the "secular state solution."

This option employs a strong centralized federal government, committed to non-sectarian toleration, that would oversee the various communities within the current boundaries of the State of Israel and the Palestinian Territories. These individual communities could be guided by various religious or non-religious rules and convictions, whether they be Jewish, Muslim, Christian, secular, or other. Each community would have wide discretion to implement their own specific laws and regulations that would be effective only within that community.

Each community could choose to be completely open to the rest of ULCIP society or closed off, partially or completely, by walls, gates, and other means. In any case, the country as a whole must be interconnected and unified by comprehensive systems of transportation and communication. All existing sectarian communities would remain with their current local governments and regulations. Any change from the status quo would have to pass through intense screening, as would any new sectarian communities that would arise in the future.

A new constitution would be written and approved that would supersede the current Israeli Basic Law. Central and irrevocable to this constitution would be the principle that the federal government would be secular and non-sectarian. The federal government could in no way promote or show preference to any sectarian group or belief system.

A new capital would also be built. This would be a planned city like Baghdad or Brasilia, and constructed in the triangle between Jerusalem, Ramallah, and Tel Aviv, east of the TLV airport in one of the contested areas between the two 1949 armistice lines.

Kenan, interesting ideas. 10 / 10
—Mr. Goldstein

Nehemyah looked up after he had finished reading Kenan's paper and said, "Amazing! He's only ten years old?"

Asher, convinced that Kenan posed a serious threat and surprised that Nehemyah appeared more impressed than concerned at what he had just read, pressed his friend further. "Nehemyah, you do see how I must protect my Benjamin from this kind of thinking, don't you? I don't want my son around that boy anymore; I want him to only have good influences in his life. But what do I do? . . . I was wondeing . . . do you think it would be possible for my family to join your kibbutz?"[46]

46. Kibbutz, from the Hebrew word meaning "gathering," is a type of settlement, unique to Israel, where members live, work, and share life in a community

Nehemyah didn't answer right away. He was deep in thought, contemplating Kenan's idea with unusual interest. It occurred to him that, though this proposal seemed to mark a step backward for Zionism, nevertheless a compromise like this might very well find popular appeal both among Jews and Arabs.

After a few moments Asher interrupted his thoughts, saying, "Nehemyah?"

"Yes?"

"What do you think about my idea?"

Nehemyah came back to the conversation at hand, saying, "What? Oh, yes! I'll look into your family receiving an invitation to join our kibbutz. Certainly, it would be an honor to have you come and live among us."

Ch 19. Hope and Life

(Jerusalem, 10 months before the Fire)

> *But he who received the seed on stony places, this is he who hears the word and immediately receives it with joy; yet he has no root in himself, but endures only for a while.*
> *For when tribulation or persecution arises because of the word, immediately he stumbles.*
>
> Matthew 13:20–21

It was dark as Khaled made his way to Omar's house. He was still thinking about Nehemyah's testimony and his words, "hope for a bright future." As he walked along, he realized his future did not look bright. In fact, he had come to the conclusion that he would have to tell Omar the bad news: he had no money and couldn't buy the scooter.

When he arrived at the door, he found that Omar had guests inside. He turned to leave, but Omar wouldn't hear of it and warmly invited him to join them. As they sat drinking tea, suddenly, one of the young men asked, "Is it true you couldn't even steal an old lady's purse without getting caught?" At that, they all burst out laughing and Khaled could feel his cheeks redden with embarrassment. He wanted to storm off in a huff, but he wasn't sure where to go. The truth was, he didn't want to go home right then in case his uncle was still angry.

The others talked among themselves for a while but eventually trickled away, leaving Khaled alone with Omar. While Khaled was still building up the courage to broach the subject of the money for the scooter, Omar surprised him, saying, "Khaled, I know you don't have the money to buy the scooter. But don't worry, I'm still going to let you have it. And if storing it is a problem, you can leave it here and stop by for it whenever you want."

He continued, "You wonder why? Because I believe in you, Khaled, that's why. Yes, I heard what happened today. Look at me. I'm not laughing at you. Trying to steal that purse was brave. It was foolish, but brave. I know it hurt you when those guys laughed at you just now, but don't worry, I can help you. I can train you. I work with powerful people. You can get the respect you deserve. Go on home for now. Let's talk on Thursday."

The next day, Wednesday, Khaled experienced an exhilarating sense of freedom as he made his way across town on his scooter to hear Nehemyah speak at the lecture hall. His smile was due to several things. One, now he had his own means of transportation. Two, tomorrow Omar was going to introduce him to his inner circle. And three, surprisingly, he was excited to hear more of Nehemyah's story.

When Khaled arrived, Nehemyah was already up in front of the room and had begun speaking. "After I got out of Dachau, I began talking with other Jews, men and women who, like me, had nowhere to go home to. I overheard two men talking about making *Aliyah*—traveling to the land of our Fathers. Since I had no better option, I thought, *Why not?* Later, I found out several reasons why not. One of the main ones was that the British—the ones who controlled access to the Holy Land at that time—were strictly limiting immigration.

"But restrictions didn't stop me. I boarded a vessel headed to Haifa. Unfortunately, like many others, our ship was stopped by the

British authorities, who considered our immigration to be illegal and sent us to a detention camp on Cyprus. But God was in charge even in that, because it was there that I met Talia, the kindest, most thoughtful person I'd ever met.

"About that time, there began a time of great change. The British Mandate over the Land was dissolved, and Israel became a state. Suddenly, Talia and I, along with thousands of other Jews in our camp who were eager to return to our homeland, were transported to Haifa.

"To mark this momentous life event, in the process of gaining my Israeli citizenship, I decided to change my name. Instead of *Ludvik,* which in German means 'glorious warrior,' I choose *Nehemyah,* a name which in Hebrew means 'God comforts.' My former family name, *Schlachtberg,* which means 'battle mountain,' I changed to *Friedenthal,* which in German means 'valley of peace.'

"And when the Holy Spirit led us to form a kibbutz here in a valley in the Judean highlands, not far from Jerusalem, we called it *Emeq Shalom*, 'The Valley of Peace.' I now consider it of utmost importance to promote an environment of calm, comfort, and peace, reflected both in my new name and the name of our kibbutz. God has brought me through many battles, but in Him I always have peace, because I serve the Prince of Peace. The events of my past—the victories as well as the defeats—have served to bring me closer to Him."

The next day, Thursday, Omar took Khaled to a meeting of the political group Al'amal wa Alhayet.[47] Khaled found himself in a room filled with men who, like Omar, were angered by the national

47. Arabic: Hope and Life

government's plan to *'Judaize'* Jerusalem, that is, maintain a Jewish majority in the city. Because the percentage of Jews in Jerusalem had continued to decline, in part because of a higher birth rate among the Arab population, the government had taken recent steps to subtly (and not so subtly) oppose the rights of Muslims.

The speaker was introduced as the *"sheikh,"* an honorific title for a religious leader considered to be a direct descendant of the prophet Mohammed. He was also the *imam*, or leader of the daily prayers at one of the mosques in East Jerusalem. His voice was forceful but steady as he laid out his grievances, saying, "Jews and even Christians keep gaining more and more power economically and politically in our land, while we Muslims, and specifically we Palestinians, are losing ground in our own homeland. Trying to keep Muslims out of the halls of power is obviously undemocratic since Muslims now outnumber Jews in Jerusalem.

"I could list all the evils the Jews have done to us, but you have seen it with your own eyes as well as I have. How many of you have jobs?"

No one raised a hand. "You see, these offspring of pigs and apes try to strangle us economically. But it won't work. They have a long history of failure. The Jews have been conquered over and over by the nations around them: the Babylonians, the Persians, the Greeks, the Romans, the Christians, and finally by us Muslims. By Allah's hand they will be annihilated."

After the meeting, Khaled was quiet. Omar invited him out for tea and asked what he had thought of the meeting.

Khaled tried to organize his thoughts. "That group," he began, "is called *Al'amal wa Alhayet,* which means 'hope and life.' But they have no *hope* and no *life*. Don't you see? They blame others for their problems. That's no way to live.

"Recently, I met a man who nearly died in prison. He lost his home, his family, everything. And you know what? His difficulties didn't destroy him. You should come and listen to him. He is the one who has hope and life."

Omar was intrigued by Khaled's description of a man who still had hope after suffering so much loss. The next day, they both attended a meeting where Nehemyah spoke. Afterwards, Khaled presented Omar to Nehemyah.

"Hearing Khaled describe you as a person who has 'hope and life,' was what caused me to accept Khaled's invitation today. You see, I'm part of a group that goes by that very name."

"It's my pleasure to talk with you, Omar."

"Thank you. It's just that I feel a bit uncomfortable talking with you. It makes no sense. You are a Jew, I am Muslim. I should be with my people. But hearing about your story I just had to come. And now, meeting you in person. I can sense the deep peace that you have."

"Well, I hope you understand that the peace I have is not mine; it comes from God."

"Yes, I see that. We all talk about peace. In Hebrew, you Jews say *shalom*. In Arabic, we say *salaam*. That is our daily greeting. And yet, Khaled is right. My friends don't have peace. They are angry at their lot in life, even though they have more money and more freedom than many others around the world. They are focused on blaming others for their problems instead of trying to do something for themselves."

Nehemyah nodded.

Omar continued, "Khaled is right. The problem isn't other people nor our circumstances. The choice to live a fulfilling life is ours if we accept it. It's an easy choice for me. I want real hope and real life."

Khaled and Omar were baptized at Kibbutz Emeq Shalom. It was a small ceremony to mark their new faith and their desire to follow Jesus, but the joyful celebration was held in secret with no friends or family invited.

Before he baptized them, Nehemyah spoke about the Parable of the Sower in Matthew 13, explaining that the seed, the Word of God, can produce a good crop, but that good crop also depends in part on the soil. In rocky soil, the seed will indeed sprout up quickly, but it will also wither quickly because there is no place for its roots to grow. In the same way, occasionally a person quickly believes, but then when they experience trouble or persecution because of the Word, their faith may wither.

After his baptism, Omar wanted to share the exciting news, but, anticipating that his family might react negatively, he decided to tell his friends from Al'amal wa Alhayet. They weren't impressed at all. Blaming Khaled for this sudden turn of events, they decided to tell Khaled's uncle about his conversion.

Khaled's uncle was livid when he heard the news and immediately kicked Khaled out of the house. Khaled, with no place to go, appealed to his new friends at Kibbutz Emeq Shalom, who took him in. After seeing how Khaled's family responded, Omar decided not to share with anyone else and became very secretive about his faith.

Ch 20. Time and Chance

(Jerusalem, 10 months before the Fire)

I returned and saw under the sun that—
The race is not to the swift,
Nor the battle to the strong,
Nor bread to the wise,
Nor riches to men of understanding,
Nor favor to men of skill;
But time and chance happen to them all.

Ecclesiastes 9:11

Nehemyah sat drinking tea in his house. The kibbutz had recently received four new residents. First came Khaled, who had been homeless after having been kicked out of his house for his faith. Next came Asher, who had come with his two sons seeking a wholesome environment for his spiritually sensitive youngest boy. Nehemyah was happy that the kibbutz was growing and that it could serve as a refuge for those in need.

He looked at Talia's picture and wept as he prayed, "God, I believe you are both good and all-powerful. But there are times when life doesn't make sense. Why couldn't I have had a chance to say goodbye to her? It feels like nothing we do on earth makes any difference. Time and chance happen to us all."[48]

He thought back to a conversation they had had a year ago. while she was still alive. Neither of them could have known that day as they held hands that they would never again sit together and talk.

"Listen to those birds, Nehemyah. It's so quiet and peaceful here."

"Yes, God told me our kibbutz would be called *Emeq Shalom*, 'the Valley of Peace.' But when I think back to our struggle to establish the kibbutz, it was anything but peaceful—there seemed to be opposition on all sides, both from the Israeli officials and from our Arab neighbors. Without Shmuel in the Ministry of Interior, I don't know what would have happened. Getting permission to start a kibbutz is hard enough, but a kibbutz for Jewish followers of Jesus?"

"And yet, thanks to your hard work, here we are!"

"*Our* hard work," Nehemyah said. "And more importantly *God's favor.* Still, you are right. It is a privilege since less than half the Jews in the world today have the opportunity to live in the Land promised to our ancestors. I am grateful to be part of creating a Jewish homeland."

"Yes," replied Talia. "But will Messianic Jews ever truly be accepted here? Jews who follow Jesus as the Messiah may be hundreds of thousands worldwide, but here in the Land among a population of nearly ten million, we are less than 20,000 total."

"You must realize, my dear, what an unwelcome complication for Israel a Messianic kibbutz is. In Western countries, Christians can freely practice their faith. In Islamic countries, Muslims have their Sharia[49] law. But Israel is the only country in the world where Judaism is actively protected and promoted. And to the government, the presence of Messianic Jews dilutes the very idea of Jewish

---

48. Ecclesiastes 9:11

49. Sharia is a system of Islamic religious law regulating private and public life that, along with common law and civil law, is one of the three most common legal systems in the world

nationalism. I only wish they could understand that we Messianic Jews are often more loyal to Zionism than many of our religious or secular countrymen."

"Nehemyah, I know you experienced resistance from Jewish officials. But I think that I felt more acutely ill will—and even persecution—from our Muslim neighbors who are grieved by our very existence, considering us outside the House of God, the *Dar Al Islam*. We belong to what they call the *Dar Al Harb*, the House of War. Even my dear neighbor Sana confides in me that there is no hope for a friendship between us simply because I am a Jew; to her, all Jews are complicit in the theft of land from the Arabs to whom God has given it by right."

"Yes, Talia," he sighed, "it is perplexing. Life for Jews in Eastern Europe a century ago was indeed as precarious as a fiddler on the roof, but in Israel today Jews have at last found a home. Even Muslims here, with dozens of Islamic countries surrounding Israel, can rest assured that their rights will be represented. But we, as Jewish followers of the Messiah, find ourselves caught in the middle, rejected by both Jews and Muslims.

"Nehemyah, I am so proud of you. Resistance and persecution have not kept you from following the vision God has given you. You believed, as Abraham did, that 'God gives life to the dead and calls into existence that which does not exist.'"[50]

"I couldn't have done it without you, Talia. When we first met in that refugee camp in Cyprus, I was not the man I am today. Being with you has made me a better person."

"Nehemyah, dear, do you think it was chance that we traveled here together from Cyprus? Did you never guess that I asked to be assigned to your group?"

"So, you had feelings for me even before we made aliyah?"[51]

---

50. Romans 4:17 (TLV)

51. The Hebrew word for the holy act of Jewish immigration to the Land of Israel

Talia laughed, "But of course! I was afraid you would never notice me. After we arrived and began working, learning Hebrew, trying to start a new life, I was afraid you'd fall for one of the other girls."

"What?! I proposed to you after only six months! Others thought I was being hasty, but I didn't care; I knew I wanted a life with you."

"Even though some didn't think of me as Jewish?"

"The war changed everything, Talia. We were starting a new life in a new land. Yes, I already knew Yiddish, but like all the rest we both had to learn the Hebrew language and Israeli culture."

Talia held his hand a little tighter. "What's your best memory of those early years?"

"The same as yours, I think."

"Rivka."

"Yes. Our beautiful daughter who grew into a perfect young woman." They both looked over at the framed photo of Rivka and Yaqov on their wedding day and their eyes filled with tears.

"I miss her. I miss them both. But they gave us the joy of our life, our little Devorah."

"Devorah's not a little girl anymore, Nehemyah. She's a graduate student in America!"

"You are right, my love. Where did the time go? What right do we have to have enjoyed such a blessed life?"

Nehemyah remembered Talia's kind smile as she said, "Yes, we are blessed. Not because life works out well. No, we are blessed because, come what may, like Job, we say, 'Blessed be the name of the Lord.'"[52]

52. Job 1:21

Ch 21. God and Evil

(Jerusalem, 10 months before the Fire)

What God means in Isaiah 46:10 is that nothing has ever happened, or will ever happen, that God did not purpose to happen.

John Piper,
The Sovereignty of God:
I Will Accomplish All My Purpose

During one of his midweek talks at the kibbutz, Nehemyah was asked to speak about the importance of faith.

"The psalmist states that the heavens declare the glory of God.[53] However, here on earth we sometimes see not *glory* but *evil*. In the concentration camp in Germany, for example, I saw so much evil that I cried out along with the prophet Jeremiah, 'Why do the wicked prosper?'[54] Another way to ask the question is, 'Why do bad things happen to good people?'

"I think we can all agree that the Holocaust was a great evil. But can we imagine God at work even in that? Let me give you one example. After the war, the need for a Jewish homeland was seen for

53. Psalm 19:1
54. Jeremiah 12:1

what it was: a matter of life and death. The tragedy of the Holocaust turned an idea, in discussion for decades and long endorsed by many Western nations, into a reality. The fact is that the creation of our own nation likely would not have happened without the Holocaust.

"Furthermore, following the establishment of the State of Israel in 1948, Germany agreed to pay reparations in the amount of over 700 million dollars, money that helped to finance the repatriation of thousands of Jews who came to live in our newly formed state.

"Oddly enough, at the time, some of our leaders opposed the whole idea of reparations. They felt that accepting money in repayment for the crimes that had been committed would serve to absolve the guilt of those who participated in the Holocaust. But Prime Minister David Ben-Gurion and his Mapai party fought for those funds, believing that financial help represented the only practical hope for our fledgling state.

"He argued that accepting the reparations was the only way to sustain our nation's economy. 'There are two approaches,' he once said. 'One is the ghetto Jew's approach and the other is of an independent people.' Then he declared, 'I don't want to run after a German and spit in his face. I don't want to run after anybody. I want to stay right here, and I want to build.'

"He was right. There is no future in the victim's approach. There is no benefit to holding on to past injuries. He asked our countrymen to take the initiative as an independent people, to settle down in this new land and to build. Ben-Gurion not only convinced the Knesset[55] to accept the reparations deal, he also worked to recover as much Jewish property as possible, so that, in his words, 'the murderers do not become the heirs as well.' Refusing to accept the victim mentality is one key to understanding God's purposes in times of evil.

---

55. Knesset is the 120-member assembly, elected by popular vote, that represents the Israeli people and functions as the legislative branch of the Israeli government

"Today," continued Nehemyah, "as I meditated again on the words from the prophet Jeremiah, 'Why does the way of the wicked prosper? *Why* are those happy who deal so treacherously?' I sensed God saying to me, 'Faith is holding on in the midst of uncertainty. When all is clear and visible, faith is not required.' I also sensed God saying to me, 'Right now, I want people to come to Me of their own free will, even when the evidence for or against Me is inconclusive. However, it will not always be so. The days are coming when I will work clearly and incontrovertibly again.'

"Romans 8:28 says, 'And we know that all things work together for good to those who love God, to those who are the called according to His purpose.'[56] God is not uncaring. He is not evil. He is not powerless against evil. He actually uses evil to accomplish His good purposes. Nothing is excluded.

"Think about what happened to Joseph, when his brothers plotted against him, threw him in a pit, and then sold him as a slave to be taken to Egypt. What they did to him was evil, and yet he could declare to them later, 'You meant evil against me, but God meant it for good.'[57] Notice that it says God *meant* it for good. It doesn't say God was powerless to stop the evil they had done. It doesn't say God merely figured a way to undo the evil they had done. No, it says, 'God *meant* it for good.' God superintended it. He planned it.

"A man may say, 'But surely God couldn't oversee or plan the horrible, wicked, evil, vile things that happened in the concentration camps.'

"I ask you to consider the torture and murder of the completely loving and perfectly innocent Son of God Jesus. In Acts 2:23, we read, 'Him, being delivered by the determined purpose and foreknowledge of God, you have taken by lawless hands, have crucified, and put to death.'

---

56. Romans 8:28
57. Genesis 50:20

"Notice that the text says this happened by God's determined purpose and foreknowledge. Indeed, there is not a single detail of life that is out of His control. Ephesians says that He works all things according to the counsel of His will.[58]

"So, if God plans everything, does that mean that God determines our decisions, and we have no real say in the matter? Not at all! For example, God puts before us the right way and the wrong way to live and then says, 'Choose life.'[59] His expectation is that we can choose—and that we will be judged according to the choices we make. At the same time, God has plans for His people which He expresses when He says, 'There is a remnant according to the election of grace.'[60]

"In other words, though real characters do make real choices—some good, some bad—it is ultimately God who writes the narrative. At times, the choices are downright evil, but God weaves even those choices together like a tapestry. In the end, history all comes together exactly as He wills it to be, to produce His story, the narrative of this world.

"Why is there evil in the world? Ultimately, because God has willed it to be so. He could have created a world that had no possibility of evil, but He chose not to. And I choose to believe that He knows best.

"God, as the good, wise, and all-powerful author of all of creation, has Himself chosen to write a story filled with tension and conflict. Since I personally enjoy reading stories with a healthy amount of drama in them, I hope I will not complain if, as one of the characters in God's drama, I myself experience a challenging moment or two.

"Especially since our suffering is not in vain. After all, when we, as God's actors, patiently endure the suffering He has allowed us to experience in His story, I believe we will receive, measure for measure, suffering's counterpoint, which is joy. And that joy will never go away, nor will it ever diminish.

---

58. Ephesians 1:11
59. Deuteronomy 30:19
60. Romans 11:5

"How can I make such a bold claim? Listen to the words of the apostle Paul:

> *Therefore we do not lose heart. Even though our outward man is perishing, yet the inward man is being renewed day by day. For our light affliction, which is but for a moment, is working for us a far more exceeding and eternal weight of glory, while we do not look at the things which are seen, but at the things which are not seen. For the things which are seen are temporary, but the things which are not seen are eternal.*[61]

"So, I have two takeaways for you today: One, take action! You can make decisions; therefore, do not think of yourself as a powerless victim, do not despair, do not think of life as out of control, because life is never out of God's control. And two, trust God! Nothing escapes His notice. He will act. He is good and ultimately will bring good from anything that happens."

Nehemyah's talk about God working through evil started a chain of thoughts in Omar. In part, this was because he was experiencing an excruciating inner turmoil mixed with a loneliness unlike any he had ever felt before.

Other than Khaled, the one person who appeared to accept Omar was Devorah, Nehemyah's granddaughter, who had recently returned from university in America. She never made him feel like an outsider. It was refreshing the way she seemed to look beyond

61. 2 Corinthians 4:16–18

Christian/Jewish/Muslim lenses to see him first and foremost as a fellow human being.

Devorah was a mature twenty-six-year-old and Omar, an immature twenty-three-year-old. From her perspective, there was no danger of romance: he was like a younger brother, and she found that they could talk together easily.

Omar shared the doubts that had begun to rise in his heart. "What if I've made a mistake? What if Islam is right and I've left the true faith?"

"Well," Devorah said, "most Jews think people should remain in the faith in which they were born. They especially despise Jews who become Christians, converting from a persecuted, minority religion to the biggest, most powerful religion in the world."

Omar could understand that perspective. "I am considered a traitor by anyone who hears of my decision to become a Christian. If there is one thing my Muslim friends hate more than anything, it's a Muslim who leaves his true religion and becomes a Jew or Christian. The constant stares, the whispered accusations; it's unbearable! I'm afraid of what they might do, I'm afraid of the evil eye."

"Yes, I know people who wear amulets to protect against that very thing."

"Yes, and it's not just that I am afraid, I feel like I don't fit anywhere. Even among Messianic Jews, I feel like a second-class citizen. No one would say it out loud, but it's obvious that Khaled and I really don't belong here at the kibbutz. Khaled is only staying here because he's your grandfather's pet project."

"Well," Devorah said with empathy, "life isn't perfect in my little world either. I grew up in my parents' faith and, after they passed away, my grandparents raised me in their strict Christian faith. But then, at school, my eyes were opened.

"For example, take the issue of equality. No offense intended, but most men, especially religious ones, are stuck in the past with outdated ideas, trying in vain to keep their patriarchal system in place as the world awakens to new realities."

She thought she would stop there, but Omar was listening quietly and didn't seem offended. Soon, other examples came to mind. Her thoughts began to form and, before she knew it, she was talking again.

"Or take evolution. Scientific evidence clearly demonstrates that the world we see around us wasn't created in six literal days or created six thousand years ago. The order we see around us is the byproduct of random chance; mutations in the DNA of living organisms over the course of billions of years, shaped by the unthinking hand of natural selection.

"So how does that fit with the Bible? For example, Psalm 19, which my grandfather mentioned today, goes on to talk about God's creation, comparing the sun to an athlete who starts at one end of a circuit and races to the other. What is that about? While my grandfather focused his talk on the need for faith, my mind went a different direction to this question: If these Holy Scriptures are written from God's perspective, why such an unscientific view?"

Omar was quiet, unsure if she was actually asking him a question. It might have helped him to know that very few people claim the Bible (or, for that matter, the Quran) are to be read as a scientific textbook, believing the Scriptures use religious language for the purpose of communicating about God in the normal way that normal people tend to express themselves.

But, thankfully, he didn't need to respond to her question because she began again, "In the 1600s, Galileo corroborated through observation and deduction what Copernicus before him had posited: that it is the earth, rather than the sun, whose movement brings us night and day. This went against the prevailing thought at the time based on Aristotle.

"We know now that the Copernican theory is true, but back then most everyone believed in Aristotle's geocentric theory. Church leaders in that day insisted Galileo recant and admit that it was the sun, rather than the Earth, that moved. Why was Galileo forced, under threat of punishment, to agree with them? Why did he have to bite his tongue and ignore his scientific proof? It makes me smile to think that he still managed to get in a jab after recanting, by allegedly saying under his breath, referring to the Earth, 'Nevertheless it moves.'[62]

"So, you see, I have doubts about the Christian faith just as you do. Because it seems clear to me that some parts of the Bible do not easily fit with our modern world."

After Omar left, Devorah began to make dinner for her grandpa. As she worked, she replayed in her mind her talk with Omar and realized their conversation had left her deeply troubled. Not only had she learned about the loneliness a Muslim might experience when he left his religion, but his situation had also reminded her of her own doubts about God and the Christian faith. She shook her head, trying to focus her mind on something else. She had, after all, returned to Israel to help her grandpa in *his* time of need. He had plenty of reasons to doubt God's love throughout his life, and she didn't want to add to his worries by telling him about her own doubts.

As Devorah and Nehemyah sat down to eat, he noticed she was unusually quiet. "Is something troubling you, my little bee[63]?" he asked.

62. In Italian, *E pur si muove*

63. The Hebrew name Devorah means "bee"

That brought a smile to her face as she said, "No, Grandpa, I'm fine. How was your day?"

"My dear one, I know life has been hard. After your mother and father lost their lives in the terrorist attack, I thought we would never recover. But one thing kept me going during that dark time. You. I know you are no longer that little girl who would run to my study to ask me questions or tell me her problems. You're all grown up now. But I do want you to know that if something is bothering you, I am here to listen."

When she didn't say anything, he added, "I know what a sacrifice it was for you to leave your studies in America and come here to take care of your *saba*.[64] At the time, you put a good face on it by insisting that it would, in fact, be a step forward, educationally, for you to transfer to the Hebrew University here in Jerusalem. But if this isn't what you really want, please let me know."

"No, Saba, that isn't it. I'm very happy to have this chance to spend time with you." After a pause she added, "It's just that I had a conversation with Omar and he seems to be doubting his decision to leave Islam."

"I see."

"He doesn't feel like he belongs in the Muslim community anymore. But he also doesn't fit in the Jewish community, and he doesn't really feel accepted in this Messianic kibbutz. Though I've been a part of the Messianic community all my life, I know what it's like to feel different from almost everyone around me, whether at school or at work. I know what it's like to not fit in, to feel like you don't belong. And I hurt for him. But what can I do?"

"You have always had a good mind, Devorah. And you have a tender, compassionate heart. It's okay to ask questions about your faith. That's how we make the faith handed down to us our own. As for

64. Hebrew: Grandfather

Omar, I pray that his questions are sincere. If they are, you can be sure that in the end God will keep him on the good path."

Ch 22. The Mole

(Shadowlands, 10 months before the Fire)

It is well understood that no alteration can be made to the status quo in the holy places.

Article 62 of the Berlin Treaty—July 1878

Qorin had successfully planted the thought in Verethragna's mind that no opinion but Nabu's would ever count for much in the Babylonian Prince's inner circle. "That group will never agree on anything anyway," Qorin assured him. "They're too afraid of upsetting the status quo. None of them understands my two keys to success: think big and take risks."

When Verethragna came up with a daring plan of his own, it was, therefore, no surprise whom he turned to. Convinced he couldn't share it with Nabu—who would merely laugh—he looked for Qorin, assured that he would understand.

After a few pleasantries, Verethragna said, "You know, Qorin, maintaining the status quo is like standing still on the escalator taking us all down to the dreaded pit. I for one, will not go down without a fight!"

Qorin was a bit jarred by this apparent reference to their ultimate defeat, but to be polite, instead of contradicting, he merely nodded. Verethragna took that as a signal he should continue and added, "I remember very well the downward spiral that marked the former Prince of Germany's tenure during what humans call the World Wars. Tyr[65] had, for all his faults, at least been a *Tsel* with clear decision-making abilities and a thirst for dominion. But Heidhr's[66] ascension after Tyr's humiliating defeat?! Heidhr! That piece of work has always been weak and submissive."

Verethragna felt inspired. He had worked out the "when" of his plan, determining that the time to act was now. Seeing that the Prince of Palestine remained limited by his incarnation as a human child, and given that nature abhors a vacuum, it was obvious that someone needed to step into the void. Adding to the urgency of the situation were the recent rumors that the enemy was stirring in Jerusalem, something that must not be allowed to continue unanswered. *No,* he thought, *waiting will never do.*

He looked up at Qorin. "After working out the 'when' of my plan, I'm beginning to see the 'how.' A year ago, I received word that my contact within the military had initiated secret talks with a member of the 'Organization.' I don't know if you have heard of it. It's a loosely connected group of humans working together with the Resistance."

Qorin nodded as if he had heard of the "Organization," and Verethragna continued. "I saw to it that my contact, Ali, was placed in a position giving him access to the deepest levels of the IDF, that is, the Israel Defense Forces. At the time, I wasn't sure what purpose this access might serve, but now the way forward has become clear to me."

And most importantly, the Prince of Persia thought to himself, *I've identified the 'what' of my plan: to obliterate the nation of Israel.* Verethragna noticed that Qorin was looking at him with a strange expression, and he thought, *Well, maybe the word* obliterate *is a bit extreme. But the other* Tselim *are driving me crazy,* tentatively *talking about* potential *alliances*

---

65. Tyr is the former *Tsel* prince over the principality of Germany
66. Heidhr is the *Tsel* prince over the principality of post-World War II Germany

that might eventually *lead to* possibly *dividing the principality up between them. What is conspicuous by its absence is any kind of* action. Verethragna looked again at Qorin and then wondered to himself, *Have I been saying these things out loud or just thinking them?*

He looked down at his own hands and his long, elegant fingers. He formed his right hand into a fist and raised it as he said, "Qorin, you know me. I am a *Tsel* of action. With help from my intelligent young mole, I've arranged for the Israeli Iron Dome Air Defense to be disarmed long enough to allow a nuclear missile strike on Jerusalem. That, together with my connections with Noor-Allah[67] will make my attack successful. True, this will end up leveling a large part of the city and even the Al-Aqsa Mosque in the process. But we must keep our focus on the prize: In the aftermath of the attack, there will be a total rewrite of the map of the Middle East. And I intend to come out on top after that gerrymandering."

Verethragna smiled as he thought about how patient he had been while viewing human events for thousands of years. *A year or even several decades with no apparent progress was not necessarily a setback. Every veteran of the Resistance knows how to play the long game. Having Ali in place reflects only the first part of my plan. With Noor-Allah involved, I now have a way to deliver the promised devastation.*

He looked up. Qorin was nowhere to be seen. Looking around he thought, *Have I been talking or just thinking? If I was speaking out loud, was Qorin here listening to me? I hope I didn't say too much!*

67.Noor-Allah is a fictional Muslim organization whose name means "Light of God" in Arabic

Ch 23. The Nuclear Option

(Shadowlands, 10 months before the Fire)

> *". . . and guard yourselves against the fire which has been prepared for the unbelievers."*
>
> Quran 3:131

Qorin had indeed been listening. To hear Verethragna tell it, the Principality of Germany had done *everything* wrong, which was, of course, preposterous. True, Tyr should not have been so rash. And Heidhr was too accommodating. But criticism of the Princes of Germany wasn't what most troubled Qorin.

He agreed with Verethragna that the Palestinian principality was weak. And he agreed, obviously, that the continued success of the Jewish experiment was a matter of serious concern. He even agreed that Heidhr bore most of the blame for this present situation: The very existence of the protection afforded by the modern Iron Dome Defense System resulted directly from the huge reparations paid by Heidhr's Germany.

What alarmed Qorin was not Verethragna's assessment of the past failures or weaknesses of other *Tselim*; he was worried about certain aspects of Verethragna's present plan of action. For example, Noor-Allah.

After meeting with Verethragna, Qorin did some research, or rather, found someone else to do some research. Apparently, that Muslim social organization's leadership had specifically chosen the name *Nóor-Allah* based on verse 5:15 of the Quran, which says,

> *O People of the Book! there hath come to you Our Apostle revealing to you much that ye used to hide in the Book and passing over much (that is now unnecessary): There hath come to you from God a new Light and a perspicuous Book.*

This organization interpreted the phrase *Noor-Allah* in Arabic to mean not *light of God* but *fire of God*, with the understanding that God promised to give them fire to defeat the unbelievers. This interpretation, though not necessarily orthodox, did fit nicely with one of the organization's main objectives: to destroy the Jewish state.

Qorin's researchers also discovered that although Noor-Allah members had jobs and families, their visible, legitimate role in society served as a cover for their involvement with Hezbollah,[68] which itself was a puppet of Iran. Qorin knew from experience that that kind of cross-principality activity created a veritable headache for all the *Tselim* in the region. Though Hezbollah's heart was in the right place—attacking and destroying Israel was a noble cause—their lack of willingness to coordinate with others had more than once set back Deywós' long-term plans. According to documents that Qorin now held, Noor-Allah might have recently obtained from Iran the "fire" they had been praying for: seven 107mm-type rockets and a type 63 mobile rocket launcher, which were now concealed in a hidden tunnel somewhere in Syria.

In addition to the involvement of Noor-Allah, there was a second item that Verethragna had mentioned that worried Qorin: a nuclear bomb. Though Qorin dismissed the possibility as mere bluster, he

68. Hezbollah is a sociopolitical and paramilitary organization associated with Iranian Shia Islam whose name in Arabic means "The Party of Allah"

was unaware of the fact that the Persian Prince really did have someone working that angle; someone who expected to take possession of the bomb in Istanbul and had already arranged delivery to Noor-Allah in Syria.

The third part of Verethragna's plan that caught Qorin's attention was the name *"Ali."* With only a first name, it took equal measures of hard work and dumb luck, but, eventually, one of Qorin's contacts approached him with news that the Prince of Persia's contact named Ali had been identified.

Qorin read the report on *Ali Khamis,* a file that included a photo of the olive-skinned twenty-eight-year-old. Qorin looked at the handsome face for a long while then moved on to a stack of newspaper articles and opinion pieces. One article decried the fact that even though Arabs comprise about 20% of Israeli citizens, they were sorely underrepresented in the national government. Another cited the passing of the recent 'Jewish Nation-State Law' which effectively made Israeli Arabs into second-class citizens. Another, written by a Jewish legal scholar, noted that Arabic had been an official language (along with Hebrew) since the founding of the Jewish nation in 1948 and that the recent removal of Arabic's legal status was nothing less than a crime. Another pointed out the racism and hypocrisy in the Israeli military where Jewish citizens over the age of eighteen were *required* by law to serve, while Arab citizens were *exempted*—although they could voluntarily join if they chose.

Qorin continued reading. In summary, the lack of political recognition, the lack of cultural/religious recognition, and the lack of linguistic recognition combined to lead a number a young people to complain that Arab Israelis, no matter how loyal they might be to the state, would never hold any real position of responsibility in Israeli society.

In light of this inequality, world leaders called for a "Two-State Solution," allowing Jews and Muslims to have two distinct, recognized countries in the Land. The majority of Jewish Israelis, however, still favored the status quo (including various levels of Palestinian autonomy under the umbrella of Israeli control), while the vast majority of Arab Muslims in Israel (and throughout the world) vowed they would not rest until the Jewish state was eliminated from the region.

A growing number of university-educated young Israelis blamed infighting in the Knesset for Israel's unjust social environment. Many called for a concession to appease the Arab minority, and a committee was formed to suggest ways to improve Arab–Jewish relations in Israel. Since many young people viewed the police and military as part of the problem rather than the solution, the committee's proposal, applauded by a large number of the Jewish and Arab elite, was the creation of a new position called a *Social Liaison,* a mediator between the Knesset and the Israel Defense Forces. And to fill that position, they proposed a graduate of the University of Tel Aviv, whose father was Arab and his mother Jewish: Ali Khamis.

Though this was a largely symbolic gesture, in theory, Ali's new position would provide the Knesset with more oversight over what some perceived as rogue operators in the IDF. To authorize his security clearance, the tall, thin, nerdy, bespectacled young man's social media postings going back to high school were carefully scrutinized to assure the government that Ali didn't hold any radical views about religion or politics.

His appointment was hailed as a win-win. Though he was Jewish, the Arabs, knowing his name was Ali and that his father was a Muslim, eagerly cheered for him, considering his placement a great political breakthrough. The fact that he was a computer genius who quickly earned accolades from his peers was mentioned over and over in the news.

According to the notes Qorin was reading, Ali's supervisors in the IDF were convinced that there were sufficient firewalls in place limiting his access to files containing any important military or strategic information. But Qorin was not so sure. If Ali fancied himself a hacker, he might very well look at firewalls not as impenetrable obstacles but instead as challenges to overcome. *And, as for getting caught,* Qorin reasoned, *it could be assumed that Ali wouldn't be a computer genius if he were sloppy enough to leave any evidence about where he had been poking around.*

Ch 24. Hebrew University

(Jerusalem, 10 months before the Fire)

The goal of our struggle is the end of Israel, and there can be no compromises . . . .

Yasser Arafat
quoted in *The Washington Post,*
March 29, 1970

It was a hot morning, and Khaled was looking for shade while sweating in the sun. Omar had asked to meet him outside the entrance to the Hebrew University for a project for the "Hope and Life" group, but he was an hour late and Khaled was getting impatient.

As he stood, shielding his eyes and scanning left and right for Omar, he realized that the more time he spent with his new friends at the kibbutz, the less he believed that the sheikh's Islamic group had anything positive to offer. Khaled was waiting by the university gate, not because he believed in Hope and Life's ideas, but because he didn't want to lose Omar's friendship. It was that simple. Omar was his only friend now that he had moved to the kibbutz. Looking at his watch, he asked himself, *Where is he?*

He called his phone again, but no answer. Just when he had decided to give up and head back to the kibbutz, Omar came walking toward him with a big smile.

"As-salamu 'alaykum."[69]

"Wa-'alaykumu s-salam."[70]

"Khaled," Omar said, greeting him warmly, "I understand we are now followers of Jesus, but we are still Arabs. I have here," he patted the briefcase, "a very important project for our people.

"Many of the best students in the country are Palestinians, but there aren't enough opportunities for them to study at the Hebrew University. Today I have a chance to meet with the director of the Admissions Department to plead our case."

Omar opened the briefcase he was carrying and took out a file folder saying, "Hold onto this briefcase while I go inside. Do you remember how I told you I have important connections? Well, I have a letter here signed by the presidents of ten European universities expressing their indignation about the lack of educational opportunities for Arabic-speaking students in Israel. Today I'm going to show you how to bring about change in society. Wait for me here and I'll be right back."

Khaled waited a short distance away, sitting on a bench in the shade, while Omar entered the gate, going through the metal detector and passing the guards with machine guns, making his way to the university administration building.

Inside, after a short wait, a secretary called Omar's name, and he was directed to the office of the Director of Admissions. As he stepped into the spacious room, the director said, "There is no need for you to sit down. I received your request to speak with me, and I've looked into this association 'Hope and Life.' I want to make it clear

---

69. Arabic: "Peace be upon you"

70. Arabic: "And upon you be peace"

that this university will not, under any circumstances, hold discussions with any organization that calls for the destruction of the state of Israel."

Omar, still smiling, said, "I realize that our politics are not in alignment. Even so, we believe that it is the right of every person to pursue higher studies, if they have the aptitude, regardless of their politics."

The director sat politely tapping his finger on the desk as if he was considering Omar's perspective. But he had already pushed a button under his desk, and, in a moment, two large security guards entered the room and stepped between Omar and the administrator.

Omar was escorted unceremoniously from the building. Once outside, he was allowed to make his own way off the campus. As he walked, he made a quick phone call, checked his phone for the time, and then looked to his right just in time to see Devorah coming out of a nearby building. Going up to her, he said, "Hey, Devorah, how are you?"

"I'm good! What are you doing here? Are you studying at the university?"

"No, I just had a meeting with the Director of Admissions. Khaled is waiting for me outside."

"Great. I just had an early morning meeting with my advisor and now I'm heading downtown."

"Maybe we can take the bus together. We're heading downtown, too."

Once they got out on the street, they waved to Khaled who came over.

"Hey, Khaled, look who I met!"

"Hi, Devorah." Turning to Omar, he said, "So, what's next?"

Omar retrieved his briefcase from Khaled and said, "I just talked with the sheikh. He anticipated my request might be denied, so this briefcase contains papers I am to take downtown to present to the Ministry of Education."

"Okay."

Their bus arrived and, as the three got on, Khaled wondered what they were getting into. *I guess this is where Omar's important connections come into play. I hope he knows what he's doing.*

Then Khaled's thoughts turned to Devorah, who was sitting near him. He had heard how Nehemyah showed her off to everyone at the kibbutz when she arrived back home after graduating from university in the United States last year. Nehemyah was even more proud of her now that she was given the opportunity to pursue her PhD at the Hebrew University. And he once mentioned that her research was so secret that even he, her grandfather, didn't know about it.

As they rode along, Omar interrupted Khaled's thoughts with a whisper, "We need to get off now."

"Here?"

The bus slowed to a stop, and Khaled and Omar stood up. The doors opened and Khaled made his way down the steps. He turned to see the doors close and the bus pull away, leaving him alone on the sidewalk.

Khaled stood in confusion for a moment, trying to figure out what was going on. The bus had turned a corner and was now out of sight. He automatically started walking in the direction the bus had gone, thinking Omar would surely get off at the next stop, when he heard and felt a huge explosion.

He looked around and thought, *What happened? Was it a bomb? It might have been close to the bus with Omar and Devorah on it.* He cautiously started jogging in that direction. Before he arrived, he could already see the smoke. Coming around the corner he stopped, unable to believe what he saw: the bus was a fireball. He was still standing on the corner stunned when the Israeli police arrived. After a couple of quick questions, they escorted him into the police car and drove away.

Khaled sat handcuffed in a windowless office of Israel's security agency, the Mossad.[71] Seated across the table from him were two silent agents, both of them young and dark, with closely trimmed hair and beards.

After a lengthy wait, a clean-shaven man in his forties, Agent Peretz, entered the room. "What were you doing on that street corner near that bus?"

"I'd just gotten off the bus. I heard the explosion, so I went to see what had happened."

"You had been on the bus? Why was it off its normal route?"

"I have no idea. I wasn't really paying attention; I was talking with my friends."

"What friends? Friends on the bus?"

"Yes. Wait a minute, what is this? What happened?"

"Answer the question. What are your friends' names?"

Khaled paused for a moment. His instinct urged him to be less than forthright, but as he evaluated the situation he could think of no reason to withhold that particular information. The police were the enemy, and information should only be given to them sparingly, but withholding the names of his friends for no reason would be unwise. "Omar Awad and Devorah Malkah," he answered, then asked, "Can you tell me what's going on?"

71. Mossad is the national intelligence agency of the State of Israel, known as the Institute for Intelligence and Special Operations, similar to the CIA in the United States

Agent Peretz stared at Khaled with unfriendly eyes. After a few seconds, he looked down at the papers in his hand as if evaluating how to respond, then glanced at the other two agents before saying, "The investigation is ongoing. There are many details that still need clarification. What we do know is that the bus was off its normal route and that it was in an area without surveillance cameras to give us intel." He looked directly at Khaled as if that had been a question.

Khaled offered, "All I know is that the doors opened and I got out. My friends stayed on the bus, and the next thing I knew, there was an explosion."

Before Agent Peretz stood up to leave, he looked straight at Khaled and growled, "Well, you'd better start remembering more than that!" Turning, he stepped out of the room and closed the door.

He motioned to the officer standing in the hallway and said, "Take him to room B, have his information entered in the system and do not release him or leave him unsupervised. A dozen innocent people were just murdered, and right now, he's our most promising lead. I want to know what happened! Why was this Khaled fellow on that bus, and why did he get off right before it exploded? Go!"

When the officer entered the room, he found Khaled with his handcuffed hands over his face, his elbows on the table, his shoulders shaking uncontrollably. At the officer's touch, Khaled started and looked up with bloodshot eyes but didn't resist. He was taken down a long hall and around several corners before being told to sit. He found himself in a room with a stern-looking brown-haired woman who was busy entering information on a computer. After she had finished, she curtly asked him to confirm his name and address, made a phone call, and then continued typing.

A short while later, Agent Peretz burst into the room with a puzzled look and asked, "You say your current address is the kibbutz Emeq Shalom? With Nehemyah Friedenthal?"

"Yes, sir."

"When did you last speak with him?"

"This morning. An agent took my phone, but if you have it, you can check."

"Not necessary. Come with me," Agent Peretz ordered as he grabbed Khaled's arm and led him away.

They went through several doors, up some stairs, then stopped at a desk where Agent Peretz's partner was waiting. After hurriedly signing the prisoner out, they exited the building and Khaled found himself in the back seat of Agent Peretz's car on his way to the kibbutz. There was no conversation during the drive, but when they arrived at the Friedenthal house, Agent Peretz parked and said to his partner, "Stay here with him for a couple of minutes. I'll be right back."

About ten minutes later, he returned to the car and motioned to his partner who opened the rear door. Khaled got out cautiously. He looked around tentatively, sensing the seriousness of the moment but unsure what was coming next.

Inside the house, Nehemyah, who had obviously been crying, started to rise to meet Khaled, but then seemed to lose strength, hesitated, and sat back down, motioning instead for Khaled to come to him. Khaled went and knelt by his chair. Nehemyah put his arm around Khaled's shoulders and bowed his head, weeping.

After a time, Khaled stood and, finding a chair a few steps away, sat down. Coffee was brought in, and they all sat listening to the sound of cicadas as their coffee cooled.

Nehemyah looked at Agent Peretz. The policeman seemed to be evaluating the wisdom of his friend's unspoken request. Finally, he reluctantly stood up, walked over, and removed Khaled's handcuffs. Nehemyah took a sip of coffee with shaking hands, then broke the silence, "Khaled, you remember the day we first met in that restaurant?"

"Yes, sir."

"Do you remember that I had two friends with me?"

Khaled nodded his head yes.

"Shmuel was one of the friends with me that day. He and I have been friends for over fifty years. He is one of the few people who was sympathetic to my dream of starting this kibbutz."

Khaled nodded his head without speaking and Nehemyah continued, motioning to Agent Peretz, "This man here is Levy Peretz. He is my friend. And he is my friend Shmuel's son. I've known Levy all his life. I would trust Agent Peretz with my own life.

"I can appreciate that you prefer to not talk with police officers. But right now, I need to know what happened to my Devorah. She is all I have left. I am begging you, Khaled, please tell him everything you know."

Khaled was quiet for a moment, then bowed his head and began to cry softly.

As the minutes went by Agent Peretz fidgeted in his seat, thinking that this was a waste of time. He looked at Nehemyah as if to say, "I knew this wouldn't work."

Nehemyah said softly, "Khaled, I just need to know what you were doing on that bus." The words somehow seemed to help Khaled compose himself and he reached for a tissue to blow his nose. Looking up at Nehemyah, he answered, "I don't know what happened, sir. Honest. Omar and I went to the Hebrew University to ask them to allow more Palestinians into study programs. After Omar met with someone at the university, he said we needed to make an official complaint at the Ministry of Education. He might have called the sheikh, I don't know."

"Who is this sheikh?" Agent Peretz asked, looking up from his notes. Khaled explained what he knew, including the mosque where he had heard him speak and Agent Peretz motioned to his partner who responded, "I'll check on him."

Turning back to Khaled, Agent Peretz asked, "What happened next?"

Khaled said, "We met Devorah as we were leaving the university, and since she was heading the same way we were, we got on the bus together."

"Had you arranged to meet with her?"

"No."

"Okay, continue."

"On the bus heading downtown, we were talking together, and after a few minutes, Omar and Devorah got into a conversation, and I started daydreaming a little.

"Then Omar nudged me and said we needed to get off. I didn't realize we had reached our stop already, but I stood up, and when the bus stopped, I got off. The door closed and I looked around to see that Omar hadn't gotten off with me.

"I stood there for a few moments, wondering what to do, and then I decided to start after the bus, which had turned the corner and was out of sight. I thought that Omar would get off and start walking back toward me. A minute or so later, I heard an explosion. It came from the direction where the bus had gone, so I started running. I went around the corner, heading toward the source of the smoke, when I saw the bus engulfed in flames. I was still standing there in shock when the police came and took me away."

Agent Peretz nodded and closed his notebook. Nehemyah stood up, and Khaled gave him a long hug before Agent Peretz and Khaled walked out to the car. Agent Peretz's partner was standing in the shade, talking on his phone, trying to track down the identity of the sheikh.

Khaled got in the backseat, but before they returned to the station to get a written statement, Peretz went back into the house to say goodbye to Nehemyah. Looking at his friend with compassion, he said, "I'm very sorry for your loss, Uncle Nehemyah. You know how much we all loved Devorah. I will need to question Khaled some more. I won't rest until I get to the bottom of this.

"Now, I know you were also close to this Omar. I've already spoken to his family, and since they aren't aware of his connection to you, it's probably better if you don't contact them. I'm sure you would like to give your condolences, but if they were to learn of his connection with this kibbutz, it would almost certainly be taken as an offense by them."

Then he turned even more serious as he said, "Losing your granddaughter is a loss for all of us. You may not be aware of it, but she was working on an important Defense Department project in her PhD studies. I can't reveal the details, but I am afraid she may have had documents of inestimable value to our enemies in her possession."

Agent Peretz looked intently at Nehemyah for a moment, bent down to give him a long hug, and left.

Ch 25. Ki El Gadol Adonai

(Jerusalem, 9 months before the Fire)

Let us come before His presence with thanksgiving;
Let us shout joyfully to Him with psalms.

Psalm 95:2

Two weeks later, the police were still searching for the sheikh. He had apparently gone underground—not literally—but hiding out with followers in the West Bank, keeping a low profile.

Khaled had been released provisionally and returned to the dorm house at the kibbutz. The next day he was supposed to meet with Nehemyah for lunch. It would be their first time talking since the bus explosion.

Nehemyah, unable to sleep, had gone with Moshe to an all-night prayer vigil at Mount Zion Church. He was in prayer, pouring out his heart to God for the loss of his granddaughter in the predawn darkness when disaster struck. It took some time for the fire brigade to locate him at the Mount Zion Church, and by the time he was alerted and raced home, very little was left of his and Talia's little wooden house.

The authorities said they suspected arson but could tell him little more.

Nehemyah collapsed to his knees, buried his face in his hands, and sobbed. Less than a year had passed since he lost his wife. Only days ago, Devorah had been taken from him. And now his house and all his possessions were gone.

Khaled and the rest of the members of the kibbutz eventually helped him to a chair in the shade. After a short while, Kaleb, one of the leaders from the Mount Zion Christian Church, came and sat with Nehemyah. Along with his consolation, Kaleb also brought an invitation for him to stay at the Mount Zion Inn, the guest house associated with the church, free of charge, for as long as he needed. Nehemyah, having no better option, accepted their gracious offer.

Once settled in his room, he asked to be left alone, refusing all offers of food and secluding himself behind his closed door. The only possession he had left was his leather-bound Bible in which he kept a five-by-seven photo of Talia.

The workers at the inn grew more and more concerned as days stretched into weeks and still Nehemyah made no contact with the outside world. During the daytime, he left his curtains open, and they could see him occasionally through the window. He seemed to be fine physically, so they continued to honor his request to be left alone.

Seven weeks later, at Mount Zion Church, less than fifty meters from Nehemyah's room, the morning Shabbat service had just begun. The worshippers—over a hundred men, women and children from over a dozen nations—filled the small sanctuary of the nearly 200-year-old church, singing the opening song. They stood, belting out the final lines of the Hebrew worship song, "Let us sing to the Lord."[72]

> *Let us come before His presence with thanksgiving.*
> *Let us shout joyfully to Him with Psalms.*
> *For the Lord is the great God.*
> *For the Lord is the great God.*

Unexpectedly, Nehemyah entered, unnoticed by most who were facing the front. Walking in, he joined with other worshippers standing near the back.

As the song ended, Kaleb stood up. Noticing Nehemyah, he said, "It's very nice to have our brother Nehemyah with us this morning." All eyes turned to look at him.

"It's nice to be here," Nehemyah responded. "God has been working mightily in my life, teaching me many things."

Kaleb paused and smiled. "Would you feel comfortable coming up to the front and sharing with us?"

Nehemyah picked up the bag he had brought and made his way to the front. He gave Kaleb a strong embrace and then turned to address the congregation. His ninety-year-old face seemed to glow with vitality.

"Good morning. Thank you for your kind hospitality, for allowing me to stay here in the inn, and for all that you have provided for me. And thank you for the opportunity to share what God has been doing in my life.

"When you first invited me to come stay here at the inn, I was in shock. I had no desire to eat. As you can imagine, I had so many questions. The verse that God impressed on me for that time was, 'Be still, and know that I *am* God.'[73]

---

72. *"Let us sing to the Lord"* by Jamie Hilsden
73. Psalm 46:10

"And so that is what I did; I remained quiet before God. I don't know for how long, but at some point, I realized that God had begun to nourish my spirit. I can't explain it any other way than to say that God showed up. It was as if I were resting beside still waters and He was restoring my soul.

"After about a week, I woke up one morning to discover a basket of bread and a pitcher of wine on the table. The Lord told me to eat and drink, so I did.

"The next day, the basket filled with fresh bread and the pitcher filled with new wine again appeared on my table. So again, I ate and drank and communed with God all day. Just as He had been nourishing my spirit beside the still waters during my fast, so He began to restore my physical strength through the meals that you—whoever it was—brought to me.

"This has been going on day after day for many weeks. Then this morning, God appeared to me and told me it was time for me to end my seclusion, to rejoin you, my brothers and sisters, in fellowship. So again, I want to thank you for allowing me to stay here and for the meals you have so graciously provided."

Kaleb, in the front row, rose and rejoined Nehemyah. "Brother, I don't know who has been bringing you food. We discussed whether we should. We wanted to honor your desire to be left alone, so we merely knocked and left it at the door. We could see you were up and about but were puzzled because it seemed the food we left each day remained untouched."

"Well, then," said Nehemyah, "That confirms my suspicions. I think I may be able to guess who provided this extraordinary bread. I've never tasted anything that can compare to it. In fact," he said as he reached into his bag and pulled out a basket, "I brought some so you can try it."

He raised the bread for Kaleb and the others to see, then lifting up his eyes, prayed a blessing on the bread, in Hebrew, "Blessed are you,

LORD our God, King of the universe, who brings forth bread from the earth."

After breaking off a piece of the bread for Kaleb, he then broke off another for himself. As they began eating the bread together, Kaleb's face turned from solemn to joyful. Then they both broke into laughter.

Nehemyah turned to the bewildered congregants. "There is enough to share."

The two of them began to break off chunks of bread and hand them out. The people sitting at the end of each row received a piece, broke off some for themselves and then passed the rest along. At first, most people only took tiny pieces, but Nehemyah noticed that the chunks of bread seemed to stay the same size, no matter how many people ate from them. He said, "Don't be shy! Eat up! There is plenty for all. This is the blessing of the Lord!" As people began to notice the multiplication of bread, amazed smiles broke out on all their faces. It became a celebration.

After everyone had eaten as much as they wanted, there was still bread left in the basket. Nehemyah, hardly able to speak because of his joyful laughter, went back up to the front and said, "I almost forgot. I have something to drink as well." He pulled out a bottle from his bag, held it up for all to see, and prayed in Hebrew, saying a blessing on the wine, "Blessed are you, LORD our God, King of the universe, who creates the fruit of the vine."

There were several cups sitting on a nearby table. Nehemyah walked over and filled each of the cups from the bottle. Then, picking up one of the cups, he took a drink. Again, a contagious grin spread across his face. "This is really good. You've got to try it!"

Nehemyah and Kaleb passed the cups row by row throughout the church and everyone took a drink. Amazingly, after everyone had drunk, all of the cups were still full.

Kaleb had prepared a sermon, but he realized that Nehemyah had more from the Lord. Nodding for him to continue, Pastor Kaleb took a seat with the congregation.

Nehemyah stood in the front of the church, still smiling. "In Psalm 46:6, we read, 'Be still and know that I am God.' During the weeks of my seclusion, God has greatly impressed these words on my heart. I've had a lot of opportunity to be still, and I can tell you that I know for sure that He is God.

"I wouldn't wish on any of you the experience of losing a loved one or the loss of all your possessions. And yet, if you do find yourself in such a dark moment, I encourage you to take the time to be still and quiet your heart before God. Because if you do, I'm sure you also will come to know for certain that the Lord is truly God, and that there is none other."

Nehemyah's words seemed to light a fire in the hearts of his listeners. As he stood looking at the congregation, he felt led to ask if anyone had something they would like to share. Immediately, a red-haired, twenty-three-year-old visitor from Los Angeles who had been sitting in the back stood up and introduced himself.

"My name is Chad and I am from the US. This is my first meeting with you all here and I want to say that it has exceeded all my expectations. I was raised in the Christian faith and attended a Christian college. After graduating, however, I realized that my life felt empty. I was going through the motions of being a Christian, but I longed for a closer connection to God. Just a month ago, I decided that my best move was to visit the very place where Jesus himself had walked. And so, I came here to Israel and to your service today.

"I've never experienced the power of God like I have here today. I feel like I want to tell everyone!"

When Chad sat down, Nehemyah had a serious look on his face. "Thank you, Chad. Yes, I too sense that this is the beginning of something new and unusual from God. One day, we may even look back on this as the beginning of a revival. And yet, I would ask you all to exercise caution. In our day of instant information, news spreads quickly and we don't yet know what God has in mind. Too often, I've seen what appears to be a work of God lose His anointing because of an emphasis on human personalities or large crowds.

"What we want here is God's glory. We do not want attention, nor do we want an invasion of curious tourists. Please, I ask you to not spread the word about what you have seen here today. Not yet, at least."

After the service, Chad found Nehemyah. "I really think there is one person I need to tell about this. The Lord revealed to me that I will meet him when I get back to LA. May I have your permission to tell him about what is happening here?"

Nehemyah was hesitant, but after seeing Chad's passion and receiving a nudge from the Lord, he grudgingly agreed. "Yes, but please only tell the one the Lord has shown you."

Part 3

The United States & Caribbean Islands

Ch 26. Those Two Impostors

(Haiti, 7 months before the Fire)

If you can meet with Triumph and Disaster
And treat those two impostors just the same;
Rudyard Kipling, *If—*

Dominic had lost track of time. When he realized it was December, it occurred to him that six months had passed since he left home. He had been angry, feeling betrayed at how they'd kept him in the dark about who his real mother and father were. After two months of searching for his real father, he had sent an email explaining that he would be a day late in arriving home. A day late. Every day since then his thoughts had turned toward home, and he wondered how they were doing. He longed to contact them, but how could he risk it? What if the police were still looking for him in connection with the death of Father Alessandro?

He decided it would at least go to the Internet café and check his email. His inbox was full with hundreds of unread emails. He scrolled back to read them in the order they were sent, starting with one from Pablo Sánchez.

August 1
Dominic,

Thanks for letting us know you are delayed in Puerto Rico. We're thankful the pilot could make an emergency landing.

I know that when you left to visit your grandparents in Germany our relationship was strained and I understand you needed to find some answers.

Thinking of grandparents reminds me of what a wise person once said, "God has no grandchildren." Each of us needs to experience God for himself, and that is what I pray for you.

We are so looking forward to seeing you tomorrow, Lord willing.
Dad

Then a day later another email:

August 2
Dominic,

Your plane arrived, but you weren't on it. I'm trying to process what is going on.

We hadn't seen your email telling us you were unwell and missed your plane, so we went to the airport expecting to meet you. We called the hotel to talk with you, but they said you had checked out and they had no idea where you'd gone.

Your mother and I are eagerly waiting for news.
Love,
Dad

After that, his email was flooded with unread messages. He scrolled down to another email, from about two weeks later:

August 16
Son,

I'm asking myself, *What else could I have done? Was there something I missed?*

We are scared out of our minds. We've been praying, we've contacted the consulate, and we're desperate to find you. I don't know what else to do. It is as if our eighteen-year-old boy has literally disappeared with no explanation!

Of course everyone is praying, but when I heard you had checked out of the hotel in Puerto Rico and not been heard from again, I jumped on a plane. I searched for a week, but I didn't learn anything I hadn't already heard from the officials on the phone. It was as if you had vanished into thin air.

Please get in touch.
Your concerned father

Again, he scrolled down to another email sent about one month later:

September 15
Son,

I am beginning to fear I will never see you again and that these letters will never be read. But I am writing anyway because that is all I can do.

I don't remember much about the time immediately following your disappearance. Your mom and I organized Sunday meetings. Your sister Olivia and her husband Pedro have been a great help leading the Friday night youth group. Your mom and I counseled a couple who were considering divorce.

We have a lot to do. But each evening, as the day's activity slows down, questions come crashing like waves on my soul. One question I have struggled with most is: *Is anything I am doing really worth it?*

I miss you,
Dad

He scrolled down to another email, sent ten weeks later:

Dec 1
Dear Dominic,

Seeing the date circled on my calendar today seemed too much. It has been four months since I last heard from you.

I think this may become a tradition for me: to write you a letter on the first day of each month. It is crushing me to realize I might never see you again this side of heaven. But writing to you helps me to feel like we are still connected somehow.

You might remember Juan, the pastor of the church in Santiago, Chile. Today I received an email from him. He wrote to thank us for our time with them and to let us know that the church's outreach to Bolivia that we started years ago is still going on. In fact, the missions team just returned with amazing news: over a thousand decisions for the Lord on their recent trip!

Also, Pastor Juan shared about the church's newest missionaries, José Martínez and family. Ten years ago, they were the ones who were going to go with us to the Middle East, but at the last minute, the church decided not to send them, and so our family went alone.

Now, a decade later, God, who is the Lord of the Harvest, is sending this family out. The crazy thing is that the political situation in the Middle East hasn't really improved. And our family's experience there was very discouraging. Chile's economy is hurting and so the idea of a church in Santiago helping to financially support a missionary at this time seems virtually impossible, humanly speaking. And yet, the Martinez family has gone out!

What's more, just today I received an email from José Martínez himself, thanking me for our example and encouragement. Dominic, I know our year in Iraq, in a war zone, was unbearably hard. And I know you were old enough to understand that painful loss of your brother Timothy. We all miss him. And Jennifer. Losing a child is unbearable, but losing three children—there are no words for that.

Still, I hold on to the fact that God is good. In his letter to me, José mentioned the village where Timothy died. Dominic, they still remember our family there. Mohammed, one of the men I visited and studied Scripture with, asked José if he happened to know "Boulos" (as they called me). When he said yes, Mohammed insisted he send their condolences for our loss.

But Mohammed especially wanted me to know that his family and two other families have been meeting together regularly since we left, following the same system of Bible study that we taught them; they read a few verses of the Injil[74] in Arabic, share a truth gleaned from the passage, and explain how they intend to put that truth into practice during the next week.

Dominic, at times like this, I remember First Corinthians 15:58, "Your labor is not in vain in the Lord." I just closed my eyes and thanked the Lord for these pieces of encouraging news from Pastor Juan and from José. When I opened my eyes, I saw above my desk the poem *If—*, by Rudyard Kipling.

This is such a powerful poem and I intended to give you a framed copy on your eighteenth birthday, but that was not to be. Instead, I have decided to email you a copy in case you are still alive and see this:

74. *Injil* is the Arabic word for "Gospel" that in Islam often refers to the book given to Jesus, but for Christians refers to the New Testament Gospels or the New Testament as a whole

IF— by Rudyard Kipling

If you can keep your head when all about you
Are losing theirs and blaming it on you,
If you can trust yourself when all men doubt you,
But make allowance for their doubting too;
If you can wait and not be tired by waiting,
Or being lied about, don't deal in lies,
Or being hated, don't give way to hating,
And yet don't look too good, nor talk too wise:

If you can dream—and not make dreams your master,
If you can think—and not make thoughts your aim;
If you can meet with Triumph and Disaster
And treat those two impostors just the same;
If you can bear to hear the truth you've spoken
Twisted by knaves to make a trap for fools,
Or watch the things you gave your life to, broken,
And stoop and build 'em up with worn out tools:

If you can make one heap of all your winnings
And risk it on one turn of pitch and toss,
And lose, and start again at your beginnings,
And never breathe a word about your loss;
If you can force your heart and nerve and sinew
To serve your turn long after they are gone,
And so hold on when there is nothing in you,
Except the Will which says to them: 'Hold on!'

If you can talk with crowds and keep your virtue,
Or walk with kings—nor lose the common touch,
If neither foes nor loving friends can hurt you,
If all men count with you, but none too much;

If you can fill the unforgiving minute
With sixty seconds' worth of distance run,
Yours is the Earth and everything that's in it,
And—which is more—you'll be a Man, my son!

This poem has always been special to me. Today these words stood out: "If you can meet with Triumph and Disaster and treat those two impostors just the same."

I have experienced triumph and disaster. The encouraging reports I received today about Chile, Bolivia, and Iraq? They feel like triumphs, but I remind myself those "triumphs" don't add to my value as a person nor are they a sign of God's approval. And as for disasters, where do I start? Jennifer's death. Timothy's death. Those events knocked me down, but they don't define who I am. And they certainly don't mean that God loves me any less.

Today, the biggest disaster I wrestle with is my uncertainty about you, Dominic. I have made mistakes, and I wonder if my mistakes have led to this disaster of losing you. I also remember that my rock-solid identity, irrespective of any triumphs or disasters in this life, is in God.

Before sending this off I decided to talk with your mom. I have been considering for months what the future might hold for us. I think it's time for your mom and I to finish our mission work overseas.

I opened the bedroom door and found her on her knees praying. She didn't hear me come in, and she was in the middle of praying earnestly for protection for you, and for strength and encouragement for me.

I knelt down beside your mom, and she looked over at me and gave me a hug. We cried together and I began to realize that I had taken for granted for many years the power of a praying woman. More than anything else, it has probably been her quiet work of interceding for me, for you, for our whole family, that has allowed us to persevere in spite of our many setbacks.

Goodbye, son. Until next time.

Love,
Dad

Dominic realized he had been crying as he read the emails. He looked around thankful that no one had noticed. He was tempted to write an email back, to say, "I'm okay, I'm alive," but he didn't want to risk it. He felt trapped and ashamed.

Ch 27. A Wind of Change

(Haiti, 7 months before the Fire)

The future's in the air, I can feel it everywhere
I'm blowing with the wind of change

The Scorpions,
Wind of Change

The next morning, Dominic and Henri went out, as was their custom, to fish. They were used to successful fishing expeditions, but this catch was bigger than anything they could have dreamed of. Over and over, they threw the net in, hauling in catch after catch until their arms ached. Even though the wind kept them right where the fish were, they were going to have to quit; the boat was full.

Then they realized that they had been so focused on their work that they hadn't noticed that a storm was brewing. The boat sat low in the water from the weight of the day's catch and the sun was edging toward the horizon, when suddenly a wave broke over the deck. The young men looked at each other and realized that the wind had taken them much farther out to sea than they had ever ventured before.

Then, as a storm descended and began tossing waves at them, the boys hung on for dear life. They realized, a little late, the great danger they were in. They were far from shore, heading north and west into open seas, and in the middle of what could be a hurricane. They sat frozen, unsure what to do next, certain the waves would wash them overboard.

Then Henri sat up straight and began to use all the voodoo prayers, incantations, and rituals he could think of to try to calm the storm. Dominic looked on, recognizing Henri's cries to the tempest for what they were: fear mixed with a bit of bravado.

But Henri soon sank down defeated as the boat began rolling side to side and all he could do was hold on.

Dominic stood up on the heaving deck. He hadn't paid much attention to Alfred's voodoo lessons, but this appeared to be a do-or-die situation. He repeated an incantation he had learned from Alfred, and then, strangely, it seemed as if he was viewing the scene from above. He could see the boat being tossed around, with Henri and himself clinging to the sides. He said out loud, "Calm down. That's enough."

Suddenly the sea was calm. After a minute or two they began to sail back to shore, their hearts still pounding. After they sold the fish, they went home. Henri was still trembling, his legs shaking after their near-death experience. Dominic walked along calmly, quietly full of confidence after facing and overcoming their ordeal.

Dominic handed Alfred the money from the day's catch and Henri explained the danger they'd been in, exaggerating the role he had played in the calming of the storm. Alfred looked to Dominic for confirmation about Henri's story, got none, and wondered whether to press for more details. He was thrilled that the boys had made it back home safely with such a great catch of fish. At the same time, he was alarmed that they apparently had been in such danger. Rather than try to pry more information from Dominic that evening, the very next day he bought and installed a gas-powered motor for the boat so that, in the event of another storm, the boys would be able to make it back to shore safely.

A week later, the boys again went out fishing, this time equipped with a motor. New horizons opened to them as they realized they could reach fishing spots they had never been able to before. At one new location they pulled in an amazing catch of fish. They threw the net several more times but got nothing. Since they were quite a distance from the shore, Dominic suggested they motor back closer to the bay, but Henri wanted to go further out.

Dominic had thought that the power struggle between him and Henri had been settled long ago. Bringing in a large catch, however, seemed very important to Henri at that point. He became so assertive and argumentative that Dominic thought they might come to blows right there in the boat.

Dominic wasn't really worried about proving he was the alpha male in that situation, but he was concerned that once again they were getting too far from land. As politely as he could manage, attempting to de-escalate the situation, he again suggested that they return closer to the shore.

Henri, ignoring him, gazed at a boat off in the distance.

When Dominic began to ask again, Henri cut him off, announcing in his most elegant French, "No, I have a better idea." Pointing to the other boat, he said, "I think I know those people. Let's head over there and see if they have any extra gas they can lend us."

As they got closer, Henri smiled, recognizing the owner, who greeted them in Creole. Henri went over to turn off the motor, and, after a brief conversation about fishing, the weather, and spare gas, climbed up into their larger boat. He spoke quietly for a few more minutes with the other fishermen, then they all went belowdecks, out of Dominic's view, in search of a gas can.

Dominic waited impatiently, getting a little apprehensive as he noticed the two boats had begun to slowly drift apart. When Henri eventually popped his head back up on deck of the other boat, Dominic yelled, "Henri, what's taking so long? Let's go!"

Henri's responded casually, "No. I'm going back with these men."

Dominic, confused, asked, "And me? What am I supposed to do?"

"Why don't you try using your voodoo powers, miracle boy?" Henri said with an evil smile. Then, to Dominic's surprise, he added, "And you better hurry, it looks like there's a storm coming." Waving his hand goodbye as the wind blew Dominic farther and farther out to sea, Henri shouted, "Au revoir, Dominic! Bonne chance!"

The big boat revved its engine and took off toward land, leaving Dominic alone, bouncing along as the wind and waves took him away from land. He looked up to see Henri's grinning face fading into the distance, then, assuring himself that Henri would pay for this trick, he leaned down and started the engine. He began chasing Henri and his companions but after a few seconds the engine sputtered. He tried pulling the starter cord various times with no luck. Only then did he discover that Henri had sabotaged the gas tank!

He looked up to see that the other boat was already just a small dot in the distance. Squinting his eyes and looking past the boat, he could barely make out Haiti's north coast on the horizon. With no other boats nearby and a storm coming in, he realized he was on his own.

It would do him no good to second-guess how he should have seen this coming, so instead he evaluated his situation. He had no food, very little water, and was steadily drifting out to sea.

The storm was gaining strength, but he knew it should be possible to slowly zigzag his way back toward shore, even against the wind. However, just as he began to pull the lines to raise the sail, a tremendous gust caught the sail and tipped the mast until it was nearly touching the water. The boat was perilously angled and Dominic, riding high, instinctively leaned his body over the side to provide a counterbalance to the wind.

The fierce wind continued to threaten to tip the boat over for several seconds. Gradually, the boat righted itself and Dominic quickly moved to grab the lines that had flown out of his hands. As he made his way forward to retrieve the ropes, the boat rocked back and forth with the waves and the storm continued battering the sail, ripping it to shreds. By the time he was able to lower the torn and flapping sail, it was beyond repair. Land was no longer in sight, and he sat down, bracing himself for what was to come, reconciled to the fact that he had no way to get out of the path of the approaching storm.

Knowing that a downpour was imminent, Dominic quickly took measures to lighten the boat. First, he threw the day's catch overboard, saving one fish in case that was to be his next meal. Then he lowered the anchor, which might have been helpful in calm weather and near the shore, but in that deep water accomplished next to nothing. Realizing it was pulling down the side of the boat, he cut it loose.

Next, he turned his attention to the motor which was also dead weight. Grabbing a wrench, he quickly unbolted it and let it fall into the sea. For a while he tried holding the tiller steady to direct the boat in a wide, easy circle but the wind was blowing so wildly, he was afraid the boat might be torn apart if he tried to apply any direction.

Adrift at sea with no prospect of getting to shore and realizing he had no life vest or other flotation device, he tried a voodoo incantation. Immediately, torrential rain began to pound him, and soaking wet, his mind went to the Bible story of Jesus' disciples in a boat during a storm. He could picture Jesus calming the storm, so he called out to God for protection. The rain suddenly stopped but the wind continued to blow, driving him relentlessly northwest, farther and farther away from the shore. With wind and waves repeatedly spilling water into the small boat, he focused his attention on bailing water out as fast as he could. But his ceaseless efforts barely kept the vessel on the top side of the fishing grounds.

It was about midnight when he realized the worst of the storm had passed and the waves had calmed. He lay down exhausted, immediately falling asleep, adrift in the open sea.

He slept for several hours, but it seemed that only minutes had passed when he was awakened by a crash. The boat was wedged between two large rocks just offshore and was being broken to pieces by the waves. It was still dark, but he could make out the shoreline in the moonlight. Quickly jumping into the water, he swam with all his might, realizing he only had seconds to get clear before the next wave came crashing against the rocks. After a few seconds of swimming parallel to the shore, he looked back to see a huge wave pick up the small boat and smash it to kindling against the jagged rocks. Adrenaline pumping through his veins, he made his way to shore and safely walked up onto the sandy beach.

Exhausted after hours at sea, he lay down and fell asleep until dawn. He awoke to the sun warming his aching muscles. Standing up to stretch, he felt hungry and thirsty and had no idea where in the world he had landed. But he was alive!

Walking a short distance inland, he came across an elderly couple out for an early morning stroll on the boardwalk. Sand in his hair, no shirt or shoes, he looked like a typical beach bum to them. When he approached and asked where he was, the man replied, "Just about a mile south of town."

"What town?"

"You know, *Matthew Town*, the only town on Great Inagua."

"*Great what?*" he asked, his face reflecting his confusion.

At this point, the man was pretty sure Dominic was high on something and motioned to his wife that they should continue their walk. But she ignored him and said to Dominic, "Honey, this is the Bahamas. Where are you from?"

Dominic, appreciating her kindness, smiled. "I've heard of the Bahamas! I left Haiti in a small boat yesterday. I got caught in the storm."

The man looked around. "Where *is* your boat?"

Dominic turned and pointed behind him. "It got ripped apart on some rocks out there last night."

The woman cried out in alarm, took Dominic's hand and said, "Oh, you poor thing! Are you hurt?"

"No. I think I'm fine. Just tired. And thirsty."

The man spoke up again. "You came by yourself from Haiti in a small boat?"

"Well, there were two of us fishing, but the other guy went back to shore with some friends, abandoning me in the storm . . . It's kind of a long story."

A little embarrassed now of his rush to judgment, the man asked, "Well, how can we help you? We'll get you some food and water."

At this point, Dominic felt a rush of emotion. He hadn't realized how much he had missed normal caring people. He felt like a hundred-pound weight was lifted off him. He was free! No longer trapped in Haiti. Eventually they guided him to the local police. There he told the officials a version of his story: that he was a US citizen who had been kidnapped in Haiti and held captive for months.

The police took him by boat to the island of Providenciales in Turks and Caicos Islands, then, contacting the US authorities, they confirmed there was a missing person report for a Dominic Sánchez dating back to August. Without delay, Dominic was flown to Miami, where his fingerprints were taken, his ID confirmed, his story believed, and his parents contacted.

The call from the FBI in Miami could not have come at a better time. Pablo and Julia had just moved back to LA from Argentina a few weeks earlier. Julia had already lined up a job at the Christian school where their son Josh and his wife were working. Pablo, nearing sixty, was beginning to gray, and though his glory days of football at UC Fresno might be a distant memory, he still had contacts at Nike who said they would be happy to have him back again. The family rejoiced with shouts of surprise, tears of joy, and prayers of thanksgiving to God when they heard that Dominic was safe and was coming home to them.

Pablo immediately flew to Miami to meet his son. He brought Dominic's birth certificate as ID, and the police made a thorough attempt to get all the relevant facts of the case, presumably to locate Dominic's captors. After completing the necessary paperwork, the authorities, along with Pablo and Dominic, took photos and had a short interview with the local press who were eager to run a human-interest story about a happy family reunited during the holidays.

Two days later, Pablo and Dominic were on a plane back to Los Angeles. At LAX his mother Julia was the first face Dominic saw. She was crying with joy. His brothers, Josh and David—the twins—were there with their wives and kids, as well as his brother Lucas, all waving banners that read, *"Welcome Home, Dominic!"*

Dominic learned that his return was setting in motion a family reunion. His sister Sara and her husband Jason, as well as his sister Olivia, her husband Pedro, and their four-year-old daughter Petronila, were all on their way up from Argentina. The whole family was going to celebrate Christmas together.

Of course, everyone had hundreds of questions for him: *"Where were you exactly? How did you escape?"* and so on. He told a version of his adventures that wasn't very close to the truth, and everybody said it was a miracle and the best Christmas present ever.

Ch 28. Christmas Presence

(Los Angeles, 7 months before the Fire)

> *Christmas is built upon a beautiful and intentional paradox; that the birth of the homeless should be celebrated in every home.*
>
> G.K. Chesterton, *Brave New Family*

On Christmas Eve, all of Pablo and Julia's children and grandchildren celebrated together and a festive atmosphere filled the room. Not only was it Christmas, but Dominic was also back safe and sound!

Dominic looked around the table at Josh and his wife, David and his wife, and Lucas, still single. Then there was Sara and her husband who had arrived from Argentina and Olivia and her husband who also traveled from Argentina. At the children's table were Josh's two boys, David's two boys, and Olivia's little girl. It was the first time these twelve adults and five children had ever been together.

After living four months with the fear of being arrested for murder, Dominic's sense of relief was overwhelming. Apparently, there was no all-points bulletin out on him for the death of the priest Alessandro. He was out of danger, and his family had welcomed him back as if nothing had changed.

But so much had changed. His real father had abandoned him. His real mother was dead. His "parents" were really his grandparents. His "siblings" were actually his uncles and aunts. Christmas with family is a wonderful thing, but he was feeling overwhelmed.

After dinner the family told the Christmas story in their traditional way. Pablo started the Bible story about Jesus' birth from memory. After a few sentences, he was told, "Stop!" Then the next person in the circle took up where he had left off until they heard, "Stop!" All the way around the room they went until everyone had shared part of the story of how the baby Jesus came to this earth as the savior of the world.

After that, the young grandkids knew they could delay bedtime by asking for a story from Grandpa, so five wiggly bodies, ages eight to three, settled around Pablo, and begged him to tell them a story. "Okay," he began. "Once upon a time there was an elephant, and he was walking through the woods, and do you know what he saw?" Silence. The older grandkids looked to three-year-old Nili, letting her answer because she was the youngest.

When Nili didn't say anything, Pablo exclaimed, "A light!" and Nili's eyes got wide at the revelation. Then he asked, "And do you know where the light was?" She shook her head, looking at him expectantly, so he said, "On a building! And do you know what was inside the building?" Again, she shook her head, so Pablo said, "Nothing!" and after a brief pause added, "So the elephant went in and lay down and went to sleep."

It sounded like that might be the end of the story, so Nili gave a polite smile and looked at the others, but Pablo continued, "And another elephant was walking through the woods, and do you know what he saw?" Nili looked at him again and shook her head no. When he said, "A light," she looked pensive.

When he asked if she knew where the light was, she said tentatively, "On a building?"

"Yes," Grandpa said, "and do you know what was inside the building?"

"Nothing!" she offered.

"No," he corrected gently, "there was *an elephant*!" Nili's eyes registered surprise, and he continued, "So that elephant went in and lay down and went to sleep too." Nili looked expectantly, and Grandpa started again, "And another elephant was walking through the woods, and do you know what he saw?"

"A light!"

"That's right! And do you know where the light was?"

"On a building!"

"Yes, and do you know what was inside the building?"

"Two elephants!"

"Yes! So, the elephant went in and lay down and went to sleep."

Pablo continued, a bit faster now, "And another elephant was walking through the woods, and do you know what he saw?"

"A light!"

"Yes, and do you know where the light was?"

"On a building!"

"And do you know what was inside the building?"

"Three elephants!"

"That's right! So that elephant went in and lay down and went to sleep."

The story might have gone on longer, but the moms and dads came in to say it was time to brush teeth and get jammies on for bed.

Being together again with his family gave Dominic a great sense of happiness. He was surrounded by good, normal people who looked after each other and tried to do what was right. As the kids headed off to bed, he sat thinking how many times he himself had heard that same silly story about the elephant walking in the woods. *Dad told me he made that story up just for me when I was about three and we were living in Chile.* He smiled at the memory as he thought, *It's fun to hear Nili call me* "Uncle Dominic."

Then he remembered he was not really her *uncle*, but her *cousin*. And it hadn't been his *dad* telling him that story so many years ago, but his *grandpa*. Anger began to percolate inside him at the thought; he was not Pablo's *youngest child* but his *oldest grandchild!* The reason he had left home had been to try to locate his real father.

He felt shame wash over him as he thought of the events over the last months. What had he become? What would his family think if they knew that he had accidentally killed someone? Or that he had lied about it? Or that he had allowed an innocent man to take the blame? He imagined how devastated they would be if they knew he had willingly participated in voodoo séances! True, his family had lied to him about the events of his birth, but now his life was one big lie.

He looked down at the new iPhone in his hand. The whole family had chipped in to get him this Christmas gift so that he could always be in touch. "Dominic," his mother Julia had said to him, "from now on, we want to make sure you can contact us at any time. We added your phone to our family plan and installed a family locator app, so you can always know where we are. I call this our *Christmas presence.*"

Later that night, he disabled the location app on his phone. He was truly grateful for their generosity, and he appreciated their concern. But after all that he had been through, that level of communication felt far too constraining. *It's one thing to be able to contact them whenever I want to. It's entirely another to allow them to always know where I am, anytime, day or night.*

Ch 29. Atlas Shrugged

(Los Angeles, 6 months before the Fire)

Money won't create success, the freedom to make it will.
Nelson Mandela, quoted in Britannica.com

After the holidays, everyone went back to their homes and their routines. The adults had work and the children had school. Dominic had neither.

Sitting in the empty house, he was happy to be home and safe, and he was glad to have spent the holidays with people who love him. But he was not the same person he had been a year ago. He was no longer a child. To be thought of as an adult he needed money, and for that he needed a job. With no work history or qualifications, he took the first job he could find: washing dishes at a local restaurant.

Months passed and though the job kept Dominic occupied, he still felt restless and ill at ease. He was determined to make a change so he surprised Pablo and Julia by saying, "There's a guy at work who's looking for a roommate and I think it would be good if I moved in with him."

An uncomfortable moment of silence followed. Pablo, trying to stay positive, asked, "Is there something that's not working out for you here? Something we could do differently?"

Dominic answered, less than honestly, "No, everything's fine here. But this way I'll be closer to work. And my coworker would really appreciate a housemate to help with the rent."

Dominic was soon settled into his new apartment. He found he could walk to work, see his family on occasion, and at the same time enjoy his own independence. It was the first time he had chosen his own living arrangements.

One day, Jorge, his roommate and coworker, overheard one of the other dishwashers at work telling Dominic, "Hey, slow it down a bit! You're making me look bad." A few minutes later, when Fredo was off on one of his many breaks, Jorge came over and said, "Man, I hope you aren't gonna listen to Fredo."

Dominic shrugged. "I don't know. It makes sense. All day long the dishes keep coming. When Fredo works slower, the dishes pile up on his side so the busboys, seeing my area has room, bring their dirty dishes over to me. Working slower means less work."

"And that seems fair to you?"

"Well, my paycheck is going to be the same no matter how many dishes I wash."

Jorge shook his head in disbelief. "Dom, did you just fall off a turnip truck?"

Dominic was still processing that humorous criticism when Jorge added, "Don't. Take. Advice. From. Losers. I know that sounds harsh, but do you really wanna end up like Fredo?

"Man, look at me. I started here as a dishwasher the same day he did. Since then, I've moved up to cook, and now I'm training to be a chef. What's he done? He's still washing dishes. And, he's gotten written up twice for taking extra-long breaks. One more write-up and he's gonna get his butt fired.

"I've gotten three raises this year, and you're going to him for tips on success? The only reason Fredo's car hasn't been repossessed is because he's never even had a car."

Jorge looked at Dominic, "I gotta to get back to work. But let me tell you just one thing. Poor people got poor ways. Think about that."

Back at the apartment that night, Jorge was checking out the news on his computer. Dominic asked, "Okay, what did you mean when you said, '*Poor people have poor ways?*'"

His roommate responded, "Dominic, I've watched people who started out poor like us and now they got everything they need. You know what I've noticed? They're careful with their money. They see a penny, they bend down and pick it up. A penny! They save money by cutting their own hair. They wash their own car. They aren't afraid to get their hands dirty. People like that gonna be rich because of a thousand small decisions they make every day.

"I've also watched people who started out life with all sorts of opportunities, and you know what? Pretty soon they don't even open their mail 'cause it's all overdue bills and credit card notices. How did that happen? It's simple, really: They spend more than they make. Again, it's a thousand little things. They could fill their bottle from the water fountain, but instead they buy a Coke from the vending machine. They think, 'It's only a dollar,' but a dollar every workday is more than twenty bucks a month. That's like two or three hundred dollars a year.

"People with no money live as if they were rich and spend more than they have. People who have money live as if they were poor and make frugal choices every day. So, the rich get richer and the poor get poorer."

Dominic nodded his head in agreement thinking the sermon was over, but his roommate wasn't done yet. "The last Powerball jackpot was worth over half a billion dollars," Jorge said. "Now let me ask you something, do you think a rich man like Elon Musk buys lottery tickets? No, he doesn't. And I'll tell you why; because the odds are horrible. The odds of winning the jackpot are one in *three hundred million*, man! Buying a dozen $2 lottery tickets costs you twenty-four dollars and only gives you a 50/50 chance of winning a *four-dollar* payout. You see what I mean? It's nuts!"

Dominic said, "Okay, got it. I'll be careful with my money."

Jorge said, "I like that you said, '*my* money' because that's another thing. This whole idea that 'If you've got a business, *you* didn't build that business.' That if you are successful, it wasn't your hard work that created your wealth. What kind of nonsense is that? In addition to this restaurant, I'm also painting houses as a side hustle because I intend to get ahead. I'm gonna have my own place someday, even if I have to move to Alaska and build an *ulax*.[75]

Picking up his copy of *Atlas Shrugged* by Ayn Rand, Jorge found a section he had underlined, and said, "Listen to this:

> *'Money is a tool of exchange, which can't exist unless there are goods produced and men able to produce them. Money is the material shape of the principle that men who wish to deal with one another must deal by trade and give value for value.'*

"It's a basic rule: you determine what a product is worth by what people are willing to pay." He looked at Dominic and, holding out *Atlas Shrugged*, added, "You should read this. Then you'll see what comes of disincentivizing the very ones who get things done." Laying the book on the coffee table, he turned back to his computer.

Dominic looked around. He enjoyed this nice apartment. He just hadn't realized a person could be so passionate about what seemed to be rather radical economic theories.

---

75. Traditional Aleut house built by digging a pit and covering it with wood and earth

Ch 30. On the Move

(FL, CA, OR, 7 weeks before the Fire)

> *My, my. A body does get around.*
>
> William Faulkner, *Light in August*

Eván slammed his fist on the table. Ten months had passed since he first saw Dominic and tracked him to Haiti. *I was so close,* he grumbled. *I can't believe I allowed myself to be chased off by that silly Haitian boy.* To this day, he could not explain why the words "*I know who you are*" and "*I will kill you*" had struck such terror in his heart. It was only after fleeing Cap-Haïtien and making his way to Miami, that he had come to his senses and realized that his fear had been irrational. *I could have stood and fought,* he reminded himself; *I am, after all, a* Tsel*!*

Many times since then, he had considered going back to Haiti to search for Dominic, but every time he thought about it, a paralyzing fear would suddenly overcome him. Having had the spiritual power of a *Tsel,* it was incredibly frustrating to now find himself cut off from the Shadowlands, trapped in a physical body bound by time and space.

Aware of how vulnerable and exposed he was, instead of returning to Haiti, he opted to search the Internet and wait for news of the boy. Days turned into months, and though occasionally there had been news about a Dominic Sánchez somewhere in the world, it was never about *his* Dominic. Eván, uncertain how to proceed, had eventually lost hope and essentially became a hermit, rarely stepping outside the apartment, and only using the Internet to buy groceries.

He hadn't searched for news about Dominic in many months, but when he did, he found an article from *Christmastime,* complete with a photo. The story explained how Dominic had escaped captivity in Haiti and been reunited with his family after being presumed dead for months.

Eván beat the table again in anger and said, "In December, Dominic was right here in Miami!" Reading the rest of the article, he saw the words "*Los Angeles*" and knew where he needed to go.

Back from the mission field and living in LA, Pablo and Julia were often invited to share with churches and even a large Bible school about their experiences overseas. It was exciting to be in the limelight and to be treated like rock stars, but what they really wanted for this next season was a quiet life in a small town.

While on one of their speaking tours, they had fallen in love with the natural beauty and relaxed lifestyle of rural Western Oregon. Then, when they heard that a small Christian school in the area was looking to fill several staff positions, they decided to investigate. They hit it off well with the school director, and he offered them both jobs starting in the fall.

Sitting at their kitchen table in LA, Pablo was dreaming about moving up to Oregon. Finally, he said out loud, "Julia, I think we should say yes to these new jobs."

After a pause, she nodded, "I agree, but I'm concerned about being so far away from our kids and grandkids."

"I'm sure they'll come to visit. Sara and Olivia came last year from Argentina and it's not much farther for them to travel to Oregon than to California."

"I'm thinking of our being away from our kids here. LA isn't the same place it was when we went to school here. Life in big cities seems to be out of control."

"That's why moving makes sense. In rural areas, there still seems to be a measure of common sense."

"Not to mention clean air and natural beauty."

"Maybe we can convince all the kids to move up with us. How about we start with Dominic?" Julia called and Dominic answered, "Hi, I'm kind of busy right now. What's up?"

"Dad and I were just thinking of you. How are you?"

"Doing fine."

"Great. Well, you know how we mentioned a couple of months ago the job offer up in Oregon. Guess what . . . we've decided to take it."

"Oh?"

"Yeah, at the Christian school we visited. It's a really nice area . . . and we're thinking how great it would be if the whole family moved up there."

"I've got a job and an apartment here."

"Okay, well, just think about it, okay?"

"Okay, bye."

The call left them feeling both uneasy and dissatisfied. They might have tried harder to convince Dominic to move to Oregon with them if they had known what his life was really like. He had told them, "I'm doing fine" and "What else could I want?" But in reality, all was not well.

Ch 31. The Hound of Heaven

(Los Angeles, 7 weeks before the Fire)

Fear wist not to evade as Love wist to pursue.

Francis Thompson,
The Hound of Heaven

Dominic had lived in many countries and experienced his share of danger. When he was only eight, while walking home from school in the Middle East, he had been suddenly forced to defend himself from two grown men. At that moment, he found in himself a reservoir of strength, daring, and cunning he hadn't realized he possessed.

Ten years later in Haiti, far away from his family, he survived for months with no one to depend on but himself. Sure, Alfred had offered him voodoo protection, but he had come to doubt Alfred's protection had much value.

Now, once again he was alone, this time among the masses of people on the streets of LA. Each time he walked to the bus stop he had an acute sense of vulnerability and fear. It wasn't just walking past aggressive panhandlers and assorted weirdos. It was gang members making drug deals in broad daylight. He kept his eyes straight ahead so he wouldn't witness anything.

Dominic had assumed that one of the benefits of having Jorge for a roommate would be that he could catch a ride with him to work. But, although he dropped hints, Jorge never offered.

The first couple of days walking to work from Jorge's house, Dominic experimented with voodoo as a way to protect himself while walking down the lawless streets. He couldn't tell if the curses had any power or effect on others, but he did notice his own sense of sadness increase, as if he were sinking into a deep, dark hole.

He was feeling especially unhappy one day when a red-headed street preacher saw him walking and began yelling to him from across the street a phrase that sounded like pure nonsense, *"Fear wist not to evade as Love wist to pursue."*

Dominic ignored his shouting, but the next day it was the same: "Fear wist not to evade as Love wist to pursue." He paused long enough to hear the preacher calling out, "Repent, for the kingdom of God is at hand!" and to hear those passing by scoff at his words.

Dominic considered that kind of open-air preaching annoying, but as he listened, he couldn't help but admire how fearless the guy was in the face of so much rejection. Curious, he stopped for a moment in front of the street preacher who smiled, stretched out his hand and said, "Hi, my name's Chad."

He decided to pass on the handshake but said, "I'm Dominic."

"Nice to meet you."

"The pleasure is all yours," he replied sarcastically.

"Yes, I'm sure. I've seen you walk by and I was hoping you'd stop by and we could talk. You seem like a nice kid. What brings you to this part of town?"

"It's a long story."

"How about the CliffsNotes?"

"I don't know anything about any cliffs, but you could say that the wind brought me here from the Caribbean."

"That sounds interesting. Care to elaborate?"

"No. Not really. Maybe another day."

"Are you sure that we will both be given another day?"

This made Dominic stop and think. "You know, I'm not sure of much of anything right now."

"Would you like to be? For example, would you like to know how you can be connected with real power?"

Dominic froze. *What is up with this guy? Is he reading my mind?* Out loud he said, "What are you talking about?"

"You've experienced power before, haven't you, Dominic? But what about *real* power? What about *good* power?"

Dominic's interest was piqued. He wanted to hear what this guy had to say, but on the other hand, something was telling him to play it cool. "So, you've got the inside scoop on power? On really good power?"

"I do."

"Okay, I'm listening. What's your story on getting real power?"

"Right. I'll give you the short version. I was raised in the church and went to a Christian college but felt like something was missing. I decided the best place to learn about the one true God would be Israel, and specifically Jerusalem, a city of great religious importance to Jews, Muslims, and Christians. So, I went to Israel and started looking around Jerusalem."

Chad could sense that he was already starting to lose Dominic's attention, so he picked up the tempo.

"Almost immediately I met some Messianic Jews. Do you know what they are?"

Dominic shook his head.

"They are Jews that believe in Jesus as the Messiah. You know, the Christ?"

"Okay."

"They invited me to one of their meetings . . . and it was amazing! Unlike anything I'd ever experienced before! I went back the next day, and the next, for about a month. I didn't know it then, but I'd stumbled upon a revival. I had never experienced such power in my whole life."

"So, why did you leave?"

"Good question. I didn't want to. But God told me to come back to the US and preach on the streets of LA because there was one special person He wanted me to meet. I've been here for months, but when I saw you the other day, I knew you were the one. God wants to give you His power."

Dominic, who had been listening intently, gave a half-hearted smile and looked away. "I hate to disappoint you, but I don't think I'm the person you're looking for. I've known Christians and it turned out they had been deceiving me the whole time. I'm done with that. I'm a lost cause. For me, there is no hope."

"There are no lost causes, and there is always hope."

"Well, let's just see how that works out . . . for both of us," Dominic said as he walked off, leaving Chad and his soapbox. But he couldn't escape the image of Chad's flaming red hair and the feelings their short conversation had triggered. Religion. God. Jesus. *I've been down that road before. There's nothing there for me.*

After work that night, dusk was coming to the streets of LA and Dominic was lost in his thoughts as he walked along the street. He was still several blocks from home when he suddenly *sensed* something. He looked to his left and out of the shadows stepped a man wearing a hooded sweatshirt and dark glasses. The stranger started toward him. Dominic's heart raced and he began walking faster.

Only a few blocks to his apartment, but he had to cross a busy street and the light was red.

A few steps from the intersection, he heard over his shoulder, "Dominic Sánchez, lately from Haiti, I need to talk with you."

He turned around, surprised. At his back was a busy street, in front of him the hooded man in dark glasses. For a moment, he considered running away, then opted to step closer and, in a threatening tone, said, "I know voodoo."

The man laughed. "Look who brought a knife to a gun fight."

Dominic took a step back, alarmed. "What are you talking about? What do you want from me?"

"I don't *want* anything from you. I've been searching for you because I want to *give* you something: I want to tell you who you really are."

Dominic stared. *Twice in the same day! First the street preacher saying God wants to give me power. Now, this hooded stranger offering to tell me about who I really am. Does he know about my search for my real father?*

Dominic was intrigued and curious, but also very much on his guard. There was obviously something off about this guy, so keeping himself an arm's distance away he asked, "You think you know who I am?"

The hooded man smiled and took a half step closer. "I know all about you, Dominic. I know that the people you call your parents aren't really your parents but your grandparents. And that your real mother is Jennifer Sánchez. And that you have been looking for your real father. I also know about the priest in the Dominican Republic."

Dominic couldn't believe his ears, but before he could respond the man continued, "I know your dark secrets, but I also know that you are destined for greatness. Dominic, do you want to know who your father really is?"

Dominic looked around. Though the street traffic was heavy, they were alone on the sidewalk. The man fixed his eyes on him and said,

"I can tell you that your father is more powerful than any priest, voodoo *houngan,* or street preacher. Dominic, your father is a god."

He took a step back. "What? You mean, like Hercules or Zeus?"

"Yes, a being so powerful that Hercules himself would have cowered before him."

"Are you saying that Hercules was real?"

"You have no idea the things that have gone on, and in fact are going on right now, in your world, do you?"

Dominic eyed the stranger suspiciously. *Who is this guy? How does he know about Father Alessandro? If he's a secret policeman from the Dominican Republic, could he arrest me? I thought I was safe in the States. I need to get out of here!*

He turned toward the street with his back to the stranger then cursed. The signal was red again—*Don't Walk!* He had been distracted and missed his chance to cross. The traffic was a steady stream, all four lanes, both directions. *And the lights on this street take forever.*

The stranger sensed Dominic's anxiety and spoke to him over his shoulder, "Dominic, my boy, you can't escape your destiny. I can take you to where you want to go."

Dominic ignored him and studied the traffic speeding by. Suddenly, he sprang into the street, running straight into traffic. Tires screeched and horns blared as vehicles sped past. Finding an impossibly narrow gap in what appeared to be a solid flow of cars, he reached the other side unharmed.

Once safely on the other curb, he turned for a moment to look back across the busy street at the stranger, who, surprised by the quick escape, was standing with his mouth agape. Wasting no time, Dominic rushed home to his apartment, slipped inside, locked the door, and sat down, still shaken from his encounter with the strange man.

Ch 32. On the Streets

(Los Angeles, 6 weeks before the Fire)

Nobody's ever taught you how to live out on the street.
Bob Dylan, *Like a Rolling Stone*

The next day was Dominic's day off. He was home alone when he heard a knock at the door. He immediately thought of the stranger from the night before. *Has he found where I live?* Looking through the peephole, he was relieved to see it wasn't him. Not wanting to take any chances, he tried to ignore the knocking, but it continued so at last he cracked open the door.

"Good morning?"

The nicely dressed man replied, "Thank you for opening the door. I just saw you through the window as I was walking past, so I knew someone was in the apartment. But I didn't recognize you, so I thought I'd better check to make sure you weren't a burglar or something."

Dominic relaxed a little and chuckled. "Oh, I see. Sorry it took me a while to open the door."

"That's okay." The man extended his hand. "I'm Mike, the apartment manager. And who are you?"

"I'm Dominic, Jorge's roommate."

"Oh. Where's Jorge?"

"At work."

"Right. Well, please tell him to come see me when he gets home today, okay?"

That afternoon when Jorge got home, Dominic told him Mike wanted to see him.

"Oh no! Dominic, you didn't tell him you are living here, did you?"

"Yes. Why?"

"Because I know what he's going to say. According to the rental agreement, only one person can live in this apartment. That's bogus. Why did you talk to him?"

Dominic realized Jorge wanted to blame him, but really, if anyone was at fault, it was Jorge. His strong opinions about free market economics were fine, but in the real world, the terms of a written agreement almost always trump one's economic opinions.

Jorge came back from his meeting with the manager and broke the bad news: according to their rental agreement, they had one week to move out.

Jorge and Dominic immediately started looking for a new place, but there was nothing available in the area that they could afford on such short notice. They needed first and last month's rent as well as a security deposit, and they simply didn't have the money.

Throughout the week, Jorge continued yelling at Dominic and blaming him for "opening his big mouth," but his anger did little to fix the problem. Finally, on their last full day in the apartment, Dominic saw Jorge loading boxes and bags of stuff into his car.

"Did you find a new apartment?"

"No, I'm just going to live in my car. I don't have that much stuff. I'm just taking down a few things at a time."

"Really? Where are you going to sleep?"

"In the car. The seat goes back pretty far. It's not that bad. I've done it before."

"I see."

"How about you, where are you going to go? Back home?"

"No, it's not that easy. My relationship with my family is kind of strained, and I already feel like I'm somewhere between a child and an adult. Besides, my parents are preparing to move up to Oregon, and I don't want to bother my siblings here in town."

"Oh, bummer! If I had a van or even a station wagon, I'd let you stay with me, but my car is kind of small, you know."

"Yeah, right," Dominic said. "Well, I need to get to work now. I'm sure I'll figure something out."

"Okay. Well, we can sleep here tonight, but we have to be out by noon tomorrow."

"Got ya. See you later."

Making his way back home after work, Dominic heard the street preacher again. He tried to ignore him, but Chad held out his hand. "Hey, Dominic. Look, I get it if you don't want to talk with me. But I just have to tell you that we never know when our time is going to come. Are you ready? Are you ready to meet God?"

Dominic couldn't decide if he wanted to ignore him and continue on his way or punch him in the face first before walking on. He took a deep breath and counted to three before turning to face him. "Look, Chad, you seem like a nice enough guy, but I am not like other people. You don't know who I am. You don't know what I've done. And you don't know what I'm going through right now."

"Dominic, you're right. I don't know much about you. And I don't know what you're going through. How can I help?"

Dominic relaxed a little. "Do you happen to know of a cheap place to rent available, say . . . starting tomorrow?"

Chad answered slowly, "Maybe . . . Why don't you come to my place this evening and we can talk about it?"

"Listen, this is my last night in my apartment. I have to move out by noon tomorrow. I don't want to be rude, but to be honest with you, I don't really have time for a social get-together. So, I guess I'll see you later."

Dominic turned to leave, but Chad said, "Wait. Then the answer is yes."

Confused, and almost out of patience, Dominic stopped and turned around. "Yes, what?"

"Yes, I know of a cheap apartment you can rent. Do you want to come and look at it?"

"Uh, I guess. When?"

"I can go right now. How about you?"

Dominic relaxed again and smiled. "Sure. Why not?"

On the way to Chad's apartment, Dominic filled him in on his housing situation. He concluded, "I don't work tomorrow. Actually, I told them that I needed some time off to sort out my housing. Anyway, so, this is your place?"

Chad opened the apartment door. "Yeah, it's not much, but I call it home for now."

"No, it's great. So, you said you know of a place for rent."

"Yes, there's a room here in my apartment."

Chad led him through the front room, past a small kitchen, and opened a bedroom door. "This room will be available."

"Okay. How much?"

Chad hesitated. "Four hundred a month. Will that work for you?"

"Yeah, that's great! And security deposit, and utilities?"

"It's all included. Nothing extra. Four hundred dollars a month. And no hurry, you can get it to me whenever you can. So, do you want it?"

Dominic stood there silent, thinking.

Chad said, "Something wrong?"

"What's the catch?"

The street preacher laughed. "The catch? Well, I guess the only catch is that you have to put up with me."

Dominic hesitated before saying, "Well, you know at my last place . . . ."

"Oh, right. Yeah, I should have thought of that," Chad said as he pulled out his cell phone, made a call, and held the phone out in front of him.

"Hey, Scott, how are you doing? Chad here. I've got you on speaker phone."

"Hey, Chad. What's up?"

"Well, I'm here in the apartment with a friend of mine, and he's interested in renting the place with me. Any issues with that?"

"That place is approved for two people, *no problema*."

"Great. I'll check back with you later to see if there's any paperwork we need to fill out."

"Roger that. Thanks for checking. Catch you later."

Chad put the phone away and said, "So, if you want to think about it . . . ."

"No. I'll take it. When can I move in?"

"Anytime. I can come pick you up tomorrow."

"Yeah. Great. Eleven o'clock?"

"Yeah, that'll work. Where are you at?"

"Buena Fortuna Apartments, off San Pedro. Number 36."

"It's a plan. See you then."

Ch 33. Choose Life

(Los Angeles, 6 weeks before the Fire)

For God so loved the world
that He gave His only begotten Son,
that whoever believes in Him
should not perish but have everlasting life.
John 3:16

The next day, the bedroom was cleared out and cleaned up when Dominic entered the apartment with a box of his belongings. "This is awesome. Thank you so much."

"My pleasure."

"I didn't really get a chance to see the whole apartment. Where's your room?"

"Right here." Chad pointed to the front-room couch. "This is where I sleep."

Dominic's smile faded as he looked around at the boxes of clothes next to the couch, and then, looking in the empty bedroom, added, "I see. This is a one-bedroom apartment and you gave me your room. That's not right."

"You agreed to the apartment. You agreed to the bedroom. You agreed to the price. I told you the catch was that you had to put up with me. You chose to accept the deal; I chose to give you the bedroom.

But, if you're really unhappy with the arrangement, I'm pretty sure I can find someone else to rent the room to."

Dominic shook his head and then smiled ruefully. "You tricked me. You know I have nowhere else to go."

Chad poured two glasses of water, handed one to Dominic and sat down on the couch. "Dominic, please have a seat in your new apartment. You can sit in the easy chair. I'll sit on my new bed."

Dominic accepted the glass and sat down. "Thank you. I appreciate it. But you don't have to give me your bedroom. I can sleep on the couch."

"No. I've thought this through. I have my things all over the apartment. It's easier for me to clear out the bedroom and let you have that as your private space, if you want it. For me, I think privacy is a bit overrated. I can just hang out anywhere."

"I don't understand. You hardly know me. You haven't asked for any references or for me to sign a contract. You're hardly charging me any rent. You don't even seem concerned if I ever pay you or not. Why are you doing this?"

"Because God told me to. It's that simple."

"So, God told you to rent out your bedroom to someone, it doesn't matter who?"

"No. He told me I'm supposed to share my apartment with Dominic Sánchez."

"Wait. So, how do you know my last name? Have you been stalking me or something?"

Chad chuckled. "Yeah, that's good. Street preacher by day, hit man by night."

Dominic wasn't smiling. "What am I supposed to think?"

"Just what I told you. God told me your name and that I'm supposed to offer to let you stay here with me."

"Well, if you really knew who I was, you wouldn't be so eager to have me here."

"Right. You said you weren't like other people."

"It's true. You don't know who I am. You don't know what I've been through. And you don't know what I've done."

"Come on, do you think you're the only person who's even done bad things? The Bible says, 'All have sinned and fall short of the glory of God.'"

"No, it's not that. I know the Bible. What I'm talking about is way past normal sin. It's way past normal anything."

"Listen, do you remember that sentence I shouted at you the first day I saw you? I said, *'Fear wist not to evade as Love wist to pursue.'* Do you know what that means?"

"Actually, no."

"It means that fear isn't as good at hiding as love is at finding. It's from a poem called 'The Hound of Heaven,' which basically compares God to a bloodhound. The idea is that you can run from Him, but all the while He is on your trail. You can hide, but He will always find you."

"What if I don't want to be found? I thought God was love. Why can't He just let me be?"

"That's just it. Someday you will understand that the thing you are running from is the very love that your heart really desires at its deepest level."

"Well, apparently, your God isn't the only one that's hounding me."

"What do you mean?"

"The other day, after I talked with you, this creepy guy started following me on my way home."

"Really? What did he want? Did you talk with him?"

"Yeah, it was weird. He knew my name—just like you did. Actually, he knew a bunch of stuff about me."

"Wow, interesting! I didn't realize there would be so much competition for the chance to spend time with you. Well, at any rate, it looks like I won that contest," he said, smiling.

Dominic wasn't in a smiling mood. "Chad, listen to me! This isn't funny and I don't think you understand. I'm beginning to think that I was born cursed, and I've been involved in some seriously strange stuff. You do not want to get mixed up in this."

Chad took a breath. "Dominic, I get it, okay? The spiritual world is real. Fighting back against the devil and his forces is serious. But though evil exists, I know one thing for sure; ultimately God is still in charge." Then he began to softly sing,

> *"This is my Father's world,*
> *Oh, let me ne'er forget,*
> *That though the wrong seems oft so strong,*
> *God is the ruler yet."*[76]

Dominic seemed to soften a little, so Chad continued, "Dominic, I do understand what's going on here, and I need you to believe me when I say that I'm okay with getting involved in your life. God has not cursed you. God loves you. John 3:16. You know that verse, right?"

"Yeah, 'For God so loved the world . . . ."

"Are you part of the world?"

Dominic hesitated for a second before answering. "Yeah, I guess."

"'God so loved the world that He sent His one and only Son . . .' What's next?"

"'That whoever believes in Him should not perish . . . .'"

"Yes, that's right. What comes next?"

"'. . . but have everlasting life.'"

"Dominic, Jesus said *'whoever believes.'* You have the ability to choose."

Chad paused for a moment then continued. "In the Old Testament, Moses told the people, '. . . I have set before you life and death, blessing and cursing: therefore choose life . . .'[77] Later, Joshua told the peo-

---

76. From the hymn "This is my Father's World" by Maltbie D. Babcock
77. Deuteronomy 30:19

ple, 'Choose for yourselves this day whom you will serve.'[78] Dominic, you have a choice. Everyone has a choice."

Dominic asked, "Does Satan have a choice? And the demons? Can they choose life?"

"They did have a choice, and they chose death. What you're telling me is that you think you were born without any ability to choose life. Merely because of how you were born. That you never had the ability to choose life. That's not the way God works. Everyone has the ability to choose. All humans can choose life. As long as they are alive, they can still choose to believe."

---

78. Joshua 24:15

Ch 34. The Wolfman

(Los Angeles, 6 weeks before the Fire)

> *There were giants [Hebrew: Nephilim] on the earth in those days, and also afterward, when the sons of God came in to the daughters of men and they bore children to them. Those were the mighty men who were of old, men of renown.*
>
> Genesis 6:4

Chad let his words sink in for a moment before continuing. "Dominic, this 'seriously strange stuff' you're talking about is supernatural. Do you think you are the only one that has been impacted by the dark realm? People have been talking and writing about these kinds of experiences for thousands of years. Many modern authors present the supernatural in a fun or playful way, like in Harry Potter, or X-Men, or the Marvel Comics series. But we've got to admit that modern science doesn't have answers for everything we experience in this world. In the distant past, as well as right up to the present day, many people have claimed to have been contacted by beings from other dimensions—sometimes in very personal ways."

"By *personal* you mean *sexual*?"

Chad said, "What can I say? I'm trying to keep this PG for you."

"Thanks."

"Dominic, can I tell you my story?"

"Sure. Go for it."

"Okay. My father was abusive and an alcoholic. My mother tried to make the relationship work but couldn't, so she raised me on her own. The only time I saw my father was on TV. He was a professional UFC fighter, maybe you've heard of him? He went by the name Wéeyekin, some Native American spirit god. He was a good fighter, but he was terrible at relationships. And when he drank, he got crazy.

"Once, when I was fifteen, I decided I wanted to see him fight—in person. I went with a group of older kids that I knew who got me into the arena. The fight was awful. I was mostly just scared to be there, but part of me was proud of him, that my father could be that tough and that famous.

"Anyway, the fight ended, and he had won. Afterward, he came out into the crowd. He was walking down the aisle, and he was going to walk right past me, when suddenly he stopped and looked right at me. It was weird, but he seemed to know who I was. He hadn't raised me. He hadn't had any contact with me at all. But, at that moment, I knew that he knew who I was.

"All at once, he grabbed my arm and pulled me out into the aisle. I was scared to death. What was he going to do? I wasn't supposed to be there. My mom didn't even know I was there.

"He walked me back to the locker room and closed the door behind us. He pointed to a chair and grabbed himself a drink. He didn't talk much—at least, not at first—he mainly asked me questions. But after he had had a few drinks, he started telling me about himself. He said he was from a different world called the Shadowlands where it's always dark. And everyone that lives there is like a god—he called them *Selleem* or something. He said he had no way to get back there, and that when he died, he would be thrown into a pit.

"I was getting freaked out, and then suddenly the door opened up and some official-looking guy came in and said I couldn't be there. I was so relieved, I hopped up and ran out of there. I never saw him again, but a couple of days later, I read that he had been shot in a street fight that very same night."

Dominic said, "Wow. Sorry."

"Thanks. But I'll tell you what, that short conversation I had with my father scared me to death—or rather, to life. You see, after he died, I decided to tell my mom all about it.

"I expected her to scream and yell and ground me for life. But she didn't. She just listened and cried. She wasn't angry, and she wasn't sad. It was like she was relieved. She said, 'I knew someday he would find you.' I told her, 'Mom, he said he was a god from the Shadowlands. That's just the hallucination of a crazy drunk who got punched a few times too many, right?'

"My mom looked at me and just shook her head and said, 'I'm sure he thinks it's true. He told me the same thing, many times. At first, I was impressed and entertained. We only slept together once, but after that one time, he was completely uninterested in me. It was like he found me repulsive.'

"Then my mom explained why she worked so hard to keep him away from us. Her lip trembled as she said, 'I know you won't believe this, my son, but I swear to you that once, before you were born, I saw him turn into a wild animal. Not figuratively. He literally turned into a wolf.'"

Ch 35. Seeing and Believing

(Los Angeles, 6 weeks before the Fire)

> *. . . blessed are those who have not seen and yet have believed.*
>
> John 20:29

Dominic seemed a little shaken, so Chad asked, "Are you alright? I shouldn't have mentioned that about him turning into a wolf. Do you want me to continue?"

When Dominic nodded his assent, Chad continued, "My mom told me that watching my dad transform into a wild animal was too much for her. She decided that to protect her unborn child, she needed to move away. But, apparently, after I was born, it was like he was stalking us. He kept turning up; we would move to a new town and there he was. He would find us, over and over again."

He paused, and Dominic asked, "So, what did she do?"

"She turned to God. She knew that she was up against something that was bigger than she could handle."

Dominic turned away. "God's always the answer, huh?"

Chad smiled calmly. "Yes. As a matter of fact, He is. Remember, you said that I wouldn't understand, that no one could help you, that

God couldn't help you, that you're so different than anyone else. Do you still believe that's true?"

Dominic got up to leave. "I don't know what I believe anymore. I just need to go out for a bit."

Chad said, "In your fear, you are running from the only one who can help you to become who you are meant to be. And your fear is unfounded. There is nothing that can separate you from the love of God. Nothing. Not death, not life, not angels, not principalities, not powers, not things present, not things to come, not height nor depth, not any created thing. Nothing can separate us from the love of God which is in Christ Jesus our Lord.[79] God loves you so much, no matter what you have done in your life. Nothing is bigger than God's love."

Dominic was still standing. He turned toward the door. "I just need some time to sort things out."

"Dominic, wait! There's something else I need to tell you. Do you remember how I asked you if you're ready to meet God?"

"Yeah."

"It's because we don't have much time. Just like the Lord told me your name, He has also revealed to me that the time is short. God told me we have less than a year. There's no time to waste. We all need to get ready."

Dominic thought about his situation. He was estranged from his family, being stalked by a weirdo, one step away from being on the streets, and now living off the charity of a Christian radical. The truth was he didn't know what to believe or whom to trust anymore.

He sat back down and looked earnestly at his housemate. "If God is supposedly all-powerful, why doesn't he seem very interested in showing His power?"

Chad replied, "Well, I guess one answer is that God does show His power, but we often take it for granted. The whole universe was created and is maintained by the power of God. But what I think

79. From Romans 8:38–39

you're asking about is God's miraculous power, something out of the ordinary."

Dominic nodded and Chad continued, "Well, we have reliable accounts of God acting miraculously, written in the Bible and other books . . . ."

"But why not nowadays," Dominic asked impatiently. "Why don't we see God doing powerful, miraculous things every day?"

"That's a good question. And I believe the answer is that God prefers people to choose Him out of love and faith. There's nothing remarkable when people believe in things like sunlight or gravity; we see or experience these things nearly all the time. We would consider it ridiculous not to believe in these things. But God doesn't force people to believe in Him. He often allows there to be other rational explanations for those who don't really *want* to serve Him."

He paused for a moment before asking, "Can I tell you another story?"

"Sure."

Chad relaxed a little and began. "Many years ago, before I was born, my grandpa, my mom's dad, was out hunting, following fresh deer tracks, when he realized he was a long way from home and it was getting dark. It had started to rain, and he began to get a little scared about finding his way back to his wife and daughter. He didn't believe in God; in fact, he was sick of religion and of people trying to pretend there was a god.

"It occurred to him that people would normally cry out to God in a predicament like his, but it felt hypocritical to ask for help from a God he didn't even believe in. So, do you know what he did?"

"What?"

"He lifted his rifle in the air and started dancing in a circle taunting God, cursing Jesus and saying, 'Why don't you strike me dead?!'"

"What happened?"

"A bolt of lightning struck him and knocked him to the ground!"

"What?"

"That's right. It didn't kill him, but it sure did shake him up. After he was able to stand up again, he started walking and eventually found his way home. Now, I have a question for you. How do you think that experience changed my grandpa's life?"

"I don't know."

"Would you believe me if I told you that even though a lightning bolt struck him at the exact moment he was taunting God, he still wasn't convinced that God existed? My grandma and my mom were devout believers, but my grandpa still refused to believe. He told them he wouldn't believe because he couldn't see God.

"You see, faith is a gift from God. A few years after that experience, my grandfather did indeed believe when he had a life-changing encounter with God. Do you know what convinced him that God was real and that Jesus was the only way?"

"No."

"He read the Scriptures. The passage he read explained how Jesus died and rose from death, and that a group of His followers saw Him after His death. When they told Thomas, who hadn't been with them, that they had seen Jesus alive again, Thomas refused to believe them. My grandpa smiled in agreement when he read that passage. He, like Thomas, was a man who needed to see to believe.

"Then he read that Jesus came to his followers again, and this time Thomas was there. He told Thomas to look at Him, to touch Him, to stop doubting and believe. Thomas worshipped Jesus saying, 'My Lord and my God!' He was convinced! But Jesus told him, 'Thomas, because you have seen Me, you have believed. Blessed *are* those who have not seen and *yet* have believed.'[80] That sentence '*Blessed are those who have not seen and yet have believed*' was all it took to change my grandfather's view of God."

80. John 20:29

Dominic was quiet. "So, your grandpa asked for a sign from heaven. In that moment, he was hit by a lightning bolt. Yet he still refused to believe. Later, he read in the Bible about Jesus' interaction with Thomas and, suddenly, he believed. That kind of belief without evidence seems, frankly, hard to believe."

"And yet," began Chad, "That is exactly what biblical faith is."[81]

"Chad, I've heard about faith and about God all my life. But, to be honest with you, I haven't seen anything that convinces me that this God is really all-powerful or that He is really involved in our lives."

"Well, Dominic, God isn't like a genie that is obligated to perform at the beck and call of any human. But I'll pray that you might see His power and the great love that He has for you. You see, what God offers to those who believe is eternal life. Not just a longer life, but a different kind of life, a life that is fulfilling and peaceful, yet at the same time exciting and challenging. It's real, meaningful life, and it only comes from Jesus."

81. Hebrews 11:1 and Romans 8:24

Ch 36. A New Start

(Los Angeles, 5 weeks before the Fire)

I believe in Christianity
as I believe that the sun has risen:
not only because I see it,
but because by it I see everything else.
C.S. Lewis, *Is Theology Poetry?*

On Sunday, Dominic decided to join Chad at his church. At first, he felt uncomfortable being there, but as the singing started, a familiar but long-absent peace came over him. He was especially touched by a song called "One Thirst:"

You say to us, "Seek My Face"
Our hearts reply, "Your Face we seek"
Come teach us Lord, reveal Your ways
Anoint us for, the greater things
We have gathered with one thirst and hunger
Here to drink of glory and wonder
Here to cry out, "Come and fill this place!"
Our single wish, our sole desire
To gaze upon Your beauty God
We will not rest, nor will we cease

Till with our eyes, Your face we see
We wait for you to come and show
Your glory here today
We wait for You . . .
Hallelujah, Come (repeat)[82]

But as the singing continued, he found himself distracted and then annoyed by several of the worshippers who were dancing around and praying loudly. Then he noticed a man wandering through the congregation, lightly touching people and praying aloud for them. As he did so, some started speaking, saying things that didn't sound like any language Dominic had ever heard before, while others fell to the ground, seemingly unconscious.

Dominic kept his eye on the man whose touch seemed to be causing these manifestations. When he approached Dominic and put his hand on his shoulder he said, "Receive the gift of the Holy Spirit." Remembering a similar experience at a church in southern Chile as a boy, Dominic's defenses went up and he pulled away, scowling at the man who shrugged and moved on.

When he felt a hand on his shoulder again, he was startled. Turning, he saw the smiling face of a woman, probably forty years old. He relaxed a little and turned back toward the front of the church. But as he did so, the scene before him suddenly changed. He could see what looked like a flame of fire above the worship leader!

He began to panic but felt the woman's hand pressing more firmly on his shoulder. He wondered why no one else seemed concerned. Did no one else see the dangerous fire? He looked quickly around and saw the man still walking around, praying for people, and noticed a flame of fire above his head as well!

82. "One Thirst," Jeremy Riddle & Steffany Gretzinger ©2011 Bethel Music

He turned to Chad, whose eyes were closed, and grabbed his upper arm, thinking, *We've got to get out of this place!* Chad turned and smiled, and Dominic could see there was fire above Chad's head, too!

He could still hear the woman's voice next to him as she prayed with her eyes closed. As he turned toward her, he noticed a flame of fire above her head and heard her saying to him, "You have been looking for the truth. I am the truth. You have been looking for a father. I am your Father. You have been looking for peace, you have been looking for power. Look at my peace and my power in this place."

The woman stopped speaking, took her hand from his shoulder, and walked over to others in another part of the room. When she left, Dominic no longer saw the flames of fire, but he did have an unusual peace in his heart.

After the church service they remained sitting and he asked Chad, "What just happened?"

"You saw it, didn't you?"

"Yes. The flames of fire. What was that?"

"The Holy Spirit. People don't always see it."

"Well, I certainly did."

As Dominic and Chad returned home after church, Dominic said, "Okay, I'll admit it. Seeing the flames of fire over people's heads at church caught my attention. I've never seen anything like that before. Let's say I'm interested in what you have to say. What would I do next? How would I connect with that kind of power?"

"Well," Chad answered, "Do you see this kitchen chair here?"

Dominic nodded.

"Do you believe it would support your weight if you sat on it?"

"Yes."

"Suppose I said, 'Come over here and sit down on this chair' and you replied, 'No, it might break.' What would that show? That even though you *said* you trusted the chair to hold you, you wouldn't *act* on that belief."

Dominic gave him a bored looked so Chad said, "Let me explain it another way. One example, Adam and Eve were ashamed and hid from God in fear; but God provided clothes made from animal skins to cover up their shame. Another example, Abraham's son was about to be killed as a sacrifice when God provided a ram to be offered in his place. A third example, a lamb's blood sprinkled on the doorframe of houses saved children from certain death in Moses's time.

"These are three of the many examples of redemption in the Old Testament. An innocent lamb sacrificed to rescue someone from guilt and death. That is why it is so important that when John the Baptist saw Jesus he cried out, 'Behold! The lamb of God who takes away the sin of the world!'[83] To remove the shame of every person and to rescue all mankind from the punishment of death, God provided his own son for our redemption.

"This applies to you, Dominic, because you've said that you've been involved in some very bad stuff. God's response is that any wrong you've ever done can be forgiven.

"There are only two kinds of people in the world: the 'haves' and the 'have nots.' If you *have* Jesus, you *have* life. If you *don't have* Jesus, you *don't have* life.[84] It's that simple. The question is, Dominic, do you have Jesus?"

None of this was new to Dominic, and yet Chad had expressed it in a way that reached his heart and he began to cry. Chad came over and sat down next to him and said, "Dominic, just talk to God. Tell Him what is going on inside of you."

Dominic continued quietly crying for several minutes before speaking. "God, you know I've done things that I know are wrong. I've hurt my family and I've pushed away people who love me. Please forgive me. I want to change. Please help me!"

---

83. John 1:29
84. 1 John 5:11

After a long moment, Dominic got up and without a word went and sat down on the kitchen chair. Chad looked puzzled until Dominic explained, "I believe."

Later that afternoon Dominic called his parents up in Oregon. "Hi, Mom and Dad. Yes, I'm doing fine. In fact, things are really good."

He wondered if they could hear the change in his voice. Probably. He was smiling because it felt like a heavy load had been lifted off his shoulders. He continued, "I met this guy and he's a really strong Christian, and I'm staying at his apartment. And, well, I just wanted to tell you that I'm really sorry for the ways I've hurt you. I want you to know that I've given my life back to God. There's more I want to tell you, but I hope to go up there soon and tell you in person. Yes, yes, I will. Okay, I have to go now, but I hope to see you soon. I love you. Bye."

As Dominic hung up, he could tell a change had taken place in his heart. Not only had he been able to call them *"Mom"* and *"Dad"* but his bitterness toward them was gone. In addition, he no longer felt angry for the way they had lied to him about the identity of his real parents.

Chad interrupted his thoughts, "Hey, I overheard your call to your parents. If you're planning on leaving soon, I'd really like to challenge you to strengthen your faith first. One of the best ways that I know to grow is to boldly tell others about your faith."

The next morning, Dominic accompanied Chad to his preaching corner downtown. As the preacher stood on a box and called out to any who would hear, several people stopped to listen for a moment.

At one point, Chad held up his phone so people could watch a well-done popular ad showing how Jesus understands us. Dominic was moved by the presentation but one of the onlookers shouted out, "Don't try to push that religion stuff. I don't believe in God."

"Oh," responded the preacher calmly, "So you're an atheist?"

"Yes, I am."

"Well, what would you say if I told you I don't believe in atheists?"

"Just because you don't believe I'm an atheist doesn't change the fact that I am."

"Exactly," Chad replied. "I can't change who you are just by saying I don't believe it. And you can't change who God is just by saying you don't believe it."

The man was quiet, then retorted, "Well, instead of telling people how good Jesus is, Christians should admit how bad they themselves are."

"I do. I admit it. I recognize I'm not yet the kind of person I would like to be. But Jesus is changing me."

The man shot back, "Well, rather than spending your time and energy pushing Jesus down people's throats, Christians should just do good things, things like feeding the poor."

Chad said, "My friend, it doesn't have to be either/or. I think if you look around, you will admit that Christians are putting time and money into a myriad of social causes. Helping the poor was a big part of Jesus' message . . . and it should be part of what we do as His followers. But if concern for others doesn't include concern for their eternal state, it isn't real love. My love for you compels me to tell you the truth you need to hear, even if you don't want to hear it."

At that the man walked away and Chad turned to Dominic, "Would you like to say something? Just tell them what you have experienced in the last few days."

Dominic stood up, looked at a man passing by and said, "I have peace in my heart. I didn't know I could feel so free. You should really listen to this preacher." Maybe it wasn't the most elegant message, but he had done it. He had shared his faith.

Chad's training program for Dominic turned out to be intense. When they weren't reading the Bible together, or praying together, they were watching a sermon online or talking together about what they were learning. Every day, they went out sharing with others on the street corner.

The next Sunday, Dominic was no longer surprised to see people at church singing, dancing, or raising their hands in praise. Chad informed Dominic that the two leaders who had flames over their heads had been to the revival meetings in Jerusalem.

Back at the apartment, Chad explained that the flame was a demonstration of God's power and Dominic knew that was what he wanted. He decided that, as soon as possible, he would go see his parents; then, after that, he would make his way to Jerusalem.

The next day, back at their preaching corner, Dominic looked at the people walking by on their way to work or school. "I want to tell you what has happened to me. I stopped running from God and I've accepted the fact that I've made mistakes in my life. Acknowledging that has brought me such relief. I now feel like a different person. That's all I want to say."

Those who walked by didn't seem to take much notice of the preaching duo. As it started getting dark, they packed up the box, the Bibles, and the Gospel presentation literature and headed home. But one man was watching in the shadows, keeping his distance.

Ch 37. Sons of God

(Los Angeles, 4 weeks before the Fire)

For I am persuaded that neither death nor life,
nor angels nor principalities nor powers,
nor things present nor things to come,
nor height nor depth,
nor any other created thing,
shall be able to separate us from the love of God
which is in Christ Jesus our Lord.

Romans 8:38–39

The next day, as they were preparing a meal, Chad told Dominic, "Habit eats willpower for lunch." Dominic looked confused, so Chad explained: "Building good practices into your spiritual life is much more effective than trying to do the right thing by sheer force of will. The things that will help you grow in your faith are: praying to God regularly, reading His Word, meeting with other believers, and telling others about your faith.

"Those kinds of activities are sometimes called 'the means of grace.' Not that we mindlessly follow rituals, but there are certain things that will help us stay connected with God. Some people say it this way, 'Neither be idle in the means nor make an idol of the means.'"

Dominic didn't have a clue what Chad was talking about, but he did understand the idea of athletes making choices to keep their body in top form: avoiding junk food, getting plenty of rest, and exercising regularly. If it made sense in the physical realm, it also made sense in the spiritual realm. Rather than rushing off to Oregon, he committed himself to learning from Chad how to prepare for this new life.

After two solid weeks with Chad, Dominic knew he still had a lot to learn but he felt ready to go visit his parents and then head to Jerusalem. The night before he left for Oregon, he and Chad stayed up all night talking. Chad explained to him everything he had seen at the Mount Zion Revival. But he also warned him to be careful. "Don't underestimate the Devil's schemes! As well-known author C.S. Lewis once wrote to a dear friend, 'The enemy will not see you vanish into God's company without an effort to reclaim you.'"[85]

That day in their Bible reading they came to Genesis chapter six. After they had read through it together, Chad commented, "This text mentions people with unusual strength and ability and calls them 'mighty men of renown.' It makes me think of the ancient heroes of Greek and Roman mythology. Some of them were said to be gods that had come down to live on earth. Some of the heroes had also supposedly been fathered by the gods. In the Bible, the fallen angels that fathered children with human women became known as Nephilim, or the Fallen Ones."

After letting that sink in, Chad read from the Book of Jude about how these fallen angels who abandoned their natural realm and cohabitated with humans were condemned to eternal confinement. He also explained that these fallen angels still exist today, and their power should not be underestimated.

---

85. C.S. Lewis's words to Sheldon Vanauken as quoted in *A Severe Mercy*

Chad then took Dominic to 1 Corinthians 8, where it says those who worship idols and give reverence to gods are in fact worshipping demons.[86]

Dominic thought about these unusual Bible passages about fallen angels and children born from them. He looked at Chad, an otherwise normal-looking guy who sincerely believed that his father was from another world. He also thought about the words of the strange man that had accosted him on the street corner several weeks earlier. He had said that Dominic's father was a god, like Zeus or Hercules. With these thoughts in mind, he decided to open up a bit more to Chad about his own life.

Looking up, he said, "I want to tell you something that I've never shared with anyone."

"Go ahead."

"A little over a year ago, I was living with my family in Argentina when I came across a Bible in our house with the name Jennifer Sánchez on the cover. Curious, I asked my parents who Jennifer was, thinking she might have been a distant relative I'd never met.

"At first my mom and dad tried to avoid the question, but that seemed weird, so I kept pressing them. After a while, they admitted that they had been keeping a secret from me. They had had another daughter named Jennifer who had died. It would have been weird enough to find out that I had had a sister I never knew about, but it was worse than that. Their daughter Jennifer was my real mom. All those years, although they had raised me as their own, they weren't my real parents, it was all a pretense!

"Next, they told me the real circumstances surrounding my birth. She had been only fifteen when she met and became friends with a young man from Italy named Alessandro. Although she swore to them that she hadn't slept with him, the fact was that she had gotten pregnant. When she died shortly after giving birth to me, with no

86. 1 Corinthians 10:18–22

father around, they stepped in and acted as my parents, never letting me discover the truth.

"That news rocked my world. I felt I couldn't trust anyone at that point. To think that I'd never known my real father and mother. And that the people I had called *'Mom'* and *'Dad'* all my life had been lying to me the whole time!

"So, I began my own hunt for the truth. I did a DNA test and surprisingly discovered a perfect match: a man named Alessandro Tarso from Italy. I eventually tracked him down where he was living as a priest in the Caribbean. He admitted to knowing my mother but also claimed that he had never had sexual relations with her.

"When I got here to LA after being away from my family for months, I was ready to leave the past behind me and start over. That's when that guy I told you about, a total stranger, came up to me, calling me by name.

"Somehow, he knew things about me there is no way he should have known. He knew that Pablo and Julia were not my real parents. More than that, he knew about my real mother, Jennifer, and even claimed that my real father was in fact a god."

Dominic sighed deeply, imagining how strange his story must sound, but when he looked up, he noticed Chad didn't appear surprised at all. In fact, his face showed understanding as he said, "It all makes sense now. I told you that I came back here to LA to meet someone. The first time I saw you, I knew that you were the one."

Dominic thought back over his life. He had always felt different from the other kids. There were times when he couldn't explain how he knew things. Or how he learned languages so quickly. Or how, when he and his siblings were attacked in Iraq, he had been able to fight off two men with his bare hands, nearly killing one in his rage. He had always struggled with faith, and he couldn't explain why something always seemed off in his life.

Chad interrupted his thoughts. "Dominic, are you listening to me?"

"Oh, sorry, what did you say?"

"I was saying that it makes perfect sense why God sent me to talk with you."

"And why is that?"

Smiling, Chad replied, "You and I, like everyone else in this world, were born sinners. We were lost, and Jesus is in the business of saving those who are lost.

"But God sent *me* to find *you* because you and I are different from most other people in a very significant way. What you recently found out about your parents is essentially the same thing I discovered about mine some years ago. It has to do with what we were talking about in Genesis six and it might explain what seems to be happening again in our days."

"Okay, go on."

"The sons of God took the daughters of men as wives."

"Yeah. You said the term '*sons of God*' refers to 'fallen angels,' right?"

"Right. And they had children with their human wives."

"Called Nephilim, right?"

"Well," Chad responded, "I think we should distinguish between the fallen angels, who chose to rebel against God, and their offspring, who had no choice in the matter. The fallen angels are the *Nephilim,* the ones condemned to the pit."

"So, what do you call the *children* of the Nephilim?"

"Good question. In Genesis six, the Hebrew uses the term *Gibborim*[87] or 'mighty ones.' I believe that that is the term to use for the children of the Nephilim.

"You see, Jesus came to save all people, even the *Gibborim,* the 'mighty ones.' Dominic, don't you see? You and I are different from

---

87. *Gibborim* is a Hebrew term that can be translated "mighty men," and can refer to the mixed offspring of *Tselim* and humans, beings with supernatural powers who are not necessarily condemned like fallen angels are

most people. God told me that I would find you; I didn't know why at the time, but now I do. God wanted me to find you, one of His lost sheep, because I can relate to you, to your story. We not only have a common faith, but we also share a common bond; we are both *Gibborim*."

Ch 38. Does God Care about Cows?

(Oregon, 3 weeks before the Fire)

For it is written in the law of Moses,
"You shall not muzzle an ox while it treads out the grain."
Is it oxen God is concerned about?
Or does He say it altogether for our sakes?
For our sakes, no doubt, this is written,
that he who plows should plow in hope,
and he who threshes in hope should be partaker of his hope.
1 Corinthians 9:9–10

The next day, Dominic took a Greyhound bus to Corvallis, Oregon, where his mom and dad welcomed him with outstretched arms. His mom hugged him so long and hard that he patted her on the back as a gentle hint that she could let go. Once they got in the car, they drove north for about thirty minutes to the place where Pablo and Julia were currently staying. The house belonged to Bill, the assistant pastor of their church, who had kindly offered to let them live there while they looked for a place of their own.

Bill was getting on in years, having been a believer longer than Pablo had even been alive. They hit it off right away when Pablo and Julia had first come to his church years before as visiting missionaries.

Although he had always believed that signs and wonders ceased with the apostles, he was intrigued when Pablo had shared firsthand accounts of miracles they had experienced in South America and the Middle East. Since that first meeting, he had spoken candidly with Pablo and Julia over the years that he was yearning for something more—more of the power of the Holy Spirit.

Pablo had been honest with him, telling him that when they first went to the field twenty years earlier, their experience with the miraculous had been pretty limited. It was only as they lived in areas where the Gospel was just making advances for the first time—among tribal people in Latin America and among the unreached Muslims in the Middle East—that they began to see more evidence of the supernatural. They had witnessed physical healings, filling with the Spirit accompanied by speaking in tongues, as well as spiritual opposition in the form of spiritual oppression and demon possession.

That evening when Dominic and his parents arrived at the house, Bill, whose day job was running his dairy farm, was already in bed. The next day at breakfast, Bill met Dominic and said, "I'm looking forward to talking with you, Dominic! But I know you all must have a lot of catching up to do, so I'll see you when I get back this evening."

After breakfast, Pablo and Julia wanted to hear more about Dominic's new experience of faith. It took time, but little by little he shared his story, including looking for Alessandro Tarso and finding him in the Dominican Republic. He thought it might be too much to tell them how he had unintentionally caused Alessandro's death, so he left that part out. Even so, they could barely contain their shock and concern about what he was saying. Their questions back and forth kept them busy talking until evening when Bill came in after work.

Julia got up to finish preparing dinner and Bill sat down with Pablo and Dominic. Dominic continued his story, "So, at church it was like my eyes were opened and I suddenly started seeing flames of fire above the heads of some of the people in the room. I asked Chad about it and he could see it too.

"But," he said, "what was weird was that most of the others around us couldn't see it. Then Chad told me that he'd first seen the flames of fire in Israel. He said that an amazing revival was happening in Jerusalem and that I needed to go there.

"In Jerusalem, God told Chad to go back to LA, with no other explanation than that he would meet someone. When Chad saw me on the street walking to work, he said he knew right away that I was the one. He invited me to stay with him. He helped me understand that I could face my fears, and that God is bigger than any problem I have. We talked about it and agreed I need to go to Israel."

This wasn't what Pablo and Julia were hoping to hear. "When are you thinking of going?" Pablo asked.

"As soon as I can get the money for a ticket."

Julia was quiet for a moment, then said, "We were hoping we could spend a bit more time with you here. And to be honest, I wonder about the timing. You've been through a traumatic year."

Pablo added, "Not only that, but US–Israeli relations have really deteriorated lately. It seems many around the world are turning their backs on Israel. And many are saying there will be no peace for the Jews unless Israel agrees to a Palestinian state with East Jerusalem as its capital."

Dominic sat thinking. He had been with his parents less than twenty-four hours, and he was already beginning to regret it. He felt like he was on a roller coaster: the joy of being back "home," and the incredible relief he felt after finally telling them the truth about the past year was now giving way to anxiety bordering on claustrophobia. He stood up and walked around the room feeling like a trapped bear looking for a way out.

The tension in the room grew as he approached the front door. When he touched the door handle, it occurred to him that the answer was not to run away again but to communicate. Turning around, he walked back to the table and said, "I'm sure about this. What I've spent this last year looking for is what I'll find in Jerusalem. I believe God wants me to go there."

An awkward silence followed. Bill, who had served many years as a lay pastor, seemed to have a knack for helping out in just such a situation.

He spoke up, not toward anyone in particular, but as if he was just thinking out loud. "You know, I always did want to go to the Holy Land. I kind of thought I just might go over there at least once before I died." His voice brought a surprising amount of calm and seemed to break the tension in the room.

When no one responded, he turned to Dominic and continued, "Yes, I believe the Land of Israel must be a very special place. Emily and I had dreamed of going—in fact, we had a trip planned—but then she got sick. Dominic, as you were speaking about your friend Chad and the pouring out of the Spirit in Jerusalem, my heart began to burn within me. I've been yearning for years for a stronger anointing from God. This may be my chance. This may be *our* chance. What do you say we pray on this for a couple of days and see if God might open up a door?"

That was the end of that topic for the night. But by lunchtime the next day, Bill had spoken with Pablo and Julia, who in turn had spoken with Dominic, and they all had spoken with the Lord.

As they sat down to enjoy home-grilled burgers, Bill joked, "I hope you all won't be offended that I can't guarantee that all of the ingredients and the utensils are certified kosher. But I believe the pickles are. At least that's what the jar claims. Maybe kosher pickles will help bring clarity about whether or not to make this trip to Israel."

Bill continued to drop hints that he would like to accompany Dominic to Israel, and Pablo and Julia seemed to be warming up to the idea. Julia said, "Well, you know Bill being with you would provide a measure of spiritual protection and add maturity to the 'travel team.'"

But Dominic wasn't really excited about Bill joining him. He wasn't convinced he needed a travel companion, nor did he think he needed his parents' permission or even their approval to go.

Pablo asked, "Dom, when were you thinking about going anyway? Have you looked into how much it will cost?"

"I've seen flights for close to a thousand bucks and I could live there for practically nothing. I should be able to stay with the people that Chad knows there. It shouldn't take me long to save up enough once I get back down to LA."

Julia spoke again, "Now, there'll be no more talk about leaving and going to LA or Israel or anywhere for now. I just want to enjoy our time together for a while."

With that, the conversation drifted to other topics. Julia asked, "Dominic, have you been in touch with Samantha or Daniel?"

"Yes."

"So, you know they're attending Bible school in Northern Ireland where your favorite high school teacher, Mr. Gallagher, is now a professor?" Dominic mused that though Samantha and Daniel were *his* best friends in high school in Buenos Aires, his mom knew more news about them than he did.

In between bites of food and answers to questions, he was checking on his phone for deals on flights. Pablo, looking over, asked, "Dom, what are you doing? I wish you weren't on that phone while we're eating."

"Oh, I was just checking something. Hey, Mom, did you say Samantha and Daniel were in Northern Ireland?"

"Yes, at Bible college where Mr. Gallagher is now teaching. Why?"

"Well, there are several really cheap flights from Portland to Dublin right now."

"But I thought you wanted to go to Israel. Now it's Ireland?"

"No. It turns out that booking two separate flights—Portland to Dublin, and then Dublin to Tel Aviv—is cheaper than when I search Portland to Tel Aviv."

"That doesn't make much sense."

"The mysteries of modern travel. The entire flight, round trip, would be less than a thousand dollars."

Bill put in, "What are the dates of that flight?"

"Leaving in ten days. Two days stopover in Ireland. Gone for just under three weeks total."

There was only a moment of silence before Bill spoke up again. "I'll take it!"

All eyes turned to him incredulously.

Dominic spoke first. "What do you mean, you'll take it?"

"I've wanted to go to Israel for a long time, and this seems like a good opportunity. And if you agree to travel with me, I'll pay your airfare."

Pablo looked at Julia and then Dominic, then said, "Well, I don't know . . . ."

Bill spoke up again, "It seems like a win-win-win to me. It's a win for Dominic because he gets to go to Israel for free. And it's a win for you because you get to keep him around here for the next week and a half rather than having him go back to LA to work. And it's a win for me because I get to fulfill a lifelong dream of going to the Holy Land."

He looked around and grew serious. "But I don't want to assume too much here. Dominic would have to be willing to put up with me on the trip, and I would need you two to hold down the fort for me here while I'm gone."

Pablo said, "Well, I think we could do our part."

Julia added, "It seems more than generous. Dominic, what do you think?"

Dominic was thinking, *Maybe I feel put on the spot a little*. But the price was right and he was eager to go, so he said, "Sure, why not?"

He messaged Samantha right away. She was thrilled to be able to see him again and even offered to pick them up at Dublin Airport. She said that she would make sure that Daniel and Mr. Gallagher knew that they were coming as well.

That settled, Dominic called Chad, who gladly passed on the contact information he had in Israel. While Julia got up to get dessert, Bill got out his credit card and Dominic clicked on the tickets he had seen advertised. By the time the ice cream was set in front of him, he had booked the flights.

The next day, Bill and Pablo discussed finances.

"You know, Pablo, First Corinthians 9:1–18 explains that those who are preaching the Gospel have the right to receive financial support. God gives examples from regular life: how soldiers get paid for what they do and how farmers get to eat part of what they grow. Paul also gives examples from religious life: how priests and those associated with the temple get to eat a portion of what is brought as a sacrifice to God.

"Then Paul mentions one of the 613 laws in the Old Testament, one that has to do with properly caring for livestock. That law talks about threshing or separating out the grain after it has been harvested. It says that if people are using an ox to thresh out the grain, they are not to muzzle it while it works. It must be allowed to eat a little bit of what it comes across while it is threshing. This is of course interesting to me as a dairy farmer. I'm around cows all day long.

"What I find interesting are Paul's words in the New Testament as he interprets this Old Testament law and asks, 'Is it oxen that God is concerned about?'[88] Do you know why that question intrigues me? Because the answer from Paul seems to be, 'No, not really.' In other words, to the question, 'Does God care about cows?' the answer seems to be, 'Not so much.'

88. 1 Corinthians 9:9

"I'm not saying God has anything *against* cows, but this law was written to illustrate a principle: that those who work should receive benefit from their work. And this applies to those who preach the Gospel. In fact, God commanded that 'those who preach the gospel should live from the gospel.'[89]

"Now you all have dedicated a lot of your time to taking the Gospel to those who have never heard. You've honored God with your lives. God in turn says, 'Those who honor me I will honor.'[90] I'm happy to help out with your son's ticket to Israel. It's a way for me to show that God values the tremendous work you all have done."

89. 1 Corinthians 9:14
90. 1 Samuel 2:30

Part 4

Jerusalem

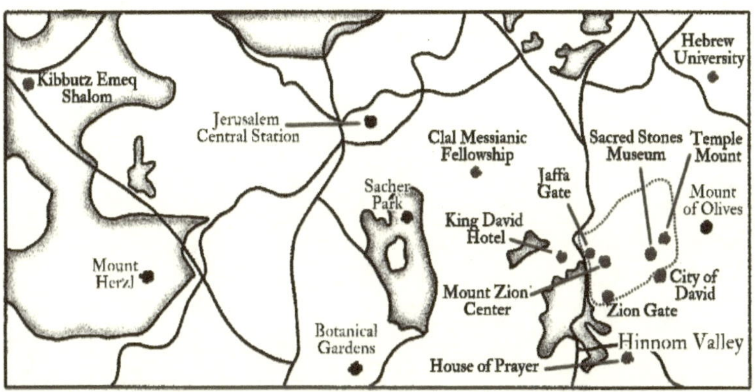

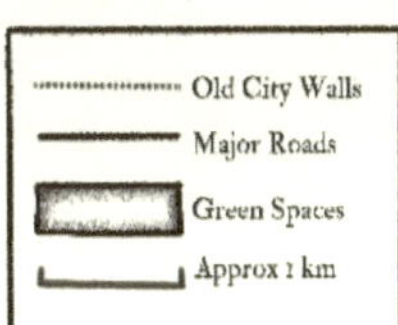

Ch 39. The Crusade

(Odessa, 8 days before the Fire)

To be able to destroy with good conscience, to be able to behave badly and call your bad behavior 'righteous indignation'—this is the height of psychological luxury, the most delicious of moral treats.

Aldous Huxley,
part of an introduction to
Samuel Butler's *Erewhon*

After months of planning and weeks of secrecy, I've done it! Andriy thought as he and Dmitry packed the Ark in its crate and stored it in the yacht. *Ten months ago, I had all but given up on life. I had nothing to live for, no reason to even get up in the morning. Now just look at what I've accomplished!*

Inside his detailed imitation of the Jewish ark of the covenant were reproductions of the traditional biblical items: Aaron's rod that budded, the two stone tablets containing the Ten Commandments, and a jar of manna. It would have been more authentic if he had used gold to cover the wooden box, but weightwise and costwise that was prohibitive, so it was bronze. Another concession he had to make in order for the Ark to fit in a four-foot-by-three-foot wooden crate for transport was retractable carrying poles and foldable cherubim. In addition, he had fitted the Ark with wheels underneath and an electric motor with a battery, making it mobile.

After they had hidden the suitcase bomb in a secret compartment in the yacht, Andriy slapped his friend's back and said solemnly, "This, Dmitry, is our final crusade. A brief stop in Turkey, then it's on to Jerusalem."

Two days sailing from Odessa got them to the Bosphorus Strait, the world's narrowest international navigation passage. Andriy, having read up on Istanbul, commented, "Did you know that the name '*Oxford*' means a low spot where an *ox* could *ford* the river?"

"No."

"And did you know that in England, the city of Oxford gets its name from the fact that a thousand years ago cattle would cross the river Thames near there?"

"No, I didn't, Andriy." Dmitri slowed down to accommodate the large number of boats on the water and asked, "But what does that have to do with anything?"

"Well, according to ancient Greek mythology, Zeus fell in love with a woman named Io who was turned into a heifer and forced to wander the earth. Eventually, she crossed this very passage right here in Istanbul to meet up again with Zeus. He turned her into a woman again and she bore him a son, making her one of the ancestors of Hercules."

"I'm sorry, you lost me. What does that have to do with Oxford?"

"This narrow stretch of water is called *Bosphorus*, because Io had been turned into an ox—*boos* in Greek—and to cross the water here she had to find a passage—*poros* in Greek. That is why the ancient

Greeks called this straight, *Bosphorus*. The Greek word means 'ox crossing' just like the English word *Oxford*."

Dmitry shook his head at his strange friend. They had spent a lot of time together these last few months, and he felt a slight twinge of guilt for having suggested this final solution. But the fact was that Andriy had willingly agreed to this plan. *It was for the best,* Dmitri told himself, *since now at least, Andriy had something to live for.*

As they slowly entered the West Istanbul Marina, Andriy paced back and forth on the deck. During the process of building the ark, he had emailed his girlfriend Niswat some pictures of his progress. When she learned he was taking it to a museum in Israel, she insisted he make time to see her in Istanbul on the way. This stop would be his first chance to meet her in person. He was eager to meet her, since he thought of her as his girlfriend, even though he actually knew next to nothing about her.

When Andriy and Dmitri finished docking the yacht, Andriy called Niswat who said she would be right down. The men had just finished cleaning up when they looked up and saw Niswat walking toward them in a pretty dress. They helped her onboard and, after a kiss on the cheek for both of them, she invited them to a restaurant for dinner.

Dmitry declined, saying he preferred to stay on his yacht, communicating to Andriy that he understood his friend would appreciate the opportunity to be alone with his girlfriend. Andriy smiled in return, communicating he was grateful that Dmitri would stay on board to guard their precious cargo. Niswat smiled as well, communicating to Andriy that she was glad they would have a chance to be alone, and communicating to Dmitri that she was glad they had succeeded in getting Andriy off the boat.

Andriy went up to her apartment after dinner and Niswat went off to the kitchen to get them some refreshments. Just then her phone buzzed with a message. He glanced down at it and was about to call to her when he noticed the message was from another man, Jafari. *How odd!* Looking at the message, he felt rage building up inside him.

When Niswat returned with their drinks, her phone was back on the table where she had left it. Andriy casually asked her who Jafari was. She looked surprised and embarrassed.

"Oh, an old boyfriend. Why do you ask?"

"You just got a message from him."

"Oh, how silly of me," she said as she reached for her phone, but he grabbed it before she could.

"Your boyfriend said something very interesting."

"Oh," she said as she glanced at the door, as if expecting someone.

"He said he would be over soon to *'help get the client to a safe location.'* But don't worry, I told him we needed more time."

At that she jumped up and made a run for the door, but he caught her and covered her mouth before she could scream. He tied her up and after a moderate amount of pain and threats of more to come, he was able to get a confession from her.

But now what? He needed to buy himself a little time, so he texted Jafari from her phone telling him there was no need for him to come over, that the job was done, and she was leaving for Tehran that night.

Then, after carefully checking she was securely tied up, he let himself out and made his way to the street where he found a taxi. By the time he reached the marina, he realized how stupid he had been to be taken in by all her interest in his personal details. He had shared his deepest secrets with her, and the whole time, she was gathering information about how to rob him. Now, he could only hope that her plans to also steal his precious ark had not been successful.

He got out of the taxi and hurried to reach the yacht. It was late and he panicked when he saw that Dmitry wasn't on watch. Checking below deck he found him lying motionless on the floor.

His first thought was, *Oh, no, they've killed him and stolen the ark.* He checked the wooden crate. The ark was still there. He checked the secret compartment in the yacht. The suitcase was still in its place. He breathed a sigh of relief.

His second thought was, *What about Dmitry? Is he alive?* Turning over his friend he realized that he was merely passed out with an empty bottle of vodka in his hand. *If he had been dead, I don't know how I would have gotten to Israel!* he moaned.

He would have preferred relaxing a little, maybe even getting a few hours' sleep, but he was eager to make his statement to the world. So, he woke his friend, who, after a couple of cups of black coffee, agreed to cast off even though it was still dark. Passing through the Sea of Marmara and then the Dardanelles, they made their way across the Mediterranean, reaching the coast of Israel without incident. They then docked at the Port of Haifa.

Andriy presented his paperwork, showing the ark was to be delivered to the new museum in Jerusalem and stopped breathing momentarily when the authorities asked to open the container for inspection. His heart raced as the wooden crate underwent not only a visual inspection, but also an X-ray and a visit from a dog who sniffed for drugs. The agents opened the ark, then held up the replicas of Aaron's rod, the golden pot containing manna, and the stone tablets on which the Ten Commandments had been written.

Despite his fear, Andriy was relatively sure their precautions would be sufficient. The ark contained nothing suspicious, and the suitcase bomb was in a secret locker back in the yacht along with the wires and mechanisms hidden in various places around the cabin.

With the ark safely stowed in their rented van, they went back to the marina and slept on the yacht. Three mornings in a row they went out sightseeing, each time smuggling out some of the parts and concealing them in the back of the vehicle. The fourth day they managed to carry the bomb itself out of the port in a backpack and, assembling it in the back of the van using the plans Yakiv had given them, they placed it in the ark.

Ch 40. The Dark Horse

(Ireland, 8 days before the Fire)

You never realize how much you like someone
until you watch them like someone else.
Author unknown

Dominic and Bill flew to Dublin, where Bill witnessed Dominic's joyous reunion with Samantha and Daniel. Bags loaded in the car, they took off driving north.

After half an hour of lively conversation, Dominic looked over and saw that Bill had fallen asleep. Then he looked out the window, a little puzzled and asked, "Where's the city? We've been driving forever and it's just small towns and fields. Don't you live in Dublin?"

Sam smiled. "No, silly! We live near the college, on the outskirts of Belfast."

"What? We have to drive to Belfast? I'm sorry, I didn't know. I wouldn't have asked you to come get us if I'd known you'd have to cross an international border."

"No worries. It's not that far. We're almost halfway there. And it's not that much of a border. You have to really pay attention to notice that you've even crossed it. You'll see. It's just a few miles ahead."

Daniel corrected, "You mean, it's just a few *kilometers* ahead. That's how you'll know you're in Northern Ireland: the signs switch from kilometers to miles."

Sam added, "Yeah, that's true. Oh, and if you guys are up for it, Mr. Gallagher said he's available and would love to meet us for a drink."

"Sure! Sounds great to me," said Dominic.

Bill woke up shortly before arriving at the Donegall Street parking lot. He stumbled out of the car and soon they were making their way through Central Belfast. They crossed the street and turned into Hill Street, a narrow cobblestone lane lined with nondescript red brick buildings.

As he shuffled along, Bill stopped to squint at a notice posted on the wall that read *"Private sign, do NOT read."* His half-asleep brain was still trying to decipher that message when he had to quickly jump back onto the sidewalk as a car approached and whizzed by. *Who would have thought people drove on this kind of narrow, bumpy path?*

From there, they turned into Commercial Court, an even narrower street, this time pedestrian-only and soon reached their destination. Bill dutifully followed Dominic and the others into a festive and creatively decorated bar called the Dark Horse Pub.

Entering, he began to shake his head, still groggy from sleep and wondering if what he saw was real. Music playing. Dozens of colorful umbrellas hang from the ceiling. Murals were painted everywhere, including one resembling Donald Trump riding a horse whose head protruded from the wall.

Dominic realized this would not have been Bill's first choice of venue; in fact, by the look on his face, Dominic guessed this might be the first time Bill had ever been in a bar. As they entered, Mr. Gallagher saw them and, jumping up, made straight for Dominic, enveloping him in a big hug.

"I'm so glad to see you, Dominic! You're looking very well, lad."

"Mr. Gallagher, I would like you to meet my traveling companion, Mr. Gilbright."

Bill stretched out his hand and said, "Bill is fine. None of this Mr. Gilbright stuff."

"Nice to meet you, Bill. And you can call me Sean."

They made their way to a table and sat down. When all the others enthusiastically ordered a Guinness, Bill was taken aback. Considering Dominic wasn't even old enough (at least by US standards) to drink alcohol, he was naturally concerned. But he held his peace and ordered himself a Coke.

Sean, eager to learn more about his new American acquaintance, asked him, "So, you're not much of a *Guinness* man?"

Bill replied with a generous dose of smugness, "I'm not much of an *alcohol* man."

Sean, without missing a beat, said, "Interestingly enough, neither was Arthur Guinness."

"And who was Arthur Guinness?" asked Bill, more out of politeness than curiosity.

Disregarding Bill's skeptical tone, Sean gladly answered. "Arthur Guinness was a Christian entrepreneur in Ireland in the 1700s. At that time, drunkenness was a serious social issue. Largely because of a lack of safe drinking water, many men and women drank gin or other alcoholic beverages instead of water. As a brewer, Guinness provided a safe, healthy alternative that was lower in alcohol. As a businessman, he made a good product that brought him a lot of money. And as a Christian, he used that wealth to improve the lives of the poor around him. Through his involvement with hospitals, he focused on health for their bodies, and through his involvement with the Sunday School movement, he focused on health for their souls."

Bill smiled politely. Guinness's efforts to minimize public drunkenness and to promote the Sunday School movement notwithstanding, he still had no intention of ordering a beer. Instead, he nudged the conversation in a different direction, asking Sean, "What is your impression of the spiritual state of Ireland today?"

While Sean and Bill conversed pleasantly on that subject, the three young friends were busy catching up. So much had happened in the last year! Their conversation, as always, flowed seamlessly between Spanish and English. Dominic wanted to know all about lives and the classes they were taking. Then Samantha asked Dominic about himself and how he was doing. "Remember high school and how we used to call ourselves the 'Three Musketeers'?"

Dominic did remember. His mind went to their friendly competitions to see who could get the best grades or who could come up with the greatest summer adventure.

Then his face got red as he remembered how, just before graduation, he found out that his parents had been lying to him all his life. Daniel and Samantha had tried to help him deal with the surprising discovery that his real mother had died shortly after his birth, but rather than accepting their kindness, he had pushed his friends away, closing them off, feeling he couldn't trust anyone anymore, and becoming obsessed with finding his birth father.

Now, back together with his friends, he was ashamed of his behavior the last time they saw him, over a year ago. He was not that person anymore: he was not even the same person he had been just one month ago!

Samantha broke into his thoughts, saying, "You are looking so good, so happy. We prayed for you when we heard about your disappearance. I can't even begin to think of what it was like to be kidnapped!"

That was his cue, and he began telling them an edited version of what he had been doing for the last year. He had already told them about meeting Chad and was just about to share about his new commitment to Christ, when he noticed Sam gently place her hand on

Daniel's. Suddenly feeling awkward and self-conscious, he stopped speaking midsentence.

Sean, though engaged in conversation with Bill, noticed Dominic's abrupt pause and glanced over at the trio. He had already wondered how this reunion might go, having observed that Samantha and Daniel had grown quite close during their time at Bible college. Looking at the three of them sitting together confirmed what he had suspected when he was their high school teacher in Argentina. Dominic had always had feelings for Samantha.

The conversation resumed as Samantha and Daniel started in on another subject and Dominic joined in, but it was obvious to Sean that Dominic felt the odd man out. He could see that despite the joy of being reunited, for Dominic, Samantha and Daniel's special connection was not only awkward, but downright upsetting.

So, Sean wasn't surprised when Dominic turned to face him and said, "There are so many things that I've experienced in this last year. So many things that I've wanted to ask you about. I hope that we will have the chance to really talk while we are here."

Sean was about to reply when Bill added, "Yeah, Dom's description of the power of the Holy Spirit in that church in LA really lit a fire within me. I feel so blessed to be able to travel at last to the Holy Land, especially at this moment in history. Why, I do believe those Four Horsemen of the Apocalypse must be chomping at the bit, if you'll pardon my pun, ready to ride on the world's stage. And of course, before any of them ride out, we the church will be raptured up. I've always believed Jesus could come at any moment, but now, I tell you, I can almost smell that 'blessed hope.' What do you think, Professor, do you think the white horse is near? Do you think the Antichrist is already living among us?"

Sean thought about Bill's questions, contemplating which of several issues he should address first. "Please, Bill, just call me Sean. But to answer your first question, I do think it's possible that the events represented by the Four Horsemen of Revelation chapter six might be quite near. But I also have a question for you."

"Shoot."

"Your question to me seemed to imply that you equate the white horse and/or its rider with the Antichrist."

"Yes, of course."

"Why do you think that?"

Bill was surprised that a Bible college professor would be unsure about such a basic detail regarding the end-times, but he relished the opportunity to explain the matter to him.

He began, "Well, for example, in Matthew 24, Jesus talked about what was going to happen in the end-times. He listed false Christs, then wars, then famines, and then pestilences. In that order. Those just happen to be the four horses of Revelation six. A false Christ, war, famine, and pestilence. Is that a coincidence? I think not. So, the Antichrist has to be the first horse of Revelation six."

Sean answered evenly, "It's true that many of the calamities mentioned by Jesus in Matthew 24 are the same ones we see in the Book of Revelation and other prophecies about the end-times. But that section of that chapter of Matthew doesn't seem to be intended as a timeline or a countdown for the end-times. Instead, Jesus' emphasis seems to be quite the opposite. It says, 'Take heed that no one deceives you,'[91] and, 'See that you are not troubled; for all *these things* must come to pass, but the end is not yet.'[92] Jesus also says, 'All these are the beginning of sorrows,'[93] and 'He who endures to the end shall be saved.'[94]

"Jesus warned his disciples that many difficulties would come, that hardships would get worse and worse, and that they would need to endure through them all. The words *'beginnings of sorrows'* are

91. Matthew 24:4
92. Matthew 24:6
93. Matthew 24:8
94. Matthew 24:13

translated in many versions of the Bible as 'the beginning of labor pains.' In fact, Paul made this explicit when he compared the end-times with 'labor pains upon a pregnant woman.'[95] Two prominent characteristics of labor pains are that they are cyclical and that they grow in intensity. That is what Jesus emphasizes here: be prepared for wave after wave of ever-increasing calamities, up until the end."

Dominic squirmed a little in his seat as Bill asked, "Are you an amillennialist? Are you trying to say that Matthew 24 and the prophecies in Revelation are all just general descriptions of conditions during the Church age and that there is no literal 1,000-year reign of Christ on the earth?"

Sean's patient voice was that of a teacher with a student he was hoping would be able to grasp a difficult point, "No, I'm not trying to force an amillennial interpretation here. I do believe that the prophecies will be fulfilled literally."

Bill followed up, "In that case, you do believe that specific events will happen in the end-times and that they will occur in a certain order, right?"

"Yes, I do. And I believe that the order of events in the end-times is significant. But in Matthew 24, Jesus predicted that there would be many false Christs, something which seems to indicate that these difficulties could happen over and over.[96] My study of history has shown me that there have been leaders who falsely claimed to be Christ, as well as leaders who were evil tyrants. In either case, what follows are often horrible wars, leading to food shortages and famines. Then war and famine often result in sickness and epidemics. This pattern has proven true time after time. Jesus warned followers to be prepared for wave after wave of hard times, to have the mindset that God is faithful, and to believe that He will be with them as they endure many persecutions and tribulations."

95. 1 Thessalonians 5:3

96. Matthew 24:5, 24

Bill asked, "But Jesus does also talk about specific one-time events in Matthew 24, right?"

"Yes, indeed. The 'abomination of desolation, spoken of by Daniel the prophet'[97] seems very much to be a specific and singular event. Also, the sign of the Son of Man, and the gathering of the elect,[98] seem to be specific one-time events at the end of this age.

"But the false Christs, wars, famines, and diseases mentioned in Matthew 24:5–7 seem to be events that will happen over and over. In fact, drawing a parallel between these verses and the Four Horsemen of Revelation six leads to several problems logically. Jesus said in Matthew 24 that *many* deceivers would claim to be the Messiah.[99] Jesus also mentioned *many* 'wars and rumors of war.'[100] That's why Jesus said next, 'See that you are not troubled; for all *these things* must come to pass, but the end is not yet.'[101] The rise of deceivers and the ravages of wars shouldn't start our countdown to the Lord's return.

"But there is something Jesus warns us to be ready for. In Luke 21, the parallel passage to Matthew 24 about the end-times, Jesus says, 'But before all these things they will lay their hands on you and persecute you . . . .'"

Bill interjected a question. "Before all *what things*?"

"Yes. That's a good question. Obviously, before the events Jesus had just mentioned: wars, earthquakes, famines, pestilences as well as fearful sights and great signs from heaven."[102]

Bill suggested, "But wasn't that persecution fulfilled already in the Book of Acts?"

"Yes. Jesus' promise to His people in time of persecution is, 'I will give you a mouth and wisdom which all your adversaries will not be

97. Matthew 24:15
98. Matthew 24:29–31
99. Matthew 24:5
100. Matthew 24:6
101. Matthew 24:6
102. Luke 21:10–12

able to contradict or resist.'"[103] This was fulfilled to some extent during the persecution against the first-century Church and their courageous witness for the Lord.

"But the Old Testament prophets speak about the 'early and latter rains,'[104] an image that the New Testament connects with the coming of the Lord[105] at the end of the age. Because of the promises of the *early* and *latter* rains, I believe that, in addition to the *early rain* that we read about in the Book of Acts, during the end-times there will be a *latter rain*. Basically, when all hell literally breaks out on earth, heaven's power will again descend and Jesus' irresistible wisdom will again be given to His followers.

"I believe that the final wave of calamities will be greater than anything the world has ever seen. It will involve one final evil tyrant called the 'man of sin,'[106] and one final war called the Battle of Armageddon.[107] But before that, and probably continuing well into those apocalyptic events, I believe the 'latter rain' will come bringing one final anointing and empowering of the Church by the Holy Spirit. To me, that is what the first horse of the Apocalypse represents."

"So," Bill asked with a twinkle in his eye, "do you believe the Antichrist is alive today?"

Dominic spoke up, "Hey, I have an idea. Why don't we call it a night? Some of us have been traveling all day and are pretty jetlagged."

"That is a very good idea. Tomorrow is, as they say, another day. My apologies, Dom," said the professor kindly. "Let's wrap things up here and I'll help you get settled into your room at the college."

---

103. Luke 21:15

104. Joel 2:23 and Hosea 6:3

105. James 5:7

106. 2 Thessalonians 2:3

107. Revelation 16:16

Ch 41. The White Horse

(Ireland, 7 days before the Fire)

And I looked, and behold, a white horse.
He who sat on it had a bow;
and a crown was given to him,
and he went out conquering and to conquer.
Revelation 6:2

At breakfast the next morning, Dominic, Sam, and Daniel were tucking in to bacon and eggs, and Bill was ready to resume the conversation again from the night before. "So, Sean, what do you think? Is the Antichrist alive today?"

Sean had had all night to think about his answer, but still he hesitated before saying, "The Antichrist? No, I wouldn't say that." Then putting down his cup of tea, he said, "I actually don't like the term '*the Antichrist.*'"

"Why is that?"

"Well, I guess because the biblical authors didn't seem to like it."

"What do you mean? The term '*antichrist*' is in the Bible—it's used several times."

"Yes, the word is in the Bible, but I don't believe it is ever used to refer to the final evil ruler that most people refer to as 'the Antichrist.' The Scriptures clearly teach that there will be a final evil tyrant, who will set himself against Christ and His Church. It's also clear that there are a variety of phrases used in the Bible to identify him: *'the little horn,'*[108] *'the man of sin,'*[109] *'the lawless one.'*[110] In the Book of Revelation, he is simply referred to as *'the beast.'*[111] But, I can state with complete assurance that the biblical authors never referred to this final adversary with the words *'the Antichrist.'*"

Bill put down his coffee cup. "And how can you be so sure?"

"Good question. I'm sure because the biblical *authors*—plural—never even used the word." Only one author did—John."

Sean paused for just a moment, then continued, "The word *'antichrist'* is used exactly five times in the New Testament, all in the letters of the apostle John. And look at how John used the term."

Sean pulled out his Bible. He pointed at an underlined verse as he slid the Bible across the table toward Bill and said, "In First John chapter two, verse eighteen, John acknowledged that the term *'antichrist'* was being used by people *in his day*. But I will reiterate, we have no record of any of the other biblical writers ever using it."

When Bill looked up, Sean continued, "What's more, the apostle John himself showed that 'antichrist' is not an appropriate title for the final evil tyrant."

"And how did he show that?"

"Well, first he wrote that there are *many* antichrists. It's not a great term for *one* specific person if it can also be used to describe a bunch of different people. Then, in verse twenty-two, he made the term even less specific, saying *anyone* who denied the Father and the Son was *an* antichrist."

Sean paused again, then added, "Next, in First John chapter four, verse three, John wrote about the *spirit* of antichrist and said that the spirit of antichrist was already in the world back then. Was John

108. Daniel 7:8

109. 2 Thessalonians 2:3

110. 2 Thessalonians 2:8

111. Revelation 13:1

saying that the spirit of the final evil ruler was around in his day? I don't think so. John wrote in this same verse that *any spirit* that didn't acknowledge that Jesus had come in a fleshly body was *a* spirit of antichrist—not very specific at all. And then in John's second letter, in verse seven, he wrote that *any person* who didn't acknowledge that Jesus had come in a fleshly body was also a deceiver and an antichrist."

Sean paused again, making sure Bill was tracking before continuing, "So, from all that, I conclude that John, the only biblical writer to use the term *'antichrist,'* clearly didn't use it to identify *one individual man* of the end-times, but rather to identify a kind of perversion of the true faith, a heresy that could be held by many different people appearing at different periods in the history of the Church. That's why I prefer not to use the term *'antichrist'* to refer to this final evil ruler."

Bill was silent for a long moment, then finally, as if rallying his courage, he queried, "Well, do you believe this final evil ruler is alive today?"

"Maybe," offered Sean.

The answer seemed to just hang in the air.

Sean was an excellent professor, a skillful communicator, one who knew how to both read and lead his audience, whether it was an audience of one or a hundred. So now, as Bill was on the verge of abandoning hope of getting a significant answer to his question, Sean began again in an upbeat voice, "But . . . Dominic was talking with me earlier this morning about the spiritual phenomena he saw in a church in California, as well as similar things his friend Chad had seen in Israel. Hearing those things makes me inclined to think that this man, referred to as 'the beast' in the book of Revelation, probably is alive today. And the reason I believe that is actually because of the white horse of Revelation six that we spoke about yesterday."

Bill perked up dramatically. "How is that?"

Sean turned and opened up one of his notebooks on his shelf. "I recently did a word study on that passage in Revelation. It helped make the identity of the rider of the white horse very clear, at least to me."

Everyone remained silent.

Sean continued, "First, the horse is white. Throughout the Scriptures, and especially in the Book of Revelation, the color white is a consistent symbol of goodness and holiness. And, of course, in Revelation chapter nineteen, Jesus himself is riding a white horse. Now, what else do we know about the rider on the white horse in Revelation six?"

Bill jumped in, "He has a bow, but no arrows. That means he has a show of strength—'saber rattling' if you will—but he lacks any substantial power, right?"

Sean hesitated, "That is . . . one idea. But the fact that *'arrows'* aren't mentioned certainly doesn't mean that he doesn't have any. My word study showed that Revelation six is the only use of the word *'bow'* in the entire New Testament. And the word *'arrow'* never occurs in the whole New Testament.

"But when we expand our search to the Hebrew Scriptures, the Old Testament, then we get a clearer picture. There, the words *'bow'* and *'arrow'* are used together either in the same verse or, at least, in the same passage, a total of eleven times. However, the term *'arrow'* is used without the word *'bow'* forty times. Furthermore, the word *'bow'* is used without the word *'arrow'* a total of sixty-four times.

"Notice that the vast majority of the places in the Scriptures—over one hundred times—when this weapon is mentioned, it is referred to by only *one* of its parts, either *'bow'* or *'arrow.'* This seems important to me and leads me to conclude that in the Bible, merely mentioning a *'bow'* or merely mentioning *'arrows'* likely includes the idea that the other part of the weapon is present as well. Does that make sense?"

Bill and Dominic nodded.

"Okay. What else do we know about the rider on the white horse?"

Bill offered, "A crown was given to him."

"Good. An important point of clarification here: Two different Greek words are both translated as 'crown' in many English Bibles. I find this very unfortunate because, although they are both worn on a person's head, they are two very different things, with two very different purposes. One word is *diadema*. It was usually made out of gold or silver, often had precious stones, and was normally worn by royalty. Jesus, in Revelation nineteen, riding the white horse, is shown wearing *many* diadems.

"The other word translated 'crown' is *stephanos*. It is a victor's wreath or garland, made of laurel or other foliage, and given to winners of the Olympic Games and other competitions. This wreath is what was given to the rider of the white horse.

"Now, my question is, 'Is this word *stephanos* used in other places in the New Testament?' The answer I found is, yes. It is used eighteen times in total: four times about Jesus wearing a 'crown of thorns,' but in almost all of the other passages, the word *stephanos* was clearly used figuratively, referring to *symbolic* wreaths, not worn by Jesus, but given to victorious Christians, specifically to Christian martyrs."

Bill said, "You said '*almost* all the other passages.'"

"Yes, there is an interesting passage in Revelation nine about horselike locusts that come out of the abyss. It says that they are wearing something like wreaths, made out of something like gold. But we might want to save that rabbit trail for another time."

Dominic rolled his eyes and said, "I can't wait."

Sean continued, "Anyway, Paul, Peter, James, and John all wrote about believers receiving victors' wreaths after they had persevered in their faith. We see these examples in First Corinthians 9:25, Second Timothy 4:8, James 1:12, First Peter 5:4, Revelation 2:10, Revelation 4:4, and more."

Bill said, "I got it."

"But wait, there's more! Revelation 6:2 says the rider of the white horse 'went forth conquering and to conquer.' The Greek word used here for 'conquering' is *nikon*, like Nike, the sportswear company named after the goddess of victory. So, the rider of the white horse, 'the conquering one,' was both victorious and was going to keep on being victorious. Or he was overcoming, and he was going to keep on overcoming. Who does the Bible describe in that way? Who is called 'the conquering one'?"

Dominic answered uncertainly, "Jesus?"

"Yes, that is definitely true of Jesus. But is it true of anyone else?" Sean waited for responses. When no one replied, he continued, "There is actually a verse that tells us the exact answer to that question."

Sean's hopeful gaze met with blank stares.

"Nothing? The apostle John, the same one that wrote Revelation, asked a question in the last chapter of his first epistle. He asked, 'Who is the *nikon* of the world? Who is the one that overcomes the world?' In the next sentence John answered the question."

Sean again waited for guesses.

"It has to be Jesus," said Dominic.

Sean was shaking his head. "Sorry, Dominic. This time we're looking for a different answer."

After another pause, Bill quoted from memory, "He who believes that Jesus is the Son of God."[112]

"Bingo," said Sean as Dominic looked at Bill and then back at Sean, who was now grinning.

"You see?" Sean asked. "Who is the one that overcomes? The one who believes. Who receives a victor's wreath? The overcoming believers. Who are given white robes to wear? The overcoming believers. Who is being represented in Revelation chapter six by a white horse and its rider? The victorious believers in Jesus. I think the Scriptures

---

112. 1 John 5:5

make it quite clear. Despite all the hardships and persecutions that the enemy can muster, the Church will triumph and 'The gates of Hades will not prevail against it.'[113] Jesus promised that before the end of this age, His followers (the Church) will be given wisdom and spiritual power that none of their adversaries will be able to resist."[114]

Bill was almost convinced, but something still didn't sit right with him. "If the white horse of Revelation six represents the believers, that is, the Church that overcomes in the midst of tribulation, is this referring to the end-times Church? Is this tribulation the *Great Tribulation?*"

"I believe everything points to that," said Sean.

Bill continued, "Then what about the Rapture? When is the Church caught up to heaven?"

Sean flipped back to the book of Matthew, saying, "I think Jesus answered that question quite clearly.

> *'Immediately after the tribulation of those days the sun will be darkened, and the moon will not give its light; the stars will fall from heaven, and the powers of the heavens will be shaken. Then the sign of the Son of Man will appear in heaven, and then all the tribes of the earth will mourn, and they will see the Son of Man coming on the clouds of heaven with power and great glory. And He will send His angels with a great sound of a trumpet, and they will gather together His elect from the four winds, from one end of heaven to the other.'"*[115]

Looking up he said, "Jesus promised to return to gather His chosen ones *immediately after* the tribulation of those days—after the *Great Tribulation*."

113. Matthew 16:18
114. Luke 21:12
115. Matthew 24:29–31

"But," said Bill, "the *elect*, the chosen ones mentioned in this verse, are *Jews*. At that point, the *Church* will have already been raptured, escaping the Tribulation."

Sean relaxed and smiled. "I think we might have to continue this another time. But I'll just mention two quick points for now. First, I see no biblical evidence anywhere for a separate rapture prior to the 'gathering together' mentioned in this passage. Second, if the *elect* in this passage are indeed Jews, then the white horse in Revelation six represents those overcoming, Jesus-believing Jews."[116]

116. Romans 2:29

Ch 42. Qorin Finds a Conscript

(Los Angeles, 7 days before the Fire)

Well, it may be the devil or it may be the Lord
But you're going to have to serve somebody
Bob Dylan, *Slow Train Comin'*

Qorin had been impulsive in his earlier days, nearly resulting in the loss of his principality. After that, he had learned to adapt and work behind the scenes, becoming adept at subtlety and discretion, staying out of Deywós' way, every one of his moves carefully calculated.

The Olam *is like a cosmic game of chess,* Qorin thought. *But most players, human and* Tsel *alike, view life from their own personal perspective. They see themselves as individual pieces on the board. Not me. By stepping back, I can focus on the big picture.*

I can see, for example, that Deywós must have calculated the high cost of sending Abdowan to Earth. He knew he was risking the loss of Abdowan, one of his most experienced lieutenants, just to obtain Dominic. But he did it anyway.

Because I know that Dominic has strategic significance in the endgame, I know the next play and where on Earth to focus my attention.

Qorin now thought of his favorite game, poker.

In the high stakes poker game for control of the Earth, Lord Deywós and the Oppressor have both begun to show their hands. They have both begun to reveal their strategies. That must mean the game is about to end. For now, I'll keep my cards close to the chest, biding my time, discreetly watching the other players at the table, avoiding anything that attracts Deywós' attention. Dominic will play a pivotal role in the Earth's final days, and I am positioned to have a crucial connection to him.

When Mombu informed him that Dominic had gone to the US, Qorin immediately worked to cobble together a spy network. His roundabout system did gather intelligence, but the information he got was almost always out of date by the time it reached him.

Always a step behind, he learned of Henri's treachery, Dominic's travel to LA, and his subsequent renewed interest in the Christian faith all at the same time. The news frustrated and enraged him.

Qorin next received a report that Abdowan had, whether by luck or by skill, located and even made contact with Dominic. He said to himself, *Well done, Abdowan! Your mistakes have unfortunately put you one step from the pit, but you're still above ground for the moment, and that's something! Maybe you could still prove useful to me.*

With a sigh, desperately in need of real-time intel about the boy, Qorin decided to make the trip himself to that region of the Shadowlands to contact that doomed *Tsel* who had lost his access to the Shadowlands and now called himself Eván Lopez.

Eván lay curled in a ball on his hotel bed in LA. His first attempt at talking with Dominic had not gone well. Expecting that Dominic would jump at the chance to join forces with him, he was surprised when Dominic seemed repulsed. Lacking any better ideas, Eván had begun to follow Dominic around, always staying in the shadows, listening, hoping for another opportunity to talk.

So, it was that Eván had been listening outside Chad's open living room window as Chad and Dominic talked all night about the Mount Zion Revival and about the 'sons of God.' When Eván heard that Dominic was leaving for Oregon, he was alarmed and wanted to follow him, but he was having doubts.

He recognized that approaching Dominic in Haiti had been a failure. And here in LA his face-to-face attempt on the street corner had not gone any better. For some reason—probably that stupid protection the enemy provided his servants—he couldn't seem to connect with the boy.

Lying on his bed in LA while Dominic was up in Oregon, Eván told himself he was trying to find an angle. He needed an edge. At that very moment, a presence appeared in the dark room and called out, "Abdowan."

"Who is that?" he responded with a trembling voice, unable to see more than a vague shape.

"Who do you think it is?"

"Wait, is this a dream?"

"Who would know to call you 'Abdowan'?"

At that, Eván grew even more anxious. Many times, over the years, he had gazed on unsuspecting humans, but now the tables were turned; his heart raced as he realized someone from the Shadowlands was watching him.

As Eván lay there motionless, Qorin shifted to a more soothing voice, "It's me," he lied, "Ghaiasha."

Eván responded, "The Prince of Palestine? Why are *you* contacting *me*?"

"Because the boy you have been following, Dominic, is an important asset. I need information about him."

Eván, alarmed that anyone was aware of his eavesdropping on Chad and Dominic, especially the *Tsel* Prince of Palestine, asked, "So you knew that Dominic was planning to go to the Mount Zion Center in Israel?"

Qorin was relieved that Eván couldn't see how much that information surprised him. He quickly composed himself. "Of course, I knew," he lied. "That's why I contacted you. You must go to this Mount Zion Center, keep an eye on Dominic, and report back to me."

"How will I report to you?"

"Don't worry, I will make contact. And Abdowan, you will be safe as long as you follow my directions."

Eván sensed a wave of relief, feeling reassured to know he would be protected if he obeyed orders. It was unbelievably tiring being completely isolated and vulnerable. "Yes, Ghaiasha, I will go to Israel, I mean, to your principality and let you know what I find out. You will not be disappointed in me."

There was no answer, and Eván realized that the *Tsel* was no longer present.

Curling his lips into a smile, a new sense of confidence replaced his loneliness and vulnerability. *To have the Shadowlands working with me, that's the edge I was looking for. Now, before I go, there's one loose end that I need to take care of.*

Ch 43. Up in the Air

(Israel, 6 days before the Fire)

. . . *with God all things are possible.*

Matthew 19:26

As Dominic and Bill boarded the flight for Israel, Dominic looked over at his traveling companion. Staying in Bill's house in Oregon for two weeks, and now this two-day layover in Ireland, he had grown to appreciate this kind and friendly old man, even if he was a little set in his ways. On the face of it, their fifty years' age difference, their completely different upbringing, and the different ways they had experienced God's grace would not seem to create the foundation for comradery or even friendship. But as they sat together talking and eating their airplane chicken, Dominic realized that he actually enjoyed Bill's company.

After the meal, he began brooding about how the time with Samantha and Daniel had gone by too quickly. His stomach got tight, his face got red, and strange feelings followed when he wondered, *Are Daniel and Samantha really together? What might have happened if I had gone to Bible school with them rather than rushing off to try and find my real father?*

He didn't realize Bill sitting beside him could tell something was up, so he was surprised and a little annoyed to hear him ask, "Hey, want to hear a joke?"

"Sure," he said not very enthusiastically, and Bill "entertained" him with what he called jokes.

"Three polar bears were having a competition to see who was the strongest. They decided to see who could throw a horseshoe into the air the highest. The first polar bear tossed it up as high as he could and they counted, 'One . . . two . . . three . . . four,' and then the horseshoe fell to the ground.

"The second polar bear threw the horseshoe even higher, and they counted, 'One . . . two . . . three . . . four . . . five . . . six . . . seven,' before the horseshoe fell to the ground.

"The third polar bear threw the horseshoe really high, and they counted, 'One . . . two . . . three . . . four . . . five . . . six . . . seven . . . eight . . . nine . . . ten . . .' Nothing. They waited, looking into the sky for a whole minute. They waited for a full hour, but the horseshoe didn't fall back down to the ground. So, they all went home."

Dominic waited for the rest of the joke. Bill said, laughing, "That's it. Isn't it funny?"

Dominic groaned, and Bill said, "Okay, how about an oldie but goodie? Many years ago, there was an agricultural student at Oregon State who went to stay with a rancher for a few days, wanting to get a bit of hands-on experience raising sheep.

"The rancher agreed, and the first day at breakfast as the student munched his toast and drank his coffee, he said, 'Mr. Gilbright, I've had enough theory about raising sheep. I would like to hear from you, a real rancher, what it's like to run a farm. Can I ask you a question or two?' The rancher said, 'Sure.'

"'For example, your sheep, how much water do they need each day?' He replied, 'Well, you know there are black sheep and there are white sheep, which do you want to know about?'

"The student looked puzzled for a moment, then said, 'The black ones.' The farmer answered, 'They drink about a gallon of water a day each.' The student asked, 'And the white ones?' He replied, 'About a gallon of water a day each.'

"He could tell his answer left the student a little puzzled. But the young man bravely carried on, 'Okay, and how much grain do you give them to eat?' He asked, 'You mean the black ones or the white ones?' The student paused and said, 'Um, the black ones.' 'They eat one quart of grain each day', the farmer said. 'And the white ones?' the student asked. 'One quart of grain each day,' was the reply.

"The poor student seemed to be even more puzzled, but he pressed on with his questions. 'Okay, so how much time do you let them graze in the field each day?' 'The black ones or the white ones?' 'The black ones.' 'They graze in the field about six hours a day.' 'And the white ones?' 'About six hours a day.'

"The poor student could take it no more. He said, 'Mr. Gilbright, each time I ask you about the sheep, you ask me to clarify if I mean the black ones or the white ones. But then each time your answer is the same. I don't understand.'

"'Oh,' said the farmer, 'that's because the black sheep are *mine.*' 'Oh, I see,' the student nodded, 'And the white sheep?' The farmer smiled, 'They're mine also.'"

Bill burst out laughing at his own joke, and Dominic smiled politely. The joke wasn't really funny, but Dominic's heart lifted as he saw how much Bill truly enjoyed life. Even if his jokes were corny.

Dominic said, "You said the farmer's name was 'Gilbright.' Isn't that your last name?"

"You are a sharp one, Dom. Yes, that story really happened. That's what makes it so funny!" he slapped his knee as he chuckled again.

After that, Dominic watched a movie while Bill slept. As they were beginning their descent into Tel Aviv, Bill woke up. Dominic was looking at the view through the window and Bill asked, "Wanna hear another joke?"

"No, I'm good. Thanks."

"Come on, it's another polar bear joke."

"Alright, go ahead," Dominic said without enthusiasm.

"A polar bear was traveling in a small airplane with his parrot. The polar bear was reading a newspaper, and the parrot was trying to sleep. The polar bear was chewing bubble gum and as he read he blew a big bubble. The bubble got so big it burst with a loud 'pop' and the noise startled the poor sleeping parrot who began to squawk furiously.

"The squawking made such a commotion that the pilot had to leave the cockpit to find out what was the matter. He found the polar bear and the parrot arguing back and forth about the noise of the popped bubble and told them, 'I don't care whose fault it is, you both need to be quiet so I can pilot the plane!'

"They quieted down for a while. Pretty soon the parrot fell asleep again and the polar bear, unaware of what he was doing, began blowing another big bubble. When the bubble burst, the loud 'pop' again frightened the parrot who began to squawk uncontrollably. The pilot again came back to them and said, 'I've told you, you have to keep the noise down. If you can't control yourselves, I'm going to throw the parrot, the bubble gum, and the newspaper all out the window!'

"They were quiet for a long time, and again the parrot fell asleep. The bear, concentrating on his newspaper, forgot what he was doing and once again blew another huge bubble. When it popped, the parrot squawked, the polar bear growled, and the pilot came rushing out of the cockpit. Grabbing the newspaper, the bubble gum, and the parrot, he threw them out of the plane.

"A little while later, the polar bear looked out the window and saw the parrot sitting on the wing of the plane. And do you know what he had in his mouth?"

Dominic said, "The bubble gum."

"No."

"The newspaper?"

"No."

"I give up. What did the parrot have in his mouth?"

"A horseshoe," said Bill smiling.

It took Dominic a moment to get it, then he started laughing as he understood the two-part joke. He was still smiling about that polar bear joke as the plane landed.

They found a shuttle bus that took them and half a dozen others from the Tel Aviv Airport to Jerusalem. As Dominic sat watching the countryside pass by, he remembered what Chad had told him. During Chad's trip to Israel the year before, he had been trying to conserve his money, so he had booked the cheapest tickets he could find without doing much research beforehand.

He told Dominic he had been pleasantly surprised to find a date that was less than half the cost of any other tickets he could find. It wasn't until Chad had arrived at the airport that he realized why. The date he had chosen to travel was a Saturday, and there was no public transportation because of Shabbat. In addition, the Muslim taxis, which usually make a lot of money on Shabbat, weren't working that day either because it was one of the most sacred Muslim holidays of the year. He had to wait three hours to finally get an overpriced taxi.

Dominic looked out the window. Compared to Chad's experience, their arrival in Israel had been easy. *It's true that passport control in the airport felt a bit like a police interrogation,* thought Dominic as he pulled out of his passport the little slip of paper given to him as a removeable visa. But he put it back between the pages of his passport, remembering how the officer had told him sternly, "Do not lose this!" He couldn't help wondering what might happen if he did.

The shuttle ride took about an hour. Arriving in Jerusalem, they passed by a bridge that looked like a giant harp. At a nearby hotel, a middle-aged French couple got out. Dominic had a passing thought, *How do we even know this driver can be trusted?* Something was making him feel uneasy, but he couldn't tell what.

In a quiet residential area in front of a bookstore, a young man wearing a kippah[117] got out. Returning to a busier street, in front of a small shop selling falafel and shawarma, another passenger left the van.

They could see the Old City walls in the distance. Noticing a sign, Dominic said suddenly, "King David Hotel! Right here, driver."

The driver hesitated for a moment. This wasn't the destination that Dominic had told him back at the airport. But Dominic pointed to an empty parking place in front of the hotel and the driver obliged by pulling over. He opened the side door for them and by the time they had climbed out, the efficient driver had moved around to the back and unloaded their bags. With a nod, he jumped back in the van and departed.

When the shuttle was out of sight, Dominic said, "Okay, now we walk."

"But I thought this was our hotel," Bill protested.

"No, not yet. I think it's better if we don't advertise to everyone where we are staying. We can walk the rest of the way. Here, I'll pull both bags." He led the way along a street that passed through an arch and into the walled city itself. At a kiosk selling fresh fruit juice, he asked, "The Mount Zion Christian Church?" The owner pointed up the street. "Stay to the right, up about one hundred meters."

117. Kippah is a brimless cap, usually made of cloth, traditionally worn by Jewish males to fulfill the customary requirement that the head be covered

They grabbed their bags and started walking again, trying to avoid getting run over by bicycles, motorcycles, cars, and even other pedestrians. After about thirty steps, Dominic asked a man standing outside a shawarma shop, "Mount Zion Inn?"

"Fifty meters. On the left. Go in the coffee shop."

The sun was dropping below the city walls as Bill and Dominic, sleep-deprived and exhausted from traveling, stood in front of the inn's closed door, trying to figure out how to enter. Finally, they saw a bell, rang it, and were welcomed in. Immediately, Dominic felt a sense of relief. They had arrived at last! They were shown to their room, choosing rest rather than food. Bill was asleep immediately, but Dominic, thinking about Samantha, decided to send her a text to let her know that they had arrived safely. Soon, he as well was fast asleep.

The next morning, they woke up refreshed and eager to meet Nehemyah Friedenthal, the man Chad had said was responsible for igniting the spark of the Jerusalem Revival. Before heading out, Dominic sent a message to his parents letting them know he had arrived safely. Then Bill and Dominic found the coffee shop associated with the Mount Zion Inn and were introduced to Aaron, one of the leaders at the church.

He showed them around the church grounds then took them into the Old City. They again asked about Nehemyah, but Aaron said, "Tomorrow," and walked off leaving them on their own to explore the myriad antiquity and souvenir shops. Bill looked at the map Aaron gave them with instructions on finding their way back to the inn, and remarked, "Well, there certainly isn't any hand holding here."

The next day, Aaron again met them in the coffee shop. "Nehemyah confirmed your story. He remembers Chad and will be happy to see you."

"Why all the secrecy?" Bill asked.

"We don't yet know what God is doing, and we don't want a whole bunch of tourists attracting attention to us. Here are directions to the kibbutz." Aaron left and they managed to find the light-rail stop just outside the city wall, taking it to the central bus station, where they caught a bus to the Kibbutz Emeq Shalom.

At the kibbutz gate they explained who they were and what they wanted. Soon they were sitting in the reception area of the guest house, and not many minutes later Nehemyah came in to greet them. He turned first to Bill and shook his hand warmly. Then, as he turned to Dominic, he hesitated for just a moment before warmly shaking his hand too. He welcomed them into his office, where they all sat and chatted over a cup of coffee.

When Nehemyah reentered the office after showing Bill where the bathroom was, he found Dominic standing by a collection of framed photographs, studying an old and worn picture.

Dominic turned and asked, "Who are those men?"

"My friend and I, shortly after the war."

Dominic appeared deep in thought but said nothing.

Nehemyah spoke up, "You know, Dominic, I must ask you. You look very similar to a man I once met. Do you have relatives from Germany?"

"Yes, I do." Then, turning back to the photo, he said, "This man here with you. I know it sounds weird, but I saw this same man in a dream. I clearly remember his face."

Nehemyah smiled. "In a dream? Really?" After a moment, he asked, "Have you ever heard of Martin Niemöller?"

"No. Why?"

He turned and pulled a book from the shelf, *Then They Came for Me*, and he handed it to Dominic. "That's Martin Niemöller on the cover."

Dominic studied the cover in silence. "Martin Niemöller. He was in my dream too."

"Amazing! And do the words '*Nein! Er bleibt da!—No. He stays there!*' have any special meaning to you?"

Dominic was stunned. Into his mind popped the words *"We all stay here,"* and he said out loud, *"Wir alle bleiben da."* Looking at Nehemyah, he said, "That's a scene from my dream. How is that possible?"

Nehemyah smiled broadly and said, "With God all things are possible."

Then, since Nehemyah had meetings to attend, he arranged for a car to retrieve their luggage from the Mount Zion Inn so they could stay at the guest house at the kibbutz. He also arranged a tour guide to take Dominic and Bill sightseeing around Israel for the next few days.

Ch 44. Entering the Kingdom

(Jerusalem, 2 days before the Fire)

> *Therefore, brethren,*
> *be even more diligent to make your call and election sure,*
> *for if you do these things you will never stumble;*
> *for so an entrance will be supplied to you abundantly*
> *into the everlasting kingdom of our Lord and Savior Jesus Christ.*
>
> 2 Peter 1:10–11

On Shabbat, Bill and Dominic accompanied Nehemyah to the Mount Zion Church. They found some seats near the front and stood with everyone else as the music started. A worship band played familiar tunes, and they joined in the singing. After several songs, Dominic suddenly realized that both he and Bill were singing *in Hebrew!* It just seemed so natural. He looked around and noticed that several others who were obviously not Jewish were also singing along.

But he noticed one man standing near the back of the church who wasn't singing. Dominic thought, *Where have I seen him before?*

Just then the music ended, and Nehemyah went forward to speak. Dominic turned to the front to listen. "As some of you may know, my only daughter Rivka and her husband were killed fifteen years ago in a terrorist attack. And I lost my beloved wife Talia nearly two years ago. Then about ten months ago my lovely granddaughter Devorah was killed in circumstances that are still under investigation. A few weeks after that all my belongings were lost when my house burned to the ground. My point today is not to focus on these sad events, but instead I want to talk to you about how God sustained me in those dark days. To do that, I need to go back many years to a Nazi prison camp.

"I found hope in God in a hopeless place. In the darkest prison, the light of the Gospel shined on me. 'How?' you might ask. In prison I managed to find a New Testament, which I read over and over again. One Scripture portion became very special to me, and so today I want to read from Second Peter chapter one, verses three to eleven."

Dominic was trying to pay attention, but as he turned and glanced again at the man with dark glasses and a hood standing in the back, he realized it was the stranger who approached him the month before in LA! At the time, fearing a police officer had found out about Alessandro's death, Dominic had run off. But now he felt more curious than afraid.

Convinced he had to investigate, Dominic got up casually, squeezed past Bill, and with his eyes lowered, slowly made his way along the aisle toward the back of the church, as if he were going to look for the restroom. Looking up, he was just in time to see the man slip outside.

He wanted to run after him immediately but instead walked respectfully to the door of the church. Once there, he saw the man heading down the street. Dominic was in dress clothes, but he didn't care. He took off after him.

He chased the stranger but soon lost him in the twists and turns of the Jerusalem streets. He stood in a doorway and looked around but could see no sign of him. Hot and sweaty, he turned and trudged back to the Mount Zion Church. Nehemyah was well into his message as Dominic sat down again by Bill who was listening intently.

Nehemyah continued, ". . . as I've said, this text has given me comfort and strength for over seventy years. We've talked about eight qualities or characteristics God wants to see in our life. The first is faith—holding on to the fact that God is good. To faith we add virtue, or 'being a good person.' To virtue we add knowledge, to knowledge self-control, to self-control perseverance. I want to remind you that perseverance is a key to success. As the great inventor Thomas Edison once said, 'Many who fail in life do not realize how close they were to success when they decided to give up.'

"Next, we add godliness. I mentioned that there is an important difference between godliness and virtue. Virtue involves those behaviors society accepts as wholesome, like being kind and fair. But godly behavior adds something more: it means obeying God's Word even when society disapproves.

"To godliness we add brotherly kindness, and finally, to brotherly kindness we add love. There is nothing to add to love because when we love as God loves, we express the clearest measure of walking in God's kingdom.

"Now, here in Second Peter Chapter one, verses ten and eleven, it says that if we add these eight qualities to our life, 'an entrance will be supplied to you abundantly into the everlasting kingdom of our Lord and Savior Jesus Christ.' You might ask, 'Does that imply that we earn our salvation by doing good works?' The answer is 'No!' We know that salvation is a gift from God. 'Well, then,' you ask, 'what does it mean when the text promises an abundant welcome into the kingdom? Some versions describe this welcome as 'rich' or 'glorious.' What does it mean that God offers us an amazing welcome into His kingdom?

"Let me give an illustration. Suppose we all attend a worship concert. A large group is gathered together singing familiar songs in praise to God. One of the songs we sing together is a very poignant testimony about being held in God's arms when life seems to be falling apart.

"I can enjoy that beautiful song of praise to God even though I myself am not an especially good singer. Now, suppose Aaron, who is your worship leader here at Mount Zion and a gifted musician, is standing right next to me at that same concert. Because of his understanding of music, he can enjoy that very same song in a richer way than I can. He can better appreciate the music, the harmony, the melody, and the chord progressions. His experience is richer and more abundant simply because of his deeper understanding of music.

"Now suppose in front of me is the very husband of the woman who wrote that worship song. That man can enjoy the song in an even deeper way than Aaron or me because he knows the backstory of the song. He remembers seeing firsthand the way God rescued his wife from despair and gave her hope.

"And suppose that the author of the song herself is there at the worship concert. She can enjoy that same song in a different, and I would suggest, more profound way than any of the others. As she sings along with everyone else, she relives the moment when she wrote that song, when God met her in her hour of need and filled her with joy. The songwriter's experience is deeper, richer, and more abundant precisely because it is *her* story, *her* song.

"Now, in that worship concert, all enjoy the very same song, but each one enjoys it in different measures. An appreciation of music adds to the enjoyment, an understanding of the backstory adds more to the enjoyment, and being the songwriter adds even further to the enjoyment.

"God's promise of an abundant entrance into his kingdom may be similar. We will all experience the presence of the Lord, but not in exactly the same way. What we bring to the kingdom may help determine how richly we experience it.

"To change the analogy, imagine in heaven that we are all holding cups filled with God's blessing. Everyone's cup will be filled to the top. But not every cup will be the same size. God delights in rewarding those who seek his favor, and He promises them rewards. We don't earn heaven by being diligent. But what we do in this life may very well influence how we experience eternity. Do you want to receive abundantly what God has for you?"

Dominic and Bill felt a longing to receive more from the Lord. They felt as if they were being pulled by a magnet, and before long they realized that they, along with most of the rest of the auditorium, were moving forward in response to Nehemyah's call to a deeper life.

On the way home, Nehemyah asked if they enjoyed the church service. Bill answered, "It was amazing. I've never felt such a powerful moving of the Spirit. The worship was incredible, and your message was also clearly anointed by God."

"So, you were able to get something out of the sermon? Did somebody translate for you?"

Bill and Dominic looked at each other, puzzled. Dominic asked, "Why would we need a translator? We understand English."

Nehemyah smiled broadly. "I'm sure you do. But I delivered the entire sermon completely in Hebrew."

After an awkward silence, Nehemyah added, "Don't just take my word for it. You can ask anybody who was there, they'll tell you the same."

They turned to Moshe who was nodding in agreement.

Bill asked, "You're saying you heard his sermon in Hebrew?"

"Yes, of course."

Dominic asked, "But neither of you seem surprised to learn that Bill and I heard the sermon in English. What's going on?"

"Because it's happened before—many times, in fact," Nehemyah answered. "It started about nine months ago as one of many signs of the 'Jerusalem Revival.'"

Dominic wasn't satisfied. "But why is this happening? Why are people able to understand Hebrew who've never learned it?"

"Some are saying it's because Hebrew is a holy language—the language of God and the angels."

"The language of angels," Bill remarked. "The aspotle Paul said in First Corinthians 13:1, 'Though I speak with the tongues of men and of angels, but have not love, I have become sounding brass or a clanging cymbal.' I've always believed that Paul was using hyperbole there. Are you saying you believe Hebrew is an angelic language?"

"Probably not an *angelic* language, but I recently read a book positing that Hebrew is a *heavenly* language, or at least the language God uses when speaking with humans."[118]

"For example?"

"In Genesis 2:22, it says that God made Eve out of Adam's rib or side. Then, in verse 23, it states that Adam called her *woman* because she was taken out of *man*. In Hebrew, the word for woman is *ishah* and for man is *ish*. They say that Hebrew is the only language in the world that the word for woman is derived from the word for man.[119]"

Dominic responded, "It seems like English might be another. You know: *man, woman*. Maybe English was the language spoken in the Garden of Eden."

"I'm not a linguist," offered Bill, "but I find the idea of English being spoken in the Garden of Eden very unlikely."

118. *Hebrew: The Eternal Language* by William Chomsky.

119. The words for *man* and *woman* tend to be some of the oldest and most basic words in any language. The fact that the Hebrew word for 'woman' is indeed derived from the Hebrew word for 'man' is apparently rare and noteworthy

"I agree, Bill," said Nehemyah. "In today's world, English is quite widely spoken, but it's a relatively recent arrival on the world stage. Hebrew, however, is known to be an ancient language."

Dominic looked up from his phone. "I just checked my online etymology website, and it turns out that the English word *man* originally meant any human, male or female. The English word for a male human back then was *wer.* So, even though the word *woman* did derive from the word *man*, it's not like in Hebrew, where the word for a female person derived from the word for a male person."

Nehemyah continued, "That is interesting. Here's one more example from Hebrew: 'In Genesis 3:20, it says that the first woman's name was Chavah because she was the mother of all living."

Bill looked confused. "Chavah?"

"*Chavah* is the Hebrew way to say the name *Eve.* And this name comes directly from the Hebrew word meaning "living."[120] So, when it says in Genesis, 'She was named Eve because she was the mother of all living,' those words actually make sense. As far as I know, Hebrew is the only language for which that is true.'"

Dominic asked, "Okay, but the Hebrew of the Bible was from thousands of years ago, right? Languages change. What does that have to do with anything today?"

"There's an interesting verse in the book of the prophet Zephaniah, chapter three, verse nine," Nehemyah said, then quoted from memory, "'For then I will restore to the peoples a pure language, that they all may call on the name of the LORD, to serve Him with one accord.'" He looked at Bill and Dominic before continuing, "What is this pure language that will be restored in the time of the end? Throughout history, many people have assumed this has to be Hebrew."

"Interesting," said Bill.

---

120. The original Hebrew name was Chawah or perhaps Chayah. In any case, it is clearly connected with *chayah*, the Hebrew word for 'a living one.'

"Yes. The revival of the Hebrew language is unique in the history of the world. For about two thousand years, Hebrew was, for all intents and purposes, a dead language, a relic of times past, used mainly in religious services. Hebrew was not used in everyday communication and not spoken by anyone as their primary language. But now, look at how all that has changed. Today, Hebrew is the official and predominate language of the State of Israel, spoken by millions of people as their native tongue."

Dominic spoke up again, "I'm not sure that's a convincing argument. Like I said before, languages change. I'm fairly sure that Modern Hebrew isn't exactly the same as the Hebrew spoken, for example, by King David three thousand years ago. How can modern Hebrew be the 'holy and pure language' that has been restored by God, when it doesn't sound today like it did three thousand years ago?"

Nehemyah was smiling. "That's a fair question, Dominic. I don't have the definitive answer for you, but you might be surprised to know that Israelis today, without any training in biblical Hebrew, can read and understand the ancient Hebrew Scriptures written over three thousand years ago. Compare that to English. A modern English speaker today, without any training in Old English, would have trouble picking out a single comprehensible word of *Beowulf*, which was written about one thousand years ago.

"Modern Israeli Hebrew is unique in several ways, but that might be a conversation for another day. What if we just consider what you yourselves experienced today. The Israelis in the audience who don't know English heard me speaking in Hebrew, while you two, who don't speak Hebrew, also understood my sermon perfectly. Was I using some kind of a restored, pure language of God? Maybe. Perhaps this is like Peter's message at Pentecost when the Book of Acts records that everyone present heard Peter's preaching *in their own language*.[121]

121. Acts 2:11

In any case, for whatever reason, what God seems to be doing here in Jerusalem is being communicated in Hebrew."

After a few moments, when neither Bill nor Dominic had any more questions, Nehemyah changed the subject. "Dominic, it seemed that you missed part of the sermon. Is everything okay?"

Ch 45. The High Places

(Shadowlands, 1 day before the Fire)

Yet I have set My King on My holy hill of Zion.

Psalm 2:6

Qorin found the Prince of Persia reclining comfortably and smoking a waterpipe. When Verethragna saw him, he motioned for him to sit down and join him. Qorin was pleasantly surprised to see that the Persian Prince's former hatred toward him had thawed so considerably as to earn him an invitation to share a hookah. He guessed that Verethragna was done with Nabu and his cohort, that their obnoxiousness had finally pushed him away.

However, Verethragna's present friendliness had less to do with hating Nabu or embracing Qorin; it had everything to do with the fact that Verethragna's secret plan was nearly complete and he wanted to share it with someone. His sense of imminent success made him giddy with excitement and willing to forget old grievances in light of the great event just around the corner.

"I hope we all agree . . ." began Verethragna, imitating Hubal's high-pitched voice as he passed the pipe to Qorin. "That's what Hubal just told us. 'I hope we all agree it's dangerous to let this so-called Mt. Z Revival continue. Over the years we've learned to tolerate *worship services* because often the leaders are living with serious unresolved relational conflict even as they offer up their gifts of worship and praise to the enemy. Thankfully they tend to disregard the Oppressor's words about reconciling with their brother,[122] and their lack of peacemaking seriously limits the effectiveness of their worship.'"

The Prince of Persia looked at Qorin. "Those were Hubal's exact words. As if His Majesty, the royal Prince of Arabia, had any experience at all with worship services in his territory! Anyway, then he warned us about an unhealthy trend toward reconciliation among the enemy's forces. He even mentioned a new and alarming feature of this so-called revival: confessing one's sins.

"Not the kind of confession we have become accustomed to hearing: confessions about ancient faults committed by others for which the confessor could really have no true sense of guilt. Nor the confession of sins to a priest, an uninvolved third party.

"No, this rumor deals with real, heartfelt confession of sin expressed in person to the injured party themself. And what's worse, this type of humble confession of actual offenses is apparently followed by the offended party offering forgiveness to the offender. Hubal claimed to have evidence that this tragedy is actually taking place among some of the enemy's troops.

"But Hubal went on to point out to us that the biggest problem, of course, with this so-called Mt. Z Revival is not the worship itself, but its proximity to the high places." Verethragna leaned closer and said with a mocking voice, "Did you know, Qorin," here he paused as he took a puff from the hookah, "that the area encompassing the Dome of the Rock, the Al-Aqsa Mosque, and the Western Wall is a protected zone? Well, Hubal was all in a dither complaining that this status quo is a double-edged sword. It protects these high places for our purposes but also protects nearby strongholds of the enemy."

122. Matthew 5:23–24

"You mentioned *'us,'"* said Qorin. "Who exactly was at this meeting?"

"Oh, Nabu, Ptah, Hubal, and I. After that last time when you happened upon us, Hubal decided it was best to meet in a remote corner of his domain where we would have guaranteed privacy."

"Right. And you all came up with some solution, I take it?"

Verethragna laughed. "Solutions? Ha! Hubal told us, 'If we allow this enemy activity to continue so close to the high places, we risk seeing our power diminish. But if we act too forcefully, we might upset the delicate status quo established by the human political powers.'

"For my part," the Persian continued, "I held my tongue as they debated dozens of ideas that would allow us to maintain our foothold in the region. Those idiots would suggest ideas, and over and over the conversation would gain strength, excitement building, until it inevitably crashed into the impenetrable wall of 'status quo.' As I listened to each suggestion, I was thinking, *Let them talk. I am taking action. In fact, my plan is already in place.*

"You see, Qorin, Hubal assumes we all have the same great reverence for the holy site and the buildings on it. I, however, have instilled doubt among my people over the years so that now, although they consider the site itself important, they see the buildings on top of it as so much wood, brick, stone, and gold. I say, 'Let it burn!'"

Qorin, deciding to change the subject, casually asked, "So how is our young prodigy Kenan?"

"Who? Oh, he's doing fine. Why do you ask?"

"Oh, it's nothing. I was just thinking that it might be interesting for him to meet that boy I was telling you about." Verethragna's face began to redden as he remembered being fooled by Qorin over that same boy a dozen years ago. But the Prince of Rome quickly soothed, "You're right to still be angry about my lack of candor back then. But, trust me now, this boy will certainly be an important part of Deywós' endgame. And unless I am mistaken, Kenan will also play an important role. Come on, if the Resistance is to succeed, we must work together."

"Actually," said Verethragna, "I'm working on something more urgent right now."

"Oh, really, what's that?"

Verethragna hesitated for a moment. His excitement and eagerness to share his plan with someone overcame his reluctance to trust Qorin. "Oh, alright," he said, "I guess I can tell you. But don't let the others know."

"Wow, it must be impressive."

"Impressive? How about missiles aimed at the Oppressor's Temple Mount? How about leveling the location of His so-called Mt. Z Revival? How about inciting years of war? How about the countless repercussions made possible by doing away with their stupid 'status quo'? How about blowing the whole area to bits?"

Qorin hid his surprise and instead feigned enthusiasm. "I would call that a veritable *coup de grace*. Especially since that know-it-all Nabu probably has no idea what's coming. Nor Hubal, for that matter. I don't suppose they're in on this?"

"No, just me."

"And of course," Qorin ventured, "the Prince of Palestine, trapped as he is in Kenan's body, must be unaware of what is happening in his realm at the moment, and in no position to stop this attack?"

"Exactly. And just between you and me," Verethragna said as he exhaled a huge cloud of smoke, "His weakness is what gave me the idea in the first place. It's just a matter of time until someone topples him. 'The early bird gets the worm' and all that."

"Yes, I see."

"I don't have all the details worked out yet, but I'm fairly certain that I can get a nuclear warhead thrown in the mix!" Verethragna boasted.

"Well, that sounds excellent," Qorin said. "And as for the other matter, I'll take the initiative myself to set up a meeting between Kenan and Dominic. And now, I'd better go before someone sees us together."

"What an idiot," Qorin mumbled as he slipped away. "Dominic is in Jerusalem and so is Kenan! Firing missiles to disrupt the Oppressor's plans? As if that has ever worked. Destroying buildings to stop a revival? How ludicrous! Has Verethragna not yet learned the most basic strategies for fighting those committed to the Oppressor? Get them to compromise, yes. But kill them? Make them martyrs? What a disastrous idea!"

Qorin realized there were three things he needed to do right away to try and protect Dominic. One, convince Nabu to try to sabotage Verethragna's stupid attack. Two, get Kenan and Dominic out of harm's way in case Nabu fails at that task. Three, try to stop the attack himself.

He decided that first he would focus on getting Dominic to safety. For that he needed to communicate with Eván.

"Abdowan!"

"What?!" Eván exclaimed as he awoke with a start from his afternoon nap.

"Abdowan, we need to talk."

Embarrassed and annoyed at being caught sleeping, he mumbled, "Okay, fine! But first, listen to me. I've found a forum on the deep web. We can send messages back and forth there. You don't have to make an appearance like this each time."

"Is this *deep web* secure?"

"I think so. The forum I'm on won't show up on any Internet search without typing in the exact address, which is thirty characters long. Even if someone were to find the forum's web page, without the password, they wouldn't be able to see anything."

"Okay, I guess that could work."

"I've set up an Internet account and signed you up. When you want to contact me, just send me a message."

"Great. Give me the account details."

"Okay, but first, I'm curious. It's just that I can't remember you ever confiding in me before."

"Your point is?"

"You're not really Ghaiasha, are you?"

"Abdowan, who I am doesn't matter. What matters is that Verethragna is attempting to pull off the biggest idiotic blunder of the century, and I want you to investigate it."

"What's in it for me?"

"What's in it for you? Are you really in a position to bargain? Admit it, you're relieved to be in contact once again with the Shadowlands. What's more, I'm offering you my protection. Don't try to negotiate with me. You don't want to lose me: You need me much more than I need you."

In the following minutes of conversation, the *Tsel* prince learned from Eván about Dominic's plans for that day. Then Qorin gave Eván two assignments: first, find out how to get in touch with Ali Khamis, Verethragna's contact at the Israel Defense Forces, and second, get as much information as possible on an organization in Syria called *Noor-Allah*.

Eván gave Qorin the account details so they could be in touch via the online forum. Though communication on the Internet forum might be easier for Eván, Qorin wasn't convinced it was any faster or better.

Qorin closed the conversation, deciding not to mention that Jerusalem, where Eván was currently located, seemed to be in danger of being obliterated. *He's destined for the Pit anyway!* thought the Prince of Rome. *What difference does it make if his demise happens sooner rather than later?*

Qorin bowed low as he saw Nabu approaching. "A thousand apologies for my earlier missteps, my Prince."

Nabu's vanity got the better of him and he deigned to give Qorin the merest passing glance. Interpreting the gesture as a hopeful sign of civility, Qorin followed up immediately with what he hoped was an olive branch. "My most esteemed Prince, ruler of Babylon! I've just become aware of a problem far too great for my limited resources."

"Ah, come to beg, have you?" sneered the Babylonian.

"Yes, my lord. I wouldn't have dared to approach you again after my egregious conduct concerning the identity of the Mahdi. But, that mistake aside, I hope you will find a way to help us now with a very crucial issue."

"Well, speak up!" Nabu shot back, his interest piqued. "What seems to be the problem?"

"My Prince," Qorin began quietly then paused to let the suspense build. Bowing his head, he continued, "Your humble servant has just learned of an attack planned against Jerusalem. I thought it my duty to bring you the news right away."

"What? I've heard of no such thing! Who is planning this attack?"

"My great leader, it is none other than Verethragna. He has gone behind our backs and set in motion a nuclear attack on the high places. He confided as much to me. And there is no use confronting him. He'll deny it, I'm sure. What can be done?"

"Done? For your part, you just stay out of the way. I will investigate this matter myself. If it's true, Deywós will know what to do." Nabu swept off without another word.

Ch 46. Tisha B'Av

(Jerusalem, 15 hours before the Fire)

You may either win your peace or buy it:
win it, by resistance to evil;
buy it, by compromise with evil.
John Ruskin, *The Two Paths*

12:00 PM

"Seven is the perfect number," Ali said to himself as he typed the English words on his encrypted phone and pushed *send*. His coded text meant, "All is clear for the plan to go forward." The message moving across the airways would inform the general that their previously agreed upon date and time for the simulation was a go.

Unexpectedly, Ali felt a chill run down his spine, and he was surprised at the sudden shiver. When the general first contacted him about this project, Ali had been dubious. A backdoor hidden deep within the Iron Dome system? Highly unlikely. But using the access information the general had given him, Ali found there was indeed a vulnerability in the software.

The general asked that he use this backdoor to insert a program to temporarily deactivate the missile defense system. For his part, the general promised to call for a simulation during a short window of time. The simulation would reveal that the system could be hacked, leading the IDF computer specialists to then locate and patch the software.

Ali shivered again. *It must just be the excitement of secretly pulling off such a great hack,* he thought. He had always wanted to do something epic, something no one else had ever done. "I hope this works," he breathed quietly to himself. From somewhere in the deep recesses of his consciousness, he heard the words, *"Be careful what you wish for."*

12:00 PM

It wasn't a general in the Israeli Army who received the text message, but rather Agent Jafari of the Quds division of Sepah, the Iranian Revolutionary Guard Corps. He immediately relayed the message to the commander of Noor-Allah, who in turn communicated with the wedding setup crew. They had chosen a prominent wedding taking place in Syria for the launch site, reasoning that a rush of activity at an outdoor wedding would seem innocuous to anyone checking satellite imagery.

The rocket launcher rested under a tarp covered by a wedding canopy, ready to be uncovered right before the launch. Seven of its twelve sleeves were filled with 107-mm rockets, more than enough to inflict serious damage. After its two minutes of activity, the "wedding organizers" would quickly wheel the rocket launcher back to its hiding place in the underground tunnel.

If the Jewish enemy retaliated in kind, Syrian news reports would be able to show the damage: bodies of innocent civilians and destroyed homes. The small Syrian village was nowhere near any military installations. The International Press would have a field day. Israel's counterattack would be seen as an unprovoked attack involving innocent civilians. That would play in the news for months to come.

2:00 PM

Qorin didn't bother with the Internet, choosing instead to appear to Eván in his hotel room. Eván, again taking an afternoon nap, thought he was having a nightmare. He woke to a feeling like a hand on his throat, making it difficult to breathe.

"Well, what have you found out?"

Eván didn't answer. He couldn't. Qorin released the pressure and Eván gasped a couple of times, then finally said, "I sent you a message! Didn't you read it?"

"No, I prefer more direct communication. What have you found out about this Ali?"

"Nothing yet, my lord. I'm still searching." He felt a sudden pressure on his chest that shoved the air from his lungs.

"Abdowan, you are of no value to me unless you can produce results."

"But I do have some information," Eván managed to get out when the weight lifted from his chest.

"Go on."

"Noor-Allah. I've done some searching. The organization is not well known, but I did find some communication online that led me to two pieces of information on what is called the 'deep web.' It's not the regular Internet that most people browse, but . . . ."

"Abdowan!" Qorin interrupted. "I'm in a hurry. What. Did. You. Find?"

"Sorry, my lord. For one, Noor-Allah is opposed to the Jewish State. They don't advertise that fact, but I discovered they pray for fire to reign down on their enemies, the Jews."

"Meaningless!" Qorin screamed. "That is no help at all!"

"But there's something else. I'm not sure how it's connected, but you are expecting a major event to happen soon, right? If this event concerns Noor-Allah, I may have a clue. Apparently, a wedding is being arranged in Syria east of the Golan Heights. A daughter of a high-ranking member of Noor-Allah is being given in marriage to a general of Hezbollah. This wedding, just like European royal weddings, ought to include a who's who of Arab guests and be a major social event. But it's barely being mentioned online."

"What does that mean?"

"It might be nothing. But you asked me to look into Noor-Allah. Why so little information online about such a major life event in the Noor-Allah community?"

"Why indeed?"

"It's possible that someone might be using the wedding as a cover to organize something else."

"Go on."

"I don't know what Noor-Allah may be planning, but it would be reasonable to expect more fanfare for such a momentous occasion. Why no important guests from Hezbollah? Searching the deep web, I found a comment about the upcoming wedding where one poster said, and I quote, 'This union will be the end of the Jewish State.' The leadership of Noor-Allah may be keeping some of their most important guests away from the wedding because they expect Israeli reprisals to the missile attack."

"Okay, that has possibilities. Keep digging. And find this Ali Khamis . . . quickly!"

3:00 PM

Kenan didn't know that Deywós had found a new portal connecting the Shadowlands and the Earth. Kenan had, in fact, never heard of the Shadowlands nor had he any idea what a portal to it could mean. He did, however, know that at a certain time each day, in a certain corner of his closet, he seemed to make contact with an intelligent being or beings. He had read about UFOs, extraterrestrials, and connecting with the divine spirits. He thought it might be something like that, or perhaps something completely new. His access to this other world was limited. He could dimly see shelves of books during his times of connection, but he couldn't read titles or reach out to touch them. He promised himself that he would keep coming back daily until he understood what he was experiencing.

Having learned that Kenan came nearly every day at the same time to Saparon's office in the Shadowlands, where Lord Deywós kept his books and scrolls, Qorin entered the *Tselim* library ready to watch. Realizing the boy could sense his presence but couldn't see him, Qorin said, "I have a message for you."

"What? For me? What is it?" the surprised boy replied.

"Go to the Mount Zion Center this afternoon and wait for a young man named Dominic. I think you will know him when you see him. When you find him, tell him that the two of you must immediately leave Jerusalem. Go together and find a place to stay in Tel Aviv until you hear from me again."

3:00 PM

Eván had no intention of spending all his time being anyone's research assistant, so after an hour investigating Noor-Allah and Ali Khamis for his new *Tsel* master, he left the hotel, expecting that Dominic might be heading to the Mount Zion Center for the evening prayers.

Eván arrived late, just as Dominic and Khaled were approaching the steps of the church. He cursed, since he had hoped to talk with Dominic before he entered the meeting. He was close enough that he could have called out to Dominic, to ask him to stop, to wait just a moment. A few days earlier when Dominic had spotted him in the church, Eván had not yet decided his best approach. Now, knowing that the Shadowlands was actively seeking to connect with Dominic, he knew what to say. He needed to convince Dominic to escape with him. He would tell him about the Shadowlands and that dangerous people were after him. Dominic might not yet know his own power, but Eván did.

Just then, a young boy who had been loitering nearby approached Dominic and Khaled. Eván stepped back into the shadows and watched as Kenan approached confidently and said, "Excuse me, are you Dominic?"

Dominic was startled and immediately on his guard. "Who's asking?"

"My name's Kenan," he said, smiling and extending his hand. "A friend of mine told me about you, and I was wondering if we could go somewhere and talk?"

A flicker of confusion passed over Dominic's face as he realized he had heard of this strange boy from his housemates at the kibbutz. Accepting the outstretched hand, he was simultaneously drawn to and wary of him, feeling at the same time exhilaration and contamination.

Khaled intervened at that moment, putting his arm around Dominic's shoulders and saying to Kenan, "Sorry, kid, not right now. We're on our way to a meeting."

Kenan, not accustomed to rejection, said, "Dominic, this is important! You and I must get out of Jerusalem now!"

Dominic and Khaled kept on climbing the stairs to the front door. As they entered the building, Dominic gave a deep shudder, and Khaled asked, "What's up, Dom?"

"I honestly don't know. For one thing, I have no idea how that kid knew my name. I had a similar experience once before with a guy in LA who was stalking me. Let's get inside and join the worship service."

Ch 47. The Rapture

(Jerusalem, 8 hours before the Fire)

> *And He will send His angels with a great sound of a trumpet, and they will gather together His elect from the four winds, from one end of heaven to the other.*
>
> Matthew 24:31

7:00 PM

That evening, after the afternoon worship service, Bill, Dominic, Khaled, and Nehemyah were standing around talking. Ever since Nehemyah's message on entering the kingdom a few days before, Bill had been talking about the end-times. He asked Nehemyah, "So, what do you think about the timing of the Rapture?"

Dominic heard the question, but his mind was elsewhere. He couldn't shake the strange feeling that came over him when he met Kenan just before the service. And he was still wondering about the man he had seen standing at the back of the Shabbat worship service four days ago.

Nehemyah responded to Bill's question, "Actually, I'm just on my way to hear a friend of mine speak on that very subject. Would you like to come with me to hear him?"

Bill said, "Yes!" and Khaled and Dominic tagged along as Moshe guided Nehemyah and the boys to the light-rail and then up Jaffa Street to the fifteen-story Clal Building. They passed through the security check and entered what looked like a mostly vacant, 1970s-style indoor shopping center. They proceeded down wide tile stairs and turned into a large windowless room—perhaps originally a clothing store or a home electronics shop. Whatever its past, the room now served as a meeting place for the Clal Messianic Fellowship—and like so many other Christian worship centers in this city, it sat hidden away without signs, banners, or advertising.

Dominic thought, *We just came from a Christian meeting. Is that all Christians do here in Jerusalem? Go from one meeting to the next?* Apparently so, because about half of the hundred or so folding chairs were already occupied, and while Dominic watched, the remaining seats quickly filled as people continued to flow in. He saw young and old, Israelis as well as visitors from around the world.

A pair of young women and an even younger man with a guitar started a Hebrew praise song as the congregants made their way to their seats, although most remained standing.

As the third song came to an end, a man with olive skin and a dark beard, only a little older than the singers, left his place in the front row and joined the trio on the stage.

He wore a smile that seemed to never fade as he said, "Shalom!"

Most in the gathering returned the greeting, and as they settled into their seats, the leader said, "*Ani Yitzhak, ani moreh poh b'Kehilat HaRoeh*. Welcome. I am Yitzhak, a teacher here at the Shephard's Congregation. *Kulam poh mevinim Ivrit?*"[123]

He waited for a moment and then added with a grin, still speaking in Hebrew, "Please raise your hand if you can't understand me."

There were several giggles throughout the room, and he broke into a hearty laugh as he looked out on the audience.

---

123. Hebrew: "Does everyone here understand Hebrew?"

When Nehemyah put his hand high in the air, Yitzhak laughed again and said, "Uncle Nehemyah, did you forget how to speak Hebrew?"

"No, my friend. By God's grace, I can still speak our beloved language. But alas, I have two guests with me this evening who have not yet mastered it."

At this, Bill leaned over and said to Dominic loud enough so that all could hear, "Not yet mastered Hebrew. Well, if that isn't the understatement of the century!"

Yitzhak led the room in another round of laughter, then continued in English, "Very well. For the sake of your two guests, as well as any others here who may be 'Hebraically challenged,' I will make my short introduction in English.

"As you may know, our congregation is part of an affiliation of Messianic Jews. At our regional administration meeting last month, we were taking a break between sessions, when a lively conversation broke out regarding the timing of the Rapture. It was just starting to get interesting when we were called back to our final session.

"I will neither confirm nor deny the accusation that my mind was not fully engaged in the budget discussion before us at that moment. I prefer to think that God gave me a divine revelation, an inspired thought, as it were. After the meeting I quickly approached the two who had been engaged in the Rapture discussion. I explained that I really wanted to hear more of what they had to say, and I thought others might be interested as well. Seeing the large number of people here tonight, I think I was right.

"Anyway, my two brothers and friends have consented to come this evening to continue their discussion; to have an open debate, if you will. At this point, I'd like to welcome up my brothers in *Yeshua Ha Mashiach*, Menachem and Shimon."

Two men walked up to the front: one, gray-haired, bearded, and wearing glasses; the other, brown-haired and clean-shaven. The three men sat down around an oval table facing the congregation.

Yitzhak continued, "I will stay up here, but please don't expect me to give my opinion or in any way contribute to the conversation. I'll just be here to facilitate the discussion as needed. I've asked Shimon to get us started. But first, let's ask the Lord to bless and cover our time together." After a short prayer in Hebrew, Yitzhak invited Shimon to begin.

"Thank you, Yitzhak. Thank you, Menachem. And thanks to all of you for coming this evening. As Yitzhak has said, we are here to speak about the end-times and specifically about the timing of the Rapture of the Church. Most Bible-believing Christians agree that the return of Christ will occur at the end of a period called the Tribulation. That's not very controversial. After all, in Matthew 24, in one of the most important texts about the end-times, Jesus said,

> *Immediately after the tribulation of those days the sun will be darkened, and the moon will not give its light; the stars will fall from heaven, and the powers of the heavens will be shaken. Then the sign of the Son of Man will appear in heaven, and then all the tribes of the earth will mourn, and they will see the Son of Man coming on the clouds of heaven with power and great glory. And He will send His angels with a great sound of a trumpet, and they will gather together His elect from the four winds, from one end of heaven to the other.*124

Shimon looked up from his Bible and continued, "The words, '*Immediately after the tribulation*' seem clear. But what about this word *tribulation*? Many students of the Bible believe it will last approximately three and a half years, others believe it will be seven years

124. Matthew 24:29–31

long. In any case, the majority of Bible-believing Christians agree that the Tribulation will last several years."

At this point, Shimon noticed that Menachem, though nodding in agreement, looked eager to get into meatier issues. Deciding he could skip past other areas of agreement, Shimon said, "However, where there *is* significant disagreement, and where the focus of this evening's discussion is centered, is whether there will also be a rapture of the Church prior to the Tribulation. Those who believe in this additional in-gathering, appropriately called a *'pre-Tribulation rapture,'* often refer to it as a *'secret rapture.'* I find this term also very appropriate; in fact, I am convinced it's such a secret that it is, in fact, taught nowhere in the Bible."

There were a few chuckles as Shimon paused to let his words sink in. Menachem, however, took advantage of the opportunity to defend his view.

"The pre-Tribulation rapture *is* taught in the Bible. In a number of places. For example, First Thessalonians 4:16–17:

> *For the Lord Himself will descend from heaven with a shout, with the voice of an archangel, and with the trumpet of God. And the dead in Christ will rise first. Then we who are alive and remain shall be caught up together with them in the clouds to meet the Lord in the air. And thus we shall always be with the Lord.*

"Then there's First Corinthians 15:51–52:

> *We shall not all sleep, but we shall all be changed—in a moment, in the twinkling of an eye, at the last trumpet. For the trumpet will sound, and the dead will be raised incorruptible, and we shall be changed.*

"It's in Matthew 24:40: 'One will be taken and the other left.' It is the 'Blessed hope' of Titus 2:13. The Rapture is taught all over in the Bible."

Shimon answered, "Amen. I believe that wonderful event *is* taught in all those Scriptures and more: but it's *after* the Tribulation. What we don't find is any indication of a secret, pre-Tribulation rapture."

"The *Rapture* occurs before the Tribulation," Menachem sought to clarify, "and the *second coming* occurs after the Tribulation."

Shimon replied, "And that is the crux of the issue. We both understand that in the end-times God will take His believers up to be with Him. That is clear. But you believe this gathering will occur in two separate events: the *Rapture,* which takes place right *before* the Tribulation and the *Second Coming,* which takes place right *after* the Tribulation. I believe that a rapture before the Tribulation isn't taught anywhere in the Bible and that the burden of proof is on the Pretribulationists to show that the Scriptures teach a rapture prior to the Tribulation."

Ch 48. A Question of Imminence

(Jerusalem, 8 hours before the Fire)

He who testifies to these things says,
"Surely I am coming quickly."
Amen. Even so, come, Lord Jesus!

Revelation 22:20

7:00 PM

It was Menachem's turn to reply. "It comes down to imminence. The Rapture must occur *before* the Tribulation because Jesus taught us that the Rapture could happen at any moment. In Matthew 24:36, we read, 'But of that day and hour no one knows, not even the angels of heaven, but My Father only.'[125] And again, in Matthew 25:13, 'Watch therefore, for you know neither the day nor the hour in which the Son of Man is coming.'[126] If the Rapture won't occur until after all the signs given in the Scriptures, then it is no longer imminent. People could reasonably say, 'I don't have to believe now; I can wait. When I see the Tribulation and the Antichrist, then I'll believe.'"

---

125. Matthew 24:35
126. Matthew 25:13

Shimon responded, "Jesus did tell people to be watchful, and He did warn of the dangers of not being prepared for His return. The Parable of the Wise and Foolish Virgins in Matthew 25 is a good example of that. But Jesus never taught that His return would be imminent, that it could happen at any moment. He didn't teach it because He didn't believe it."

Menachem countered, "And why do you think that Jesus didn't believe that His return was imminent?"

"Well, let me ask you this: 'When Jesus said that nobody knows the day or the hour, do you think He meant that He could have returned at any point after His ascension to heaven?'"

"Yes," Menachem responded. "Just like us today, the first disciples were anxiously awaiting the Lord's return every day."

"But just prior to His ascension, Jesus promised that His disciples would soon receive supernatural power from the Holy Spirit and that they were to remain in Jerusalem until that happened.[127] So, during the days immediately following Jesus' ascension, His followers must have been anxiously awaiting Jesus' promise of the Holy Spirit, not His glorious return, right?"

Menachem answered, "That's true, but the promise of the coming of the Holy Spirit was fulfilled on Pentecost, just *ten days* after Jesus' ascension.[128] After that, they could expect Jesus' immediate return any day."

Shimon was shaking his head. "No. Not if they had been paying attention to what Jesus had said. Shortly before His ascension, Jesus predicted that Peter would one day be killed as a martyr.[129] According to Early Church writings, Peter was martyred about *thirty-five years* after Jesus' ascension. So, during all those years while Peter was still alive, should Jesus' disciples have expected His immediate return? Again, no. How could they expect Jesus' immediate return to rapture

127. Acts 1:5
128. Acts 2:1–4
129. John 21:18–19

the Church, when that would have contradicted His own prediction about Peter's martyrdom? Therefore, when Jesus said 'nobody knows the day or the hour,' the disciples must have understood that some things still had to happen before Jesus' return."

Menachem responded, "Yes, that is true. But we also need to understand that *now* there are no more prophecies or promises to be fulfilled before the Rapture happens."

"I disagree. I believe there are, and we can look at those. But in any case, first we need to understand that one can't use Jesus' words to prove that His coming was imminent, that is, that He could have returned *any* time after His ascension."

"I will grant you that." Menachem answered, "But there are many other passages throughout the New Testament that teach that Jesus could come back at any time. These were likely written after Peter's martyrdom, or possibly just shortly before."

"For example?"

"I'm glad you asked," Menachem said, opening his Bible. "In First Corinthians, the apostle Paul wrote that they were '. . . eagerly waiting for the revelation of our Lord Jesus Christ.'[130] Another way to say this is 'eagerly expecting.'" Menachem flipped his Bible to another passage. "In James 5 we read,

> *Therefore be patient, brethren, until the coming of the Lord. See how the farmer waits for the precious fruit of the earth, waiting patiently for it until it receives the early and latter rain. You also be patient. Establish your hearts, for the coming of the Lord is at hand.'*[131]

"James made it very clear: Jesus is coming back soon. We have to be patiently waiting because it could be at any time. That's why Jesus Himself in the last verses of the whole Bible said, 'Surely I am coming

130. 1 Corinthians 1:7

131. James 5:7–8

quickly.' And John's very appropriate response was 'Amen. Even so, come, Lord Jesus!'"[132]

Shimon sat back a little and asked, "Brother, can I ask you a personal question?"

"Sure."

"Do you have children?"

"Yes, four. Between the ages of two and eight."

"Wonderful. And does your family celebrate Christmas?"

"Yes. We feel, being followers of *Yeshua Ha Mashiach*, it's right to celebrate his birth."

"I agree. But your children, do they enjoy Christmas?"

"Of course, they understand we are celebrating Jesus' birthday, and they love the presents, the food, the fun family gatherings. We love Christmastime."

"Lovely. And when does *Christmastime* start for your family?"

"We celebrate pretty much the entire month of December. Sometimes even starting in November."

Shimon sat up. "Yes, one of the beautiful aspects of being a Messianic Jew is that we celebrate our traditional Jewish holidays as well as the Christian holidays. Christmas is a wonderful time in my family as well. I think my wife Anna would begin celebrating Christmas in *July* if she could. She talks about Christmas all year long. She waits for it—sometimes not so patiently—all year long. But her eager anticipation of Christmas does not mean that Christmas could actually come in March or July or even November.

"My point is that it's the same with the rapture of the Church. It's a future event we are encouraged to look forward to and to eagerly await, but that does not imply in any way that the Rapture could come at any moment."

Menachem didn't jump in, so Shimon continued. "This idea of a future event that can be eagerly anticipated is conveyed in the Bible.

132. Revelation 22:20

You mentioned Revelation 22:20, where Jesus said He is coming quickly. That word *'quickly'* is *taxu* in the Greek and means 'without unnecessary delay.' For example, Paul used this same word, *taxu*, when he wrote in First Timothy, 'These things I write to you, though I hope to come to you shortly . . .'[133] And in Romans, he says, 'And the God of peace will crush Satan under your feet shortly.'[134]

"Paul's hope to see Timothy 'shortly' and the promise that God will 'shortly' crush Satan under our feet do not imply imminence or immediacy so much as they imply 'without unnecessary delay.'

"If the New Testament writers wanted to communicate *immediacy* regarding the Rapture or the Lord's return, they could have used *euthys* or *eutheos*. These words occur eighty-seven times in the Greek New Testament, but only once regarding the Rapture or Christ's coming, in the verse I quoted earlier, 'Immediately after the tribulation of those days.'[135] So the only verse in Scripture linking imminence with the Lord's return uses the words *immediately after the tribulation*, a phrase that doesn't help the case for the pre-Tribulation rapture at all."

Shimon continued, "Let's examine what we do know to be true about Jesus's return to rescue his people. First, no one knows when it will happen. Second, it will happen at a time when people don't expect it. Third, Jesus said that people should stay prepared for it at all times, so that they don't get caught unready. Those three things are taught in the Scripture. It does not teach that the coming of the Lord is *imminent*, meaning that it could happen at any moment. There are other prophecies that must still be fulfilled before Jesus returns."

Menachem sat up a little straighter and countered, "There certainly are events that must occur before Jesus' return to earth, but not before the Rapture. Jesus is going to rescue His beloved Church from the horrors that will take place during the Tribulation. The believers

133. 1 Timothy 3:14–15

134. Romans 16:20

135. Matthew 24:29 uses *eutheos* for "immediately"

will be caught up to be with Jesus while all hell breaks out on earth. The apostle Paul wrote that we are not appointed to wrath.[136] God wouldn't subject His children to all of the horrible things that we read about in the Book of Revelation. That's why Jesus encouraged His disciples to be watchful and to pray that they may be counted worthy to escape all those things.[137] But if there is no rapture before the Tribulation, what is the point? Worthy or not, ready or not, believer or not—all will be forced to endure the atrocities of the Antichrist during the Tribulation, all will be subject to the wrath of God."

Menachem relaxed and Shimon answered, "Let's be clear: trials, tribulations, and persecutions we experience by the hands of men or the machinations of demons are not the same thing as the wrath of God. It's true, we, as believers, are not appointed to God's wrath. But Jesus said very clearly to His disciples, 'In the world you will have tribulation.'[138] Let me assure you, there are other prophesied events that must happen before the Rapture. At this point, it might help us to hear a story about a prison camp escape."

Yitzhak stepped in. "Yes, that sounds exciting! But first, we will take a fifteen-minute break. Please do come back on time to hear this exciting prison camp escape story. You don't want to miss that!"

---

136. 1 Thessalonians 5:9
137. Luke 21:36
138. John 16:33

Ch 49. The Great Escape

(Jerusalem, 7 hours before the Fire)

Because you have kept My command to persevere,
I also will keep you from the hour of trial
which shall come upon the whole world,
to test those who dwell on the earth.

Revelation 3:10

8:00 PM

The audience stood up, stretched, and mingled in small groups. Nehemyah, Bill, and Khaled were talking with a few others, but Dominic excused himself, saying he needed to use the restroom. But what he really wanted was some fresh air. He made his way outside and wandered about, looking at the shops along Jaffa Street. Suddenly, he sensed someone following him and turned to see the young boy who had approached him earlier that day on the steps of the Mount Zion Church.

"Hello, Dominic."

"You again."

"Yes, I'm Kenan, remember? We need to talk. They told me that the name 'Alessandro' might mean something to you."

Dominic looked intently at him. "*Who* told you about Alessandro?"

"It's complicated. All I know is that our destinies might be intertwined and that we have to get out of Jerusalem immediately; it's a matter of life and death."

At that moment, Dominic heard steps and looked up to see a man striding purposely toward them: the same man who had been watching him during the Mount Zion Church meeting two days before.

Dominic asked the boy, "Is this the guy who said we have to go?"

Kenan glanced at the man. "No, I've never seen him before. But, really, Dominic, we've got to get out of here!"

Dominic stayed put, his countenance stern. He watched as the stalker approached them. Dominic asked coldly, "Can I help you?"

"Dominic, I'm here to help *you*."

"No, thanks. You tried to offer your help in LA last month, and I told you I wasn't interested. Two days ago, when I noticed you staring at me in the church service here in Jerusalem, you ran away. I don't know who you are, but if you want to talk, show me your face."

The man slowly removed his sunglasses and pulled back the hood that had kept his features in shadow. Dominic gasped in surprise, "How is it possible?"

Kenan asked, "What? Is *this* Alessandro?"

"I don't know. He looks just like him . . . but it can't be." He asked the stranger, "Are you?"

"Am I what?" came the reply.

"Are you Alessandro Tarso?"

"No."

"Well, then who are you?"

"Listen, Dominic, we don't have time for this. I'm not Alessandro, but I *did* know him. I can explain everything, but not here. Come on, I have a car." He took a step, but seeing that Dominic made no move to follow, he turned back and added, "Listen. Surely, deep down, you must realize that you are different from the others around you. You are part of another world . . . and I've been sent here from that world to rescue you."

Kenan spoke up, "Dominic, I think he's right. I knew we needed to leave Jerusalem immediately, but I wasn't sure how. Now this man arrives with the means of our escape. Let's go!"

The stranger shifted his gaze from Dominic to Kenan, studying the boy who couldn't be more than twelve and yet who had the confidence and bearing of a mature adult accustomed to giving orders. The stranger asked, "Have we met before? What's your name?"

"They call me Kenan. What about you?"

"You can call me Eván. But where I come from, I'm known as Abdowan."

At those words, a chill ran down Dominic's spine.

Nehemyah and Bill were concerned. While Bill craned his neck to look around the room, Nehemyah consulted his watch, uneasy about the fact that Dominic still hadn't returned after the break.

Just then, Yitzhak began the meeting again, saying, "Welcome back. Please find your seats and sit down. Before the break, our guests were discussing the topic of imminence, and Shimon promised us an exciting story." Then, gesturing to his left, he said, "Brother Shimon, please continue."

"Yes. Thank you, Yitzhak. As promised, now we are going to hear the harrowing story of how our friend Yitzhak once escaped from prison camp."

Yitzhak looked at Shimon with raised eyebrows. Shimon nodded to the audience, and Yitzhak turned to face the group for a moment as if he was going to speak. Everyone was quiet.

Shrugging his shoulders, Yitzhak said good-naturedly, "I'm sorry, my brother. I'm not sure what you are after. I have no such story to tell."

Shimon feigned disappointment, "Are you saying that you've never escaped from a prison camp?"

"No, I've never even been in one before."

"Well, do you hope to escape from one someday?"

Yitzhak shook his head, "Uh, no. I don't actually ever plan on being *in* one."

Shimon said, "Well, in that case, let's read from Luke 21, one of the passages Menachem referred to earlier." Opening his Bible, he read,

> *'But take heed to yourselves, lest your hearts be weighed down with carousing, drunkenness, and cares of this life, and that Day come on you unexpectedly. For it will come as a snare on all those who dwell on the face of the whole earth. Watch therefore, and pray always that you may be counted worthy to escape all these things that will come to pass, and to stand before the Son of Man.'"*[139]

Shimon turned to Menachem and asked, "What is Jesus encouraging His disciples to pray for?"

"That they would get taken up to heaven in the Rapture and miss all of the evil that will happen during the Tribulation."

"But," Shimon countered, "the word Jesus used was *ekphygein*, 'to escape.' Now, I apologize to my brother Yitzhak; it wasn't fair to put him on the spot, but I am trying to make a point. He doesn't have a story about *escaping* from the horrors of a prison camp because neither he nor I have faced that particular evil. You can't 'escape' a dangerous or evil situation that is not already upon you. Jesus believed that His followers would experience the evil of the Tribulation, if not, He wouldn't have spoken of them escaping from it.

139. Luke 21:34–36

"Are believers expected to avoid tribulation? No. In fact, Paul wrote to the Romans that 'We glory in tribulations, knowing that tribulation produces perseverance.'[140] And again, Jesus said, 'In the world you will have tribulation; but be of good cheer, I have overcome the world.'"[141]

Menachem countered, "We may not be expected to avoid it, but in the Book of Revelation, it promises we will be *kept from* the Tribulation. It says, 'Because you have kept My command to persevere, I also will keep you from the hour of trial which shall come upon the whole world, to test those who dwell on the earth.'"[142]

Shimon responded, "Yes, but we need to ask ourselves, to whom was this promise made? Who are the people who will be kept from the Great Tribulation?"

Menachem answered, "This is a promise to all believers; it says, '. . . hear what the Spirit says to the churches.'"[143]

"The promises in this text apply to all believers?"

"Yes," Menachem said.

"And God always keeps his promises? They always come true?"

"Absolutely."

"Okay, so when did those so-called Jews come and worship at *your* feet?" Shimon asked.

"What do you mean?"

"You know, Revelation 3:9. The same chapter, the same letter to the same church contains this promise:

> *I will make those who are of the synagogue of Satan, who claim to be Jews though they are not, but are liars—I will make them come and fall down at your feet and acknowledge that I have loved you."*

140. Romans 5:3
141. John 16:33b
142. Revelation 3:10
143. Revelation 3:13

Shimon continued, "Has that happened yet to you? Have false Jews come and fallen before you to acknowledge that God loves you? Because that hasn't happened to me yet."

"No," Menachem said, feeling a little entrapped. "That hasn't happened to me either."

Shimon said, "Okay. And yet the promise that members of the synagogue of Satan will come and acknowledge their error to the believers comes right before the promise that the believers will be kept from the Tribulation coming on the whole world."

Menachem countered, "But that part about the synagogue of Satan, that's figurative language; it doesn't literally happen."

"And yet," Shimon asked, "You believe that the part about being kept from the Tribulation is completely literal?"

When Menachem didn't speak up right away, Shimon continued. "Here's another idea. What if the promises to the churches in Revelation 2 and 3 don't necessarily apply to all believers at all times? What if those promises were given to those specific believers at that specific time, including the promise that they would be kept from the Great Tribulation? Let me ask you this: Did the Christians of the first-century church of Philadelphia go through the Great Tribulation?"

Menachem said, "No, obviously not. It hadn't happened yet. It still hasn't happened."

Shimon responded, "Precisely. So that promise, like the other promises to the churches in Revelation 2 and 3, was fulfilled nearly two thousand years ago. And once again, we see another Scripture that gives no support for a pre-Tribulation rapture of the Church."

Just then, Dominic came in and sat down. Nehemyah looked over at him, but Dominic gave him a sign that they would talk later.

Ch 50. Watch and Pray

(Jerusalem, 6 hours before the Fire)

If I believe in God and life after death and you do not, and if there is no God, we both lose when we die.
However, if there is a God, you still lose and I gain everything.

Blaise Pascal, *Pensées*

9:00 PM

Menachem took up the microphone. "I'd like to share something from my personal testimony, because maybe that will help explain why I feel it is important to believe in a pre-Tribulation rapture.

"I first heard the Gospel forty years ago when I was a university student. At the time, I was an agnostic, thinking maybe God existed, maybe he didn't. Belief in God mattered little to me. A fellow student, a friend of mine explained to me that Blaise Pascal, a famous French mathematician from the seventeenth century, had an explanation as to why belief in God must always be the most rational choice for every person.

"Pascal's wager is an argument that goes something like this: If eternal life with God isn't real, then a person who believes in God doesn't gain anything. Neither the believer nor the unbeliever lives with God in eternal happiness if, in fact, God doesn't exist.

"On the other hand, the argument continues that if God *is real* and if the promise of eternal life with God *is real*, then the choice to believe or not becomes of supreme importance. Believing or not believing becomes a matter of gaining or else losing eternal happiness.

"The point of Pascal's wager is that only one choice gives a potential benefit. Believing in Christ offers the only possible opportunity for gaining eternal happiness. If the Gospel is wrong, we all lose. But if the Gospel is true, those who believe *gain* eternal happiness and those who don't believe *lose* eternal happiness.

"As a young man, that presentation impressed me as a strong argument. I wondered, *Was it worth taking the risk of missing eternal happiness?* On the other hand, in the back of my mind, I was thinking, *I'm young and I have lots of time. Someday I'll decide.*

"It was at that point that my friend shared with me Jesus' words about the Rapture of those who believe, and the terrible events to follow for those who are left behind. When he explained to me that no one knows the day nor the hour when this event will occur, I realized I didn't dare risk waiting even one day to make my decision. I didn't want to be left behind to face all the chaos and confusion of the tribulation period.

"Realizing that I had everything to gain and nothing to lose by trusting Christ, I made my choice that day. So, you can see why I am so passionate about the pre-Tribulation rapture. Without the imminence of the Lord's return, how will people sense the urgency of their precarious situation without Christ?"

Shimon replied, "Thank you, Menachem. Your testimony is very moving, and I praise God that He was able to use the idea of an imminent rapture to help you make your choice to follow Christ. However, I believe the pre-Tribulation rapture view actually provides a stronger reason to *not* believe in Christ and to *not* be prepared."

Menachem gave a puzzled look. "How do you figure that?"

Because the pre-Tribulation rapture view suggests that the unbelievers will be given a second chance during the Great Tribulation. That's something that the Bible simply doesn't support.

Anticipating Menachem's opposition, Shimon opened up his Bible again and continued, "In First Thessalonians five we read:

> *But concerning the times and the seasons, brethren, you have no need that I should write to you. For you yourselves know perfectly that the day of the Lord so comes as a thief in the night.*
>
> *For when they say, "Peace and safety!" then sudden destruction comes upon them, as labor pains upon a pregnant woman. And they shall not escape.*
>
> *But you, brethren, are not in darkness, so that this Day should overtake you as a thief. You are all sons of light and sons of the day. We are not of the night nor of darkness.*
>
> *Therefore let us not sleep, as others do, but let us watch and be sober. For those who sleep, sleep at night, and those who get drunk are drunk at night. But let us who are of the day be sober, putting on the breastplate of faith and love, and as a helmet the hope of salvation.*
>
> *For God did not appoint us to wrath, but to obtain salvation through our Lord Jesus Christ.*[144]

"This text explains that the day of the Lord will come as a thief in the night and that at that time unbelievers will face sudden

144. 1 Thessalonians 5:1–9

destruction and God's wrath, and that they won't escape. Do these words offer a lot of hope of a second chance to the unbeliever?"

The room was silent for a moment, then Shimon continued. "Menachem, didn't you suggest earlier that if there were warning signs before the Rapture, potential believers would simply wait until it was almost the time of the Rapture, and then decide to believe?"

Menachem nodded, "Yes. That's why the Rapture has to be a surprise. Otherwise, Jesus' emphasis on the need to stay ready doesn't make much sense."

"It would make sense," countered Shimon, "if Jesus knew that the window of being able to repent would come to an end at the beginning of this future period called the Great Tribulation."

"What? Are you saying there will be no conversions during the Tribulation?"

"That's right. The Scriptures teach that it will be too late at that point—the unbelievers' fate will be sealed."

"Okay, Shimon, what kind of scriptural evidence do you have for that?"

"Well, first, Jesus taught this truth in Matthew 25, right after talking in depth about His coming and why it's important to stay ready.

Shimon opened his Bible again and read,

> *Then the kingdom of heaven shall be likened to ten virgins who took their lamps and went out to meet the bridegroom. Now five of them were wise, and five* were *foolish. Those who were foolish took their lamps and took no oil with them, but the wise took oil in their vessels with their lamps. But while the bridegroom was delayed, they all slumbered and slept.*
>
> *And at midnight a cry was* heard*: 'Behold, the bridegroom is coming; go out to meet him!' Then all those virgins arose and trimmed their lamps. And the foolish said to the wise,*

> *'Give us some of your oil, for our lamps are going out.' But the wise answered, saying, 'No, lest there should not be enough for us and you; but go rather to those who sell, and buy for yourselves.' And while they went to buy, the bridegroom came, and those who were ready went in with him to the wedding; and the door was shut.*
>
> *Afterward the other virgins came also, saying, 'Lord, Lord, open to us!' But he answered and said, 'Assuredly, I say to you, I do not know you.'*
>
> *Watch therefore, for you know neither the day nor the hour in which the Son of Man is coming.*[145]

Shimon continued, "Notice that the 'midnight cry' did not signify the end of the age, but rather the end of the time for preparation. It didn't mean that the Church had been taken to heaven; the bridegroom didn't come then. But rather, after the midnight cry, it was no longer possible to get ready for what was to come. Those who hadn't prepared themselves beforehand were left out, and the door was shut.

"Jesus said in John nine, 'I must work the works of Him who sent Me while it is day; *the* night is coming when no one can work.'[146] This means that those who have not stayed vigilant during the day, during the time of work, will find that it is impossible to make up for their lack of preparation by trying to get ready during the night. Many people don't realize this frightening truth: The day will come when it is too late to get right with God.

"God calls people to seek Him while they can find Him and call upon Him while He is near.[147] We have an example in the life of Esau,

---

145. Matthew 25:1–13
146. John 9:4
147. Isaiah 55:6

who chose a bowl of lentils instead of his future blessing. When the time of inheritance came, he regretted that foolish choice, but by then it was too late. The Scripture says that he found no place of repentance, and even though he desperately wanted the blessing, he was rejected."[148]

Shimon continued, "Quite honestly, the pre-Tribulation rapture view paints too rosy a picture for those who don't make their decision for God soon enough. It gives them the false hope of a second chance to turn to God. Yes, they may have to endure some physical suffering for a short time, but after that, they will enjoy eternal life with God. It teaches that persecution is a consequence of not being ready, but Jesus taught his faithful followers that 'in the world you will have tribulation.'[149] In the Book of Acts, being persecuted wasn't looked upon as a punishment but a privilege.[150]

Menachem had been waiting patiently, but was now eager to jump in. "But there *will* be conversions during the Tribulation—many of them. When the unbelievers see all the Christians disappear, when they see the Antichrist come on the scene, when they see the signs and plagues happening, they'll realize they've made a huge mistake, and they'll turn to God. Those are the ones that meet Jesus in the air at His second coming."

Shimon said, "Well, that's the way it's portrayed in some popular novels and movies, and huge conversions during the Tribulation are needed for the pre-Tribulation view to work. But what kind of scriptural evidence do you have that all these people will repent and turn to God during the time of the Great Tribulation?"

Menachem opened his Bible and said, "Revelation 11:13. It says,

> *In the same hour there was a great earthquake, and a tenth of the city fell. In the earthquake seven thousand people*

148. Hebrews 12:16–17
149. John 16:33
150. Acts 5:41

> *were killed, and the rest were afraid and gave glory to the God of heaven."*[151]

Shimon was quick to respond, "Well, being afraid and giving glory to God isn't the same thing as repenting or being converted. Most people that give glory to God do so because they are already believers. But even if we assume for now that these people in Revelation chapter 11 had previously been unbelievers and then they repented and gave glory to God, is this evidence of mass conversions worldwide? No. This passage speaks of a very limited number of Jewish people, living in or around Jerusalem.[152] Menachem, are there any other passages that give any indication of large-scale conversions, or even any conversions at all during the tribulation period?"

"Nothing is coming to mind."

"I haven't found any either. This seems to be the only scriptural evidence that even hints at people repenting or being converted during the Tribulation. What we find instead is that during the time of Tribulation people continually refuse to turn to God. They hide from God.[153] They prefer to die rather than repent.[154] They refuse to leave their idolatry, murder, witchcraft, immorality, and thievery.[155] They are deceived by the beast and worship him as god.[156] Their response to God's judgement is to become angry,[157] to blaspheme the name of God, and to refuse to repent of their evil deeds.[158]

"So, we see that there is an abundance of evidence that people do *not* repent during the Tribulation, but on the other hand, we've found only one verse that *possibly* describes the conversion of a small

151. Revelation 11:13
152. Romans 11:25–27 and Zechariah 13:7–9
153. Revelation 6:15
154. Revelation 9:6
155. Revelation 9:20
156. Revelation 13:8 and 14
157. Revelation 11:18
158. Revelation 16:9–10

number of Jews in Jerusalem. In any case, we can clearly see that the idea of large-scale conversions during the Tribulation is not supported in the Scriptures. In fact, not only do we not see people coming to faith, but the Bible also specifically says that during the end-times many people will turn away from the faith.[159]

"And yet, we see in the Book of Revelation that there are many believers during the Tribulation. They are said to be persecuted by the devil[160] and by the beast,[161] and many will be killed for their faith.[162] These believers are made up of not only Jews but are specifically called 'a great multitude which no one could number, of all nations, tribes, peoples, and tongues.'[163] Some people understand this multitude to be the martyrs killed during the Tribulation. Others believe they have been raptured sometime after the midpoint of the Tribulation. But what is not possible is that they were raptured before the Tribulation, because the text specifically states that they came *out* of the Great Tribulation.[164] And remember, you can't come out of someplace if you have never been there.

"To me, the pre-Tribulation rapture is not only unscriptural, but also completely illogical. It suggests that the Tribulation begins with zero believers on earth, and yet, after a few years of intense persecution and martyrdom, widespread rejection of the faith, and few if any conversions, there are somehow multitudes of believers from every nation on earth."

Shimon continued, "I have just one more thing to add. Menachem, you mentioned Pascal's wager, the idea that believing in God is the better option because there is everything to gain and nothing to lose.

---

159. 1 Timothy 4:1
160. Revelation 12:17
161. Revelation 13:7
162. Revelation 6:9–11; 13:7
163. Revelation 7:9
164. Revelation 7:14

"That got me thinking. The same is true about the end-times. Because of the possibility that the Church might go through the Great Tribulation, every believer should prepare for that event. In preparing, there is everything to gain and nothing to lose. The possibility of being unprepared for the difficulties Jesus said are coming upon the earth is not a safe risk."

The room became quiet again, and this time Yitzak spoke up. "I think this has been great. Unfortunately, we will need to bring our discussion to a close here shortly, but before we leave, I'd like to ask both of our guests if they could share with us a few ways that we can be more prepared for the days ahead and the Lord's return?"

"Well, I can tell you what God has been showing me," began Menachem. "God has been teaching me about orienting my life around obeying Jesus, especially in the area of stewardship. I need to keep my focus on the fact that I am only a steward of the possessions God has given me. For example, giving to the poor,[165] not storing up wealth for my own security or comfort,[166] and practicing being content with what I have."[167]

"Wow, that's good," said Shimon. "And on a similar note, I'd say God has been teaching me about how I use my time. I've been striving to seek first His kingdom[168] and orient my life around His will,[169] recognizing that *people*, not *things* have ultimate value.[170] Putting the needs of others ahead of my own needs,[171] trying to not judge nor criticize my brother,[172] nor treating others with anger."[173]

165. Proverbs 19:17
166. Luke 12:13–21
167. Hebrews 13:5
168. Matthew 6:33
169. Matthew 6:10
170. Mark 8:36
171. Philippians 2:4
172. Romans 14:13
173. Ephesians 4:26

Yitzhak smiled and stood up, "Some very good words from both of you. Thank you, Shimon, and thank you, Menachem. This is not the end of the conversation, but it is where we need to end tonight. May we all be like the Berean Jews mentioned in Acts 17:11; they listened to the message but also examined the Scriptures to see if what was being presented was true."

Afterwards, as Nehemyah and the others traveled back to the kibbutz, Dominic was wondering to himself, *If the Tribulation is a period of up to seven years that happens before the Rapture of the Church, how does that fit with Chad's certainty that God told him the end would come before another year had passed?*

At that point, Bill said out loud, "Shimon's arguments made sense rationally, but I just know that I'm not going to be around during the reign of the Antichrist. I've never been so certain of anything in my life."

Nehemyah responded, "I don't doubt your sincerity, Bill. I've never seen in the Scriptures that God promises to remove His Church from tribulation in general or the Great Tribulation specifically. But God alone knows what the future holds for each one of us, and I believe it is best to trust in His loving plan."

10:00 PM

While the rest of the kibbutz had settled in for the night, Dominic lay in his bed thinking. Unable to sleep, he wandered over to the main cabin, where he found Nehemyah sitting in the same room where they had met just ten days earlier. Nehemyah had been about to go to bed, but seeing that something was on his young friend's mind, he put down his book and asked, "What's up, Dominic?"

"Could we talk for a moment . . . here in private?"

"Sure."

Dominic came and sat down. After a short pause, he said, "I met Kenan."

"Who?" Nehemyah asked.

"The boy that Benjamin's father doesn't like."

"Oh, I see. From what I've heard, this Kenan sounds like a very odd ten-year-old."

"Yes, Benjamin described him as 'ten going on thirty.' And I'd say that's pretty accurate."

Nehemyah nodded, and Dominic continued, "Actually, I met him twice today. The first time was this afternoon, going up to prayers at the Mount Zion Center. He approached me and told me his name. He knew my name before I said anything, which was quite odd. After introducing himself, it seemed like he wanted to talk, but I was in a hurry, so Khaled and I left him and went to the meeting.

"Then, this evening during the talk on the Rapture, I went out to get some fresh air at the break. As I walked along Jaffa Street, I met Kenan again. I intended to ignore him, but he surprised me by asking me about Alessandro, someone from my past that I've never told anyone here about."

"Yes?"

"It's a long story. Basically, I went through a difficult time about a year ago when I learned that I'd been adopted. I got this idea in my head that I had to try and find my birth father. I did some research, learned his name was Alessandro Tarso, and that he was from Italy, so I left home to search for him. After discovering that he had become a priest, I eventually tracked him down in the Dominican Republic. As I said, no one here knows about any of that, so why would Kenan mention that name to me? Who is this Kenan?"

"I really don't know, other than he is the adopted son of a rabbi here in Jerusalem. Where he is originally from or who his birth family is, I have no idea."

"Well, after he asked me about Alessandro, I looked up and there was a man coming right toward me."

"And?"

"He looked just like Alessandro."

"Your father?"

"Yes, but it wasn't him. And I realized this man had been following me around back in LA."

Nehemyah looked surprised and alarmed. "Someone was following you back in LA? Did you talk with your parents about it?"

"No, at the time I wasn't really talking with my parents. And when I left LA, I put it out of my mind."

"But now he's here?"

"Yes, you remember a few days ago you spoke in church about entering the kingdom?"

Nehemyah nodded and Dominic continued, "Well, he was there in the meeting, sitting in the back of the church, watching me. I tried to make my way over toward him, but he jumped up and ran out."

"And that's the same person you saw tonight?"

"Yeah. He said he knows who I am and what my destiny is. And he said his name was Eván. He gave me a weird feeling."

"Dominic, thank you for telling me about this. Can you give me a description of this fellow? I'll let Moshe know to keep his eyes open for him. Any idea where he's from?"

"Well, he's medium height, olive skin, curly dark hair. He spoke English, but I don't think it's his first language. He said that where he comes from they call him Abdowan. What kind of a name is that?"

"I don't know. Dominic, I think you should call your parents. Tell them about this Eván, and let them know we are aware of the situation and are on full alert. And promise me that if you feel you are in any danger, you will call me immediately."

"Okay, I will."

11:00 PM

Dominic returned to bed and fell asleep. He was soon experiencing a vivid dream similar to the one he had while living with Alfred in Haiti. He was walking through the prison camp again, but this time the air was hot and stifling, and the camp seemed deserted.

Suddenly, he heard a muffled scream coming from the building next to him. He ran inside and stood listening. He heard the scream again—louder this time. It was coming from below him. He found the stairs and rushed down. He was in a dimly lit hallway; the rock walls felt like a cave. He heard another voice growing louder as he moved quickly through the tunnel, around corners, and down more stairs. Then, he saw two figures at the end of the hallway: a woman, tied up, wearing torn clothes, and a man looming menacingly above her.

Dominic attempted to reach the woman to help her, but no matter how hard he tried, he couldn't actually get any closer. It was as if he were running on a treadmill. But even from a distance, he could hear the woman's voice saying, in barely a whisper, "God, please free me from this hell."

The man looked down at her with his cruel eyes and said, "You know, God will never come for you."

Ch 51. The Best-Laid Plans

(Shadowlands, 4 hours before the Fire)

> *And the smoke of the incense, with the prayers of the saints, ascended before God from the angel's hand.*
>
> Revelation 8:4

11:00 PM

Qorin found Verethragna pacing nervously as smoke rose from his territory. Both of them knew what that foul smoke meant; enemy agents were sending up their appeals to the Oppressor, prayers that to Him were like the sweet aroma of burning incense.

Tselim usually reacted to counter these efforts the moment they first appeared, but Verethragna had been so focused on attacking Jerusalem that he had not been paying enough attention to his own principality. It was clear that he had let the enemy's efforts get out of hand, and it was going to require some serious attention to bring this insubordination under control.

As he and Qorin continued to scan the horizon, the smoky incense ascending to the Oppressor was becoming more dense. Worse, it appeared to be coming in waves, crashing, as it were, against the shores of the Shadowlands.

Verethragna stood for a moment, undecided. On the one hand, he wanted to focus his attention on defending his principality. On the other hand, he had an important attack to coordinate. Offense or defense?

"What do you make of this smoke?" he asked, comfortable enough to almost completely forget his former antagonism toward Qorin.

"May I offer some counsel?" the Prince of Rome ventured, then without waiting for Verethragna's reply, he said, "The smoke? That's just the work of some of the low-level slaves of the Oppressor. Don't let it bother you. Do you know what you need?"

"What?" the Prince of Persia asked, distracted.

"You need to free yourself from your entanglement with one geographic area."

"And why is that?"

"Because you are limiting your potential. You can fight for that little bit of real estate, if you want. Or—" continued the Prince of Rome, fully extending his wings to illustrate his point, "you can join me and raise your sights higher."

"Of course I want to expand, but I want to expand while maintaining this principality too," replied Verethragna. "And that means finding a way to deal with this foul smoke disrupting my dominion."

As Verethragna watched, he was unable to discern the smoke's origin. As near as he could tell, it was an entire network of dots blanketing the country. He guessed that the enemy's forces were not relying on the few authorized places of worship but were once again operating out of their homes. He sighed as he realized this contamination was so widespread that its cleanup would require a massive amount of effort.

No, he decided, *I don't have time for this right now. I can't afford to divert my attention from the attack on Jerusalem. I'll have to deal with this mess later.*

Sighing deeply, he complained, "You know, Qorin, a *Tsel's* work is never done. One week, it's rallies and protests by political movements with their calls for freedom! The next week, it's traitors appealing directly to the Oppressor. Either way, I expect them to run out of steam once people realize there's no use trying to fight the inevitable."

The idea of fighting the inevitable started him down a train of thought he did not particularly enjoy. His eye began twitching, always a sign that he was nervous. *Why should I worry?* he asked himself. *Everything will be all right.*

He turned to ask Qorin for counsel, but the winged *Tsel* was gone.

Verethragna, having made the decision to focus on attacking rather than defending, contemplated his next steps. Unfortunately, the smoke was interfering with his communication with Noor-Allah. Without receiving any confirmation from them, he would have no way of knowing if the plan was going ahead.

He decided to use one of his back channels.

Ch 52. Secret Contacts

(Middle East, 4 hours before the Fire)

Never, never pin your whole faith on any human being:
not if he is the best and wisest in the whole world.
There are lots of nice things you can do with sand;
but do not try building a house on it.

C.S. Lewis, *Mere Christianity*

11:00 PM

The Israeli government's evaluation of Ali's social media habits indicated that he displayed no special interest in religion. The researchers—mostly secular Jews, with a few Orthodox Jews, moderate Muslims, and atheists—failed to identify Ali's religious tendencies since they themselves were unaware of their built-in prejudice about religion, assuming, as they did, that a religion had to include a supernatural higher power. What the government investigators didn't realize was that Ali's higher power was himself; his religion was humanism.

Ali wouldn't have called his belief system a religion. He had no room for what he considered superstitious nonsense. His creed could be summed up by the statement *Man is the measure of all things.* Looking up at his framed copy of Da Vinci's *Vitruvian Man,* he thought,

They talk about the image of God. Why? Man isn't made in the image of God; Man himself is God.

He smiled as he sat at his desk in his office, located in his apartment in Tel Aviv. Connected by the Internet to the entire globe, he was like a spider spinning his web. *Yes,* he thought, *the* World Wide Web *is an appropriate name.*

As a computer geek, he was aware of the *dark web,* the cyberspace most regular Internet users don't even know exists. The dark web held all kinds of interesting places to explore—chat rooms, websites, forums, and even online banking—invisible to search engines or web browsers. He knew that users could only find dark websites on their computer by typing in the exact IP address and that, even then, in many cases, a password or even special software was needed to gain access.

Ali enjoyed exploring the Internet, jumping from site to site and asking questions on the surface web. His exploration eventually led him to the dark web and to a quasi-religious site called *Shadowlands,* where he found fellow chess aficionados, many of whom were witty, cynical, and refreshingly inappropriate.

While playing chess online, he would also chat about religion, politics, or anything else that came up. He gave out no personal information, only ever saying he was somewhere in the Middle East and never using his real name. Being anonymous was so freeing.

His favorite chess opponent went by the screen name *Prince of Persia.* Though Ali was careful with his own online information, over the months he began to pick up information about him. Once, his opponent let it slip that he was a general. Another time, he mentioned a name that led Ali to speculate that he was also connected with the IDF.

After months of chess and chatting together, one day the general mentioned to Ali that he had a complex computer issue he was looking to solve. It took Ali less than an hour to troubleshoot and fix the problem for him. The next day, the general transferred the equivalent of 10,000 shekels worth of Bitcoin into Ali's secure online bank account. After that, at least once a month, the general brought him similar odd jobs and paid him handsomely. This present job Ali was doing for his secret contact was set to be the most lucrative.

Ali frowned as he realized he was still waiting to hear back from the general after communicating to him the timing for the simulation. Something must be wrong.

Deciding to log in to the online forum, he saw the user prince of persia was already there. Entering a private chat room, he was eager to confirm that plans for the simulation were going forward and that his payment would soon follow.

11:10 PM

prince of persia: *How are plans looking on your end?*
Alibaba: *All ready. You will have about a twenty-minute window during which the Iron Dome will be down.*
prince of persia: *That's not going to work.*
Alibaba: *What do you mean? Everything is already arranged.*
prince of persia: *Plans have changed. Abort the mission.*

Ali sat back and considered for a moment. In his excitement, he hadn't followed their agreed-upon protocol of using a *palindrome* (a word or phrase that reads the same forward or backward) as a way to authenticate their messages.

Alibaba: *Abort what mission?*

> **prince of persia:** *Don't waste my time! Stop with the questions, and just send word, the attack is off.*

Ali was puzzled. *Was this really the general? If so, why was he calling it an* attack *rather than a* simulation? *And why didn't he use our agreed-upon password system?* He looked again at the chat and noticed that the name *'prince of persia'* wasn't capitalized. "Aha," he said out loud, concern evident in his voice. Squinting, he removed his glasses and slowly cleaned them as he evaluated the situation. Putting his glasses back on, he concluded, *It appears we have a hacker trying to impersonate the general.*

He considered typing *"was it a rat I saw"* or *"tacocat,"* but rejected both ideas, figuring it was better to just close the chat and leave the forum.

11:20 PM

Leaning back in his desk chair, Ali laced his fingers behind his head and tried to think. The problem with the *invisible web,* as it was sometimes called, was that even for an expert like him, it was virtually impossible to verify who was actually on the other end without expending an inordinate amount of effort. He expressly did not want to know Prince of Persia's real identity, just as he did not want his own identity to be known. The point was to do occasional technical computer work as a side hustle while remaining completely anonymous.

The creases in Ali's furrowed brow got deeper as he tried to evaluate what to do next. Should he try to undo his work? Maybe it was a mistake to facilitate a temporary shutdown of the Iron Dome system? If he wanted to try to cancel the simulation, could he even get back into the program? And who was this *prince of persia* (with a lower case "*p*") who was trying to masquerade as the general?

He and the general originally found each other on the forum when they noticed that their screen names, Alibaba and Prince of Persia, both came from Disney's *Aladdin*. After chatting a few times, they decided they should employ a simple "handshake" at the beginning of each chat to authenticate their conversations. Prince of Persia had suggested the old typist's sentence, *"The quick brown fox jumped over the lazy dog."* Ali thought that was too common and suggested, *"Bright vixens jump; dozy fowl quack."* Prince of Persia had to agree, that sentence wasn't as well-known; on the other hand, he wasn't sure he himself could remember it. They needed something commonplace and yet easy to remember. In the end, they decided to each use palindromes.

Ali's computer beeped to let him know he had a new message. It was a request from Prince of Persia to join him in a chat room.

Prince of Persia: *How's the radar?*
Alibaba*: Is this on the level?*

Having authenticated the conversation with their palindromes, they were ready to discuss business.

Prince of Persia: *Talk to me. Have you heard anything?*
Alibaba: *Only from someone trying to impersonate you.*
Prince of Persia: *What?!*
Alibaba: *Yeah. Someone calling himself* "prince of persia."
Prince of Persia*: Oh?*
Alibaba: *He said we need to abort the mission.*
Prince of Persia: *An impostor, huh? What'd you tell him?*
Alibaba*: The truth. The plan is in motion and can't be stopped.*
Prince of Persia: *Good.*

Alibaba: *From my side everything is a go. It will look like a computer glitch that can't be traced to anyone. You assured me that no one will lose their job over this, right?*
Prince of Persia: *Don't worry. Only my friend and I know about this. I bet him that the Iron Dome could be disabled. When it goes down, researchers will find that vulnerability and a patch will be created, making the country safer. And my friend will pay up on his bet. We'll both be 50,000 shekels richer.*
Alibaba: *Nothing to do now but wait.*
Prince of Persia: *Okay, bye for now.*

11:30 PM

The wedding celebration neared the end of its third and final evening. The first two days, the bride and groom had celebrated in their respective homes: the bride and her family in their house, and the groom and his relatives in his family's house. This third day brought everyone together.

The groom left his father's house slowly, making his way down the road in a beautifully maintained vintage, convertible Mercedes decked with white roses. A great entourage of cars followed, honking and flashing their headlights. Heads turned to watch as they left the city and made their way slowly toward the village and the bride's house.

The bride, for her part, was patiently awaiting her bridegroom at her father's house. Her family was all prepared with their cars to accompany her back to her new home, located right next to his parents' place, a house that her husband had built just for her.

But two very different events were planned for that night. The father of the bride happened to be a ranking member of Noor-Allah, and the groom was a leader of Hezbollah. This wedding would symbolically unite the two groups in their stand against Israel. And the marriage celebration itself would provide the perfect cover for a clandestine missile strike that would inflict untold pain on the Jewish scourge.

The bridegroom arrived, accompanied by shouting, honking horns, and much rejoicing. The bride, ready and waiting, was guided to her husband's side in the lead car and, as the entourage began its return journey, fireworks exploded overhead.

That was the signal to begin the final preparations for the missile launch. As the wedding procession slowly made its way back to Damascus and safety, the fireworks continued in the village. The missiles were loaded, ready to be launched at the exact moment the Iron Dome missile defense system went down.

11:40 PM

Eván was once again amazed at his own intelligence. Searching the Internet, he had come across some conversations about a website called *Shadowlands*. After asking around and following quite a few links, he eventually found the site. Figuring that if he was searching for information regarding some plot that Verethragna was involved in, it might be helpful to choose a screen name that would appeal to the *Tsel's* vanity, he chose *"prince of persia."*

What luck that Alibaba found him at that moment in the chat room! What are the odds that he would be browsing the Shadowlands website at that exact moment that Ali also logged in and sent him a message? Well, he chalked that up to chance.

Now he had information to pass on to the Prince of Palestine. Ali had found a way to override the Israeli defense system, making Israel vulnerable to a missile attack. It was not difficult to guess that

Noor-Allah would attempt to bring down "fire" on Israel. Eván knew he had some pretty solid intel.

But how to deliver his information? He checked the online forum he had set up to communicate with Ghaiasha. No new messages. He stood up to think. His Shadowlands contact insisted on calling himself Ghaiasha, but Eván was beginning to suspect it wasn't really the Prince of Palestine. He wondered if it might even be Qorin. Whoever it was, he didn't seem to be getting the messages on the Internet forum. Eván paced back and forth, checking every few minutes to see if a reply had come. But soon, exhausted, he collapsed on his bed and fell asleep.

The contact came just before midnight. Eván was suddenly wide awake and pouring out information as fast as he could. Afterwards, he realized he couldn't explain why he had been so terrified, or why he hadn't put up any resistance, or why he hadn't had the pluck to at least ask who it was he was talking with. Lying in bed, shaking, he considered what the consequences might have been if he hadn't had any intel to give. He had a feeling it would not have gone well. He hoped he hadn't slipped and mentioned the fact that he had met and talked with Dominic.

Ch 53. A Cry for Help

(Jerusalem, 3 hours before the Fire)

Be still, and know that I am God;
I will be exalted among the nations,
I will be exalted in the earth!

Psalm 46:10

12:00 AM

It was nearly midnight in the cabin where Dominic, Khaled, Joseph, and Benjamin were staying. Dominic was dreaming again and the scenes before him felt incredibly real.

He could once again see a woman sitting, tied to a chair. He couldn't see her face, but he was sure it was the same woman he had seen before in his dream. She might have been in her late twenties, but at that moment, he couldn't guess her age. Her clothes were torn, and the man standing over her looked down on her with indifference.

"Now that you have told me everything, you know you have to die, don't you?"

She said nothing.

"Let me ask you something. Your God is ultimately in control, isn't that right?"

He paused for an answer, but she just continued to look at the floor.

"Everything is *maktub*,[174] ordained by God, isn't that so? Even the fact that I have no friends or family. That everyone has rejected me. That I don't fit in with Christians, Muslims, or Jews. That no one wants me.

"At first, I was in despair, but then it struck me; this is not a bad thing. It's my destiny."

He paused merely for effect; he knew he would get no response from her.

"Think about it. If there is a God, He can work His will through any situation. Atheist, Muslim, Christian, Jew, any vessel will serve Him because 'He works all things for good.' That was how my secret plan began. I cast aside despair and envisioned a plan so ingenious that it actually surprised me. I'll bet you didn't realize you're the one who gave me the final push I needed to take action."

Dominic watched the young man in his dream pause his monologue to again look over at his captive, spitting out the words. "Can you understand how hard it was for me to learn you only pretended to listen to me? How do you think I felt when I realized you were never honest with me? I shared my secrets with you, but you didn't share yours with me. Do you know what it was like for me to learn I was only someone's project?"

The man wasn't really asking her. He was hardly even looking at her. He went on, "Then I realized our relationship afforded me a very interesting opportunity: a chance to show the world that I am someone, that I matter. And along the way to get my revenge for your betrayal."

At that moment, Dominic moved in his bed, and the man stopped as if to listen. "What was that?" he asked. "I thought I heard a noise."

174. *Maktub* is an Arabic term that literally means "written" and refers to the Islamic view that God has preordained or "written" everything that will happen, leading some to teach that there is nothing humans can do to change their circumstances

He looked around suspiciously while his captive sat unmoving, looking more dead than alive.

The man in Dominic's dream continued, "For months, I worked diligently. Sometimes, I'll admit, it felt impossible. But you see, I will not abandon my destiny!"

12:10 AM

Dominic awoke in a cold sweat.

He got up and was on his way to the kitchen for a glass of water when he heard Benjamin and Joseph in the front room. In spite of their hushed tones, he could tell there was an argument brewing. Entering the room he said, "Hey, guys, what's going on?"

Joseph answered, "Benni had a dream. I'm just trying to calm him down."

"Really?" said Dominic. "So did I. And boy was it creepy."

"Did you see her?" Benjamin blurted out.

"Did I see who?"

"The woman. I couldn't see her face, but she was dressed in rags."

Dominic looked at him in surprise. "Actually, yes. I did see a woman in rags."

Benjamin, determined to obey the vision, started moving toward the door. "Joseph, I am going, with or without you."

Joseph responded as calmly as he could, "Benni, I told you, we're not going to leave at this time of night. Let's go back to bed and we'll talk about it in the morning."

"No, I need to go up to Jerusalem. I need to go now."

Catching his brother by the arm before he could make it to the door, Joseph said, "What are you going to do, walk to Jerusalem?"

Benjamin, still trying to reach the door, said, “I will if I have to. She’s in danger and needs my help.” Then, turning to Dominic, he pleaded, “Would *you* come with me?”

When Dominic didn’t answer, Benjamin continued. “What did the woman say in your dream?”

Dominic shrugged. “Nothing this time.”

“What do you mean *this time*?” asked Joseph.

“Well, I had a similar dream a while back.”

Benjamin looked over at Joseph and then back to Dominic. “What did she say before?”

“That she needed help.”

“But what were her actual words?” Benjamin persisted.

“She said, ‘God, please free me from this hell.’”

Benjamin looked at his brother as if to say, “I told you so.”

Dominic asked, “Okay, what does *that* look mean?”

Joseph admitted, “The woman in Benni’s dream said the very same words.”

Dominic’s interest was now piqued. “Really? Did she say anything else?”

Benjamin answered, “Yes, she said, ‘Come up to the Holy City! Help me! Hurry.’”

Joseph, trying to keep his voice low, said, “Benni, we’ll go up first thing in the morning.”

Benjamin struggled toward the door again, saying, “She needs us to go now!”

Dominic spoke up. “Joseph, I think we should go. You have to admit, it’s pretty weird that I dreamed about someone who said the very same words.”

“Dominic, stay out of this!” growled Joseph.

“No, Joseph, listen! When I was a little younger than your brother, two ruffians attacked my older brother right in front of my eyes. They were after me, but he protected me, holding them off long enough for me to escape.

"They took him and beat him trying get information about me. When they carried him off, I followed at a distance. When one of them went off looking for me, I slipped in and, knocking out the other guy, rescued my brother. I tried to get him safely back to my family, but I couldn't. I didn't know where I was, I didn't know who I could trust, and he was too heavy for me to carry. We hid from our enemies behind a broken-down wall that night and waited for daylight, but by morning, when we were finally found by my parents, Timothy was dead. I had tried to save him, but I couldn't. I was too little.

"But I'm not too little anymore. I want to look into this. Maybe there's nothing to these dreams we had. But how can you explain two people having nearly identical dreams on the same night? And the woman crying out for help using the very same words in both dreams?

"If we investigate and don't find anything, we will have missed a few hours of sleep. So what? But if I find out that I stayed in bed while someone really was out there crying for help, I will never be able to live with myself. I think something seriously evil may be happening right now and God might have told us about it so we can stop it."

At that moment, Khaled sleepily joined them in the front room. "What's happening?" he yawned.

"Nothing, go back to sleep," said Joseph.

Khaled was confused. He looked at Dominic and then back at Joseph who was holding Benjamin as he kept trying to get to the door.

Joseph could see that neither Dominic nor Benjamin was about to back down, so he finally relented, "Okay, we'll go."

"Where? I want to go too," said Khaled.

Joseph sighed as he looked from Benjamin to Dominic to Khaled. "Okay, but quietly or you'll wake up the whole kibbutz."

Ch 54. Where Is the Holy Place?

(Jerusalem, 3 hours before the Fire)

See! Your house is left to you desolate.

Matthew 23:38

12:20 AM

As the boys drove away, Nehemyah was awakened. He got up and walked into his small kitchen for a glass of water. Surprised to see Bill sitting at the table in the dark, he asked, "Everything okay, brother?"

"Yes, I'm fine. I couldn't sleep and the Lord prompted me to get up and pray."

"I see. Well, sorry to disturb you. I'm just getting a drink and heading back to bed."

"No. Please stay. I believe the Lord has finished telling me what He wanted to say. I think that He sent you to me just now."

"Well, in that case . . ." Nehemyah pulled out a chair to sit down.

As he did, Bill pushed back his chair and stood up, saying, "Actually, do you think we could go for a drive?"

Nehemyah looked at his new friend with surprise. After a moment, he said, "I suppose we could . . . but may I ask *why*?"

"I just have something I want to check out," answered Bill enigmatically.

Nehemyah looked up at the clock. It was after midnight. He looked at Bill whose eyes held a hopeful gleam. "Sure," he responded. Let me wake up Moshe so he can drive us. Then I'll grab my shoes and keys."

Fifteen minutes later, Bill was anxiously looking at his watch as if he had an appointment to keep when Moshe said he was ready to go. As they were leaving the kibbutz, Nehemyah asked, "Is there a direction you'd like to go, Bill?"

"Yes. The Lord has told me to go up to the Holy Place."

As they headed out, Nehemyah asked, "To which holy place were you thinking of going? The churches will be closed, of course, as well as the Temple Mount."

"To Mount Zion."

"To our church? Okay, we can do that. I have a key."

"Actually, I don't think that the place I'm looking for can be opened with a key."

The car was quiet for a moment, and then Bill spoke again. "You know, I think I've been wrong about the whole idea of 'holy places' for most of my life. I've always discounted the idea of one place being more holy than another. I thought, maybe that was true in the Old Testament, like the burning bush. But I couldn't fathom a physical location being considered intrinsically holy now that Jesus, who is God Himself, had come and lived among us."

"And what changed your mind?" Nehemyah asked.

"Two things. First, God brought to my mind how, in the Gospels, Jerusalem is still called the Holy City both before and after Jesus' death and resurrection.[175] And also in the Book of Revelation, the city

175. Matthew 4:5; 27:53

of Jerusalem is called 'holy' by Jesus and by His angel even before the New Jerusalem comes down out of heaven."[176]

"Okay, and the other thing that caused you to change your mind?"

"This second thing is not a logical argument. It's this: I've found there are certain places here in Israel that to me just *feel* holy. I can't prove it, but I sense that it's true."

"And Jerusalem *feels* holy to you?"

Bill remained silent for a moment and then spoke. "Yes, but until last night, I was still very wrong in my thinking about this as well. To tell you the truth, God began to open my eyes about this last week, when we went up to the Temple Mount. I was so eager to go there—the actual location of both Solomon's Temple and Herod's Temple, the very place where Jesus stood and taught. But when I got there, I felt nothing—only sadness and depression. I thought, *How could this be God's holy hill, when false worship and two unholy buildings are located there?*"

"And God answered your question?"

"Yes, but not immediately. After being up on the Temple Mount, I began thinking that God would somehow destroy the Dome of the Rock and the Al-Aqsa Mosque—you know, just wipe it clean."

"Many people think that will happen."

Bill paused for a moment. "Yes, I suppose God himself could destroy the Temple Mount and everything on it or even allow someone else to do it. But last night, He showed me that I was still thinking wrongly about holy places. I had assumed that if there were still holy places on Earth, they would be places that had always been holy. In other words, once a place had been designated as a holy place by God, it would always remain a holy place. Last night I realized that's simply not true."

"Okay . . . ."

176. Revelation 11:2; 21:2; 22:19

"Think about it. The place in the Sinai Desert where Moses saw the burning bush, is that still *holy ground?*"

"Well, I don't know."

"How about Bethel? Jacob called it 'the house of God.' He saw angels going up and down a ladder there and said that God Himself was in that place.[177] Later on, in the days of Samuel, Bethel was considered a holy place, where people met with God.[178] But what happened to that 'holy' place? It became a place of idol worship[179] and God condemned Bethel in judgment.[180]

"And then there's Shiloh. In the days of Joshua, the holy tabernacle was set up there, including the ark of the covenant, representing the very presence of the Lord.[181] For many years, the 'house of God' was there,[182] but eventually, Shiloh also became a place of false worship and, as a result, God abandoned it."[183]

Nehemyah asked, "God showed you this last night?"

"The Holy Spirit and the Bible concordance you have in the room. God brought verses to my mind, and I looked them up. But that's just the beginning. The Lord told the prophet Jeremiah that in the same way He had rejected and brought judgment on Shiloh because of Israel's sin there, so He would do to Solomon's Temple in Jerusalem."[184]

Nehemyah agreed, "And that happened when the Babylonians came and destroyed it. However, that temple was rebuilt in the days of Ezra, and God promised through the prophet Haggai that the

177. Genesis 28:12–19
178. 1 Samuel 10:3
179. 1 Kings 12:28–30
180. Amos 5:5–6
181. Joshua 18:1, 10
182. Judges 18:31, 21:19; 1 Samuel 1:24
183. Psalm 78:56–60
184. Jeremiah 7:11–14; 26:4–9

glory of that new temple would be greater than the first one, that is, Solomon's Temple."[185]

"True," said Bill. "They were given a second chance. But did the people learn their lesson? Did they serve God wholeheartedly in this second temple?"

"No," Nehemyah said with a sigh, "they didn't. As I read the Scriptures, I am amazed at both the patience of God and the stubbornness of my people."

"Yes, and trust me, I am not trying to point blame at God's chosen people. I'm just showing what God revealed to me." Bill paused for a moment before continuing. "Jesus the Messiah entered the temple, worshipping there and teaching there. He referred to it as 'God's house.' But at the same time, He shocked the religious leaders by claiming they had turned God's holy house into a 'den of thieves.'[186] Jesus' words, *'den of thieves'* is a quote from the prophet Jeremiah. And what I found interesting is that, in that very passage, Jeremiah predicted that the holy temple at that time, Solomon's Temple, would be judged just as Shiloh had been."[187]

"Yes," Nehemyah said, familiar with that passage, "Jeremiah chapter seven."

"Exactly," Bill replied. "So, Jesus was predicting here the same condemnation for the second temple. Why? Because His people hadn't learned. Although I believe God still has a bright future for the people He has chosen,[188] when Jesus, their Messiah, arrived, they rejected Him, and as a result, Jesus said to them, 'See! Your house is left to you desolate.'[189] God abandoned His temple a second time, and later allowed it to be destroyed again. But do you know what God revealed to me is the worst part of this second temple's destruction?"

185. Haggai 2:9
186. Matthew 21:12–13
187. Jeremiah 7:11–12
188. See Romans 11:25–36
189. Matthew 23:37–38

"That, as Jesus predicted, the Romans did not leave one stone upon another?" offered Nehemyah.

"Worse than that."

"That the Jews were banished from Judea, their homeland?"

"Still worse."

"What?"

"God showed me that His presence never returned. This Temple Mount has remained a spiritual wasteland. At one point, the Romans built a temple there to their false gods, but it was torn down and left in ruins. As you probably know, by the fourth century, Jews who had returned to the land tried to rebuild a temple—not once, but twice. But each attempt failed."

Bill continued solemnly. "Then the spiritual landscape changed considerably in the seventh century when the Muslims conquered the land. They cleared away centuries of rubble and erected the Al-Aqsa Mosque. Later, they built another abomination on the same hill: the shrine called the Dome of the Rock. And that is how it has remained until the present day: a spiritual wasteland, a place devoted to the worship of a false god."

Nehemyah nodded. Bill saw tears in his eyes and sensed how deeply it affected his friend to revisit this tragic history. After a moment, Nehemyah said, "You know this is very interesting timing, don't you?"

"What do you mean?"

"You don't know the significance of today's date, do you, Bill?"

"No."

"Today," Nehemyah explained, "is Tisha B'Av. This is the ninth day of the Jewish month of Av, a date that has witnessed tragedy on our people throughout history. Many Jews here in the Land observe Tisha B'Av as a solemn day of prayer, fasting, mourning, and repentance. You see, it was on this date in 586 BC that Solomon's Temple in Jerusalem was destroyed by the Babylonians.

"Seventy years later, Ezra led the people in rebuilding the temple. That second temple, later expanded and renovated, became known as Herod's Temple. Then, in AD 70, on that exact same day, Tisha B'Av, the Roman army destroyed Herod's Temple.

"We hold onto our belief that God is good in spite of these and many other tragedies that have occurred to our people. Accepting that these punishments are the result of our leaving His path, each year, beginning at sunset of Tisha B'Av, until an hour after sunset the following day, we remember our sins and humble ourselves before God."

Bill was amazed. "I had no idea, brother. And yet, this fits perfectly with what the Lord has been showing me," he continued, more passionately than before. "My brother, forgive me for saying this, but Sinai did not remain holy ground forever. When Bethel and Shiloh became corrupted by false worship, God placed them under a curse.[190] God's holy presence left Bethel, and God's holy presence left Shiloh. And it didn't return. So it is with the Temple Mount; God's presence has left. It is no longer God's holy place."

"But Jerusalem is and will remain the Holy City," Nehemyah interjected. "Surely you see that? The psalmist declared,

> *For the Lord has chosen Zion,*
> *He has desired it for His dwelling place:*
> *This is my resting place forever;*
> *Here I will dwell, for I have desired it."*[191]

Bill chose his words carefully. "Yes, Jerusalem is God's holy city. And His eternal dwelling place is Zion. But . . ." he looked at Nehemyah for a second, "I believe God's holy place is no longer the Temple Mount."

190. Jeremiah 26:6
191. Psalm 132:13–14

"Zion is the Temple Mount," Nehemyah countered. "They are one and the same."

"That's what I used to think, too," Bill said. "But the Lord showed me that Zion and the Temple Mount haven't always been the same location."

"What do you mean?"

"Is the section of Jerusalem that is known as the 'City of David' the same as the Temple Mount?"

"No, of course not. The City of David is the ancient Jebusite fortress that David conquered. It's located below and to the south of the Temple Mount."

Bill asked, "And yet, when is the first time the Scriptures mention the word *Zion?* It's when David conquered that fortress of Zion, and Second Samuel 5:7 clearly says that Zion was the City of David.[192] In addition, years later, when Solomon brought the holy ark of the covenant up to what is presently the Temple Mount, the Scriptures say he brought it up *from Zion*."[193] So at that time, Zion was associated with the location that is today called the City of David and not the location called the Temple Mount."

Nehemyah countered, "But over and over in the Old Testament, the term *Zion* refers to Jerusalem."

"I agree with you."

"And, specifically, the Temple Mount."

"Again, I agree. Over and over, we see that the term "Zion" referred to the Temple Mount. But as we just saw, Zion could also refer to somewhere else in Jerusalem."

"What are you saying?" Nehemyah asked, as Moshe dropped them off just inside the Jaffa Gate, then went to park nearby.

As they stood, waiting for Moshe to rejoin them, Bill explained, "Zion can refer to Jerusalem in general. But Zion also refers to the

192. 2 Samuel 5:7
193. 1 Kings 8:1

specific location in Jerusalem that is God's holy place. In David's time, Zion was located in the City of David. In Solomon's time, Zion became the Temple Mount."

"Zion moved?"

"It does seem like it has moved at least once," answered Bill. "From the City of David to Temple Mount."

Then he turned and pointed up the cobblestone street toward the ancient church buildings of the Armenian Quarter and said, "Many early Christians believed Zion was right there. There is evidence that starting as early as the first century, Jewish believers chose that hill as their place of worship, and they, along with the renowned Jewish historian Josephus, identified it with Mount Zion."

"Yes, but calling it Mount Zion was simply a mistake, right?"

"I've heard that too," said Bill. "But I'm beginning to think they had a spark of divine insight. The truth is, we don't know exactly how this area came to be known as Mount Zion."

He stopped walking and pulled up a verse on his phone. "But here's something else that's interesting. I saw this verse displayed on a sign when I was at the Western Wall, below the Temple Mount. 'In the last days the mountain of the Lord's temple will be established as the highest of the mountains; it will be exalted above the hills, and all nations will stream to it.'[194] Out of curiosity, I googled the highest point in the original city of Jerusalem. Do you know what I found?"

"Let me guess. Mount Zion."

"Correct. Higher than the City of David. Higher than the Temple Mount. Right here, not far from where we're standing. Near Mount Zion Church. The same place where the early Jewish Christians used to gather. The same place where you have seen this new movement of the Holy Spirit."

---

194. Isaiah 2:2 NIV

"This is indeed interesting, Brother Bill. Perhaps God has prepared a new holy place for us Jewish believers during this period of time."

"Perhaps."

"So, what does this all mean?"

"For me, discovering the true location of Mount Zion is not merely an academic pursuit. Earlier, right before you came into the kitchen and talked with me, the Lord brought Psalm 23:6 to my mind. Paraphrasing that verse, He said to me, 'Surely my goodness and love will follow you all the days of your life, and you will dwell in my house forever.' Then the Lord told me to come here—to Mount Zion. I've never heard anything more clearly from the Lord than this."

Just then, Moshe joined them. Bill paused a moment, then continued. "Brothers, I believe the Lord wants me to stay here indefinitely. I don't know exactly how that's going to work. I'm supposed to fly back to the US soon. I could change my flight. But then, after my 90-day tourist visa expires, I'll become an illegal alien, and I bet Israel isn't quite as accommodating about that as the US is."

As they approached the gate to the Mount Zion Center, Nehemyah said, "What if we just cross one bridge at a time. The Lord has called you to Mount Zion, and now here we are. There's an office inside where we can sit down and see where the Lord leads us next."

They went in and sat down in the office. After about a half hour of prayer, Bill announced, "The Lord has called me to step outside into His presence." Giving Nehemyah and Moshe a hug, he turned and went out into the night.

Ch 55. The Ark of Power

(Jerusalem, 90 minutes before the Fire)

Then He struck the men of Beth Shemesh, because they had looked into the ark of the Lord.

1 Samuel 6:19

1:30 AM

Andriy glanced at his wristwatch. It was almost time. After months of planning and weeks of secrecy, he had done it. He took a deep breath. That morning, Jerusalem city officials were intending to add the final touches to the Sacred Stones Museum at the Western Wall. *Opening another tourist attraction to use religion to fleece gullible people? Not on my watch.*

The plan to deliver destruction upon Israel wouldn't have been possible without his friend, Dmitry. Andriy wished he could have been here for this great moment, but as agreed, his part was finished once the bomb was assembled and loaded into the van in Haifa. And so they had parted, Dmitry heading back to Odessa in his yacht and Andriy traveling by road up to Jerusalem.

Andriy's hired driver knew that the rented van with its important delivery had to arrive at the museum in Jerusalem first thing in the morning. Andriy's donation of the priceless replica of the ark of the covenant had to be in place for the opening ceremony.

As they got close to Jerusalem, Andriy told the driver to pull over. Out of an abundance of caution, he explained, he would ride the rest of the way in the back of the van next to the ark with the doors secured. It might sound paranoid, but he could not take the chance that thieves might break in and steal the treasure while they were stopped at a traffic light, for example. Hopping out, he checked that both the driver and passenger doors were locked, then climbing into the back, he closed and secured the cargo door from the inside.

The ark was no longer packed in its crate but was out of the box and fully assembled. Andriy checked one last time the secret compartment where the bomb was hidden, and then, in case the authorities decided to block cell phone signals, he physically connected the wires to himself. The original idea had been to present the ark at the opening ceremony, using the battery to not only move the ark into position but also to set off the explosion. But his request to the Ministry of Culture had been denied, so now he was improvising.

As the van reached the plaza area near the entrance of the museum, the driver was stopped by several Israeli soldiers armed with automatic rifles. Before the driver could even roll down the window, a loudspeaker blared from the vehicle.

"I have a bomb that will explode if I release the trigger. In addition, the bomb is wired to my body, so if I am shot or if any of the doors are opened, it will detonate.

"Here is my demand: I want to talk with the Prime Minister himself. I'm not interested in the death of any innocent people. However, if you can't get me in touch with him, I'll detonate this bomb, and you'll have no one to blame but yourselves."

The driver sat frozen with fear. If Andriy was telling the truth, then just opening the door to escape would set off the bomb. Israeli negotiators began to assemble, bringing lights and promising over their own loudspeakers that they would meet his demands; they just needed time to make sure civilians were safely away before they would begin negotiations. Meanwhile, they called for troops to quietly gather near the plaza.

The entire area was cleared to keep journalists' cameras away, and snipers moved into position. Spotlights focused on the van. Soldiers radioed in their reports. The question was, *Could they get a clear shot?* Some worked to determine if the driver was indeed wired to the bomb, while others used AI-powered surveillance software to try to ascertain exactly what was hidden in the back of the van.

The standoff had gone on for thirty minutes when the lead negotiator was informed of new military intel on the situation. Intercepting fragments of chatter on a frequency coming out of Iran, military decryption experts said that Hezbollah was claiming to have obtained a nuclear device. From what they had gathered, a suitcase nuke had been smuggled into Syria via Turkey, though they were still unclear as to how it had been accomplished.

News of this magnitude temporarily paralyzed the negotiating team. A conventional bomb was one thing, but what if there was a nuclear device poised to detonate inside the city itself? The stakes were too high.

Pressure built as, despite the security force's best efforts, news of a standoff near the Western Wall somehow began to trickle out. If reporters or even civilians with cell phones found their way into the area, it could be a PR disaster. The loss of life would be devastating enough if a bomb were to go off in the old city of Jerusalem. The only thing that could make it worse would be if the whole world were watching as Jerusalem was obliterated in a mushroom cloud.

But the coolest heads were convinced this was a bluff. If Iran had indeed obtained a nuclear device, there was no way they could have smuggled it, undetected, into the very heart of the city. No, they said, with all the safety measures in place at borders and throughout the country, it is a statistical improbability that a nuclear bomb could have crossed into Israeli territory without being detected.

In addition, the army captain on the ground had just managed to get a Geiger detector known as a *"hot spot"* into position. With its detector tube on the end of a long pole, the "hot spot" was now close enough to the van to confirm there was no significant gamma radiation emanating from the vehicle.

At that point, one of the sharpshooters radioed that he had a clear shot on the terrorist. Scanning devices showed no sign of wires attached to the driver. Leadership's best guess was that they were dealing with a madman, so the commander made the call and the sniper took the shot.

The tinted glass windshield shattered, the driver slumped onto the steering wheel of the van, and everyone held their breath. But no explosion followed.

After a long, tense moment, a cadre of elite soldiers was slowly approaching the van when the voice on the loudspeaker spoke up. "Congratulations, you've just shot an innocent man. I am Andriy, the one with the detonator, and I'm sitting right next to a nuclear bomb in the back of this van. I'm trying to negotiate, but you obviously aren't acting in good faith. However, I will give you one more chance. You have sixty minutes to bring the prime minister here with a TV camera so I can make my demands known to the world. If you don't comply within an hour, there will be no reason for me to continue these negotiations, and I will be forced to bring an end to the apostate Israel."

Ch 56. Down to Gehenna

(Jerusalem, 60 minutes before the Fire)

> *It is better for you to enter the kingdom of God with one eye, rather than having two eyes, to be cast into hell fire [Gehenna]—where 'Their worm does not die And the fire is not quenched.'*
>
> Mark 9:47–48

2:00 AM

After twenty minutes driving on mostly deserted roads, Dominic spoke up, "Okay, Benjamin, where to? The House of Prayer? We've almost reached the Old City."

"I don't know. We're close, but I just can't tell which way to go."

Joseph made a lap around the Old City walls. "What do you think, Benni?"

Benjamin, visibly agitated, answered, "I don't know."

"Well, we can't drive around forever. Dominic, why did you mention the House of Prayer a while back?"

"I don't know, it just kind of came out. Nehemyah told me it's open 24/7."

"You think we should see if our woman in distress is there?

"It's an idea," answered Dominic, ignoring the sarcasm.

Joseph parked in front of one of the many apartment complexes along the street, and the four young men walked half a block to the unmarked House of Prayer. They entered the building and had just climbed the stairs to the meeting room when Benjamin doubled over in pain.

"Hey, Benni, what's wrong?" Joseph asked his brother.

"She's hurting, Joe," he managed to say.

"What do you mean? The woman?"

"Yes, the one we need to rescue."

"Okay. So, where is she?" Joseph said, scanning the dozens of people in the room, "This is a big turnout for the middle of the night. Is she one of the people here?"

"No," Benjamin said, with his face still near the floor. "She's not here, but close by . . . she said she's in hell."

"Okay, she's in torment someplace nearby, but where?" Joseph asked.

"That's just it. She's trying to tell us. She told me that she's in *hell*."

"But what is that supposed to mean?" asked Khaled. "Is she already dead?"

"No, that doesn't make sense," said Joseph. "Then there'd be no point in us trying to rescue her."

Dominic was thinking, *Hell . . . hell-fire . . . Gehenna*. Then he spoke up excitedly, "Hey, guys, isn't the Valley of Gehenna somewhere near here?"

"Dominic, what are you talking about?"

"In Jesus' time, Gehenna was a garbage dump and a place to throw dead bodies. It was thought of as an evil place, a place of divine punishment, a smoldering heap whose fire, it was said, never went out. When Jesus spoke of punishment in unquenchable fire in hell, he used the word *Gehenna*.[195]

---

195. Mark 9:48 and Isaiah 66:24

Joseph asked, "Are you trying to say that hell is really just a place here on earth?"

"Well, the Valley of Gehenna was a real place here in Jerusalem. I think now it's called the valley of Hinnom."

"The Valley of Hinnom?" Khaled spoke up. "Yeah, it's really close. In between here and the Temple Mount," he said, pointing.

Looking out the large windows of the House of Prayer toward a rounded rooftop glowing golden in the moonlight, Dominic offered, "The Dome of the Rock there on the Temple Mount looks so close."

"But if our destination is the Hinnom Valley," Khaled said, "it's closer yet. Probably less than five hundred meters. We could easily walk there."

Dominic agreed, "And since we don't know *where* in the Hinnom Valley we might need to look, exploring the area on foot would be best."

"Okay," Joseph sighed as he put his arm around Benjamin, whose face showed he was still in pain, "It's two in the morning. If we're going to do this, let's get moving." He guided his brother toward the door, and the others followed.

Out on the sidewalk, the four boys went down several dozen stairs, through a park, and onto another street. The street took a sharp turn, then a steep downhill, and they soon found themselves in the valley.

Joseph looked to their left, up the narrow valley. A few meters away, he saw an outdoor party venue. It was dark, shut down for the night. "Food and drink, Party Central. That looks like the sort of place where a girl could be trapped. Maybe abducted, who knows?"

Benjamin paused for a moment as if consulting his memory. "No, that's not it. It's further down."

They looked the other way, down the valley. It was an open space with occasional grass and scrub brush. A sign was posted, stating that the area was part of the Jerusalem Walls National Park. They started walking down the Valley of the Son of Hinnom Street. In the moonlight, they could see small caves in the rock walls on the other side of the narrow valley. "She's probably around here, trapped in one of those caves."

Benjamin stopped and looked around. "No, she's not here either. She's still farther down."

They kept walking down the valley. On their left, they could see a grassy field rising up toward the Temple Mount. On their right, the valley rose to a rocky hillside with caves.

"Benni, what do you think?"

"Farther down."

Another one hundred meters found them standing at the corner of Valley of Hinnom Street and City of David Street.

"Okay, Benni, if we go much farther, it won't be the Valley of Hinnom anymore, it'll be the Kidron Valley."

On the left, the fields were giving way to a few trees and scattered houses of Upper Silwan, a mostly Arab part of town. On their right, the valley had narrowed slightly. More grass and rocks, a couple of trees, and small caves in the rock wall. An ancient building, a Greek Orthodox Church, towered above them on the hillside.

Benjamin sat down on a rock next to the sidewalk, as the others stood looking around, unsure what to do next.

2:20 AM

Just as Joseph was about to make a suggestion, suddenly, the earth shook violently. Rocks began cascading down to the valley floor. They heard a crash and looked to see one of the walls and part of the flat roof of a nearby house had collapsed. Joseph, Khaled, and Dominic regained their balance and then slowly sank to the ground next to Benjamin, sitting in stunned silence.

In the ensuing quiet, moonlight began to illuminate the dust in the air and revealed a deep crevasse in the street extending into the nearby field. Suddenly, they heard a low whimper coming from the damaged house.

Benjamin was the first to move.

Joseph yelled after him, "Benni, wait! Be careful!"

They could see dust rising from the fissure in the ground. They picked their way across the street to the house and looked inside with the aid of the flashlight from Dominic's cell phone. The house looked as if it had been abandoned for years.

They carefully made their way around the house, finding nothing but rubble. The back wall was still standing intact, but next to the wall was a two-meter-wide hole in the ground. Shining the light down into the hole, they could see a small room. Against one of the walls, they could barely make out what looked like a person sitting in a chair, partially buried in the rubble.

Benjamin said confidently, "That's her."

Dominic was the first to let himself down into the room, stepping carefully, trying to make sure that more rubble would not tumble down from above. He was followed by Khaled, then Benjamin, who was being helped down by Joseph.

Dominic shone his light at the person in the chair. "It *is* a woman," he said quietly, looking back up at the others.

Joseph asked in equally hushed tones, "Is she alive?"

Dominic took another step toward her and said, "Hey, you're safe now."

Her eyes fluttered open. Her mouth opened too, but no words escaped.

He asked, "Are you hurt?"

She raised her head slightly and stared at him.

Khaled approached her. "She might not speak English." Turning to her, he said, "*As-salamu 'alaykum.*"[196]

Her gaze remained fixed on Dominic as the others gathered around.

Benjamin touched her filthy matted hair and said, "She's the one I saw. We need to get her out of here."

Khaled was busy examining the ropes that bound her hands and feet securely to the chair. "Do any of you have a knife? These ropes are strong, and it'll take forever to untie the knots."

Dominic remained motionless before the woman, so Joseph took the light out of his hand and bent down to help Khaled with the ropes. After thirty seconds of grunts and struggles, he stood up again. "I can't untie her. Dominic, what do you think? What are we going to do?"

Dominic's gaze went from the woman to Joseph to Khaled, who was still trying without any success to loosen the ropes. "Let me try," he said. "Anyone have a knife?"

They all shook their heads as Joseph said in exasperation, "Dominic! No, we don't. Khaled already asked that. We're wasting time! Someone might be coming back for her at any moment!"

Dominic bent down to look at the thick ropes and tight knots, shaking his head. *Think!* He stood back up. The chair was solid metal and bolted to the floor. The ropes were the weak point. He looked around for something to use as a lever.

In the corner, he saw a wooden broom. Running over, he grabbed the broom and broke it over his knee. Rushing back to the prisoner, he inserted the piece of wood between the ropes tied to two legs of the chair.

He then rotated the broom handle repeatedly, tightening the rope, until the joints of the chair creaked from the pressure. The ropes around the woman began to tighten as well and she grimaced,

196. Arabic: "Peace be upon you"

but at that moment, the chair legs themselves gave way, bending under the strain of the rope. Dominic quickly released the pressure on the rope by spinning the broom handle in the opposite direction. The slack in the ropes that had been created by the bent chair legs allowed the boys to hurriedly free her legs.

But her hands were still securely tied to the back of the chair. There was no way to try to repeat the process without injuring her hands in the attempt. He grabbed one of the damaged chair legs and frantically twisted it back and forth until it broke free from the chair. Then, turning the sharp edge to the ropes that bound her hands behind the chair, he worked the metal back and forth like a saw.

The other three boys could only watch and try to stay out of Dominic's way. Before long, he had cut through the rope binding her hands and freed her from the chair. He picked her up and said, "Someone climb out and make sure the coast is clear. The rest of you push me from behind as I carry her up and out!"

Khaled clambered out first, then reached down and grabbed onto Dominic's shirt to help pull him up. Joseph and Benjamin pushed and steadied Dominic from below as he scrambled up with the woman in his arms. After they had all emerged from the underground, cell-like room, they sat on the ground catching their breath. Joseph and Dominic were on either side of the woman, keeping her upright. She was dirty and bruised. Her hair was cut short, and in the dim light they couldn't even tell what color it was.

Ch 57. Changing Alliances

(Shadowlands, 20 minutes before the Fire)

We may even con ourselves into believing the threat has gone away.
It never will.
Never, never, never.

John le Carré, *The Russia House*

2:40 AM

Qorin's main worry about Verethragna's plan to attack Jerusalem was that it endangered Dominic. He thought, *This is ridiculous! Lord Deywós himself should be looking out for the boy. Isn't Dominic an integral part of his end-times plan? Sometimes our fearless leader of the Resistance seems to care so little about those under his control. I know it's risky to meddle in Deywós' affairs, but obviously, there are times when it has to be done.*

Qorin reviewed his two approaches for stopping the attack. First, engaging Nabu. He was sure the Prince of Babylon would expend every effort to warn Lord Deywós, not because he cared about Dominic, but because delivering valuable intel might earn him a reward. The problem was, Qorin hadn't heard back from Nabu yet.

His other approach had been to tell Abdowan to find a way to stop the missile launch. Abdowan had indeed reported that he had spoken with Ali and convinced him to abort the mission. Unfortunately, Qorin wasn't sure he could trust that wretched and vulnerable *Tsel* who might say anything to stay connected to the Shadowlands.

In the event that both Nabu and Abdowan failed, Qorin had initiated a backup plan: giving Kenan a message to meet with Dominic and get him out of the city. That way, if the attack on Jerusalem were to succeed, at least Dominic would be safely away from the danger.

Qorin had positioned himself behind Verethragna so he could laugh at him unnoticed when the missile launch failed to take place. However, so much was at stake. What if Nabu, Abdowan, and Kenan all failed? What if Jerusalem were indeed destroyed and Dominic killed? He decided to fly down and join the Persian.

Verethragna didn't move as Qorin landed beside him. The Persian prince's eyes were focused, a smile creasing his *Tsel* face. Without turning to face the Roman prince, he said, "The launch is scheduled and cannot be stopped. The timing will be perfect. The Iron Dome defense will be down and inactive for several minutes. There will be seven missiles total, all fired in rapid succession. The first six contain powerful warheads, aimed at various targets around Jerusalem. Then, saving the best for last, the seventh missile, which I obtained from Ukraine, contains a nuclear device capable of leveling the entire city. It will detonate directly above the Al-Aqsa complex, obliterating the most holy sites revered by Jews, Muslims, and Christians."

They stood in silence for a minute as Verethragna rubbed his hands together in excitement. Then he began to softly sing one of the *Tselim* songs of triumph:

What a delight it is to meddle
To plot and plan and scheme
We are a fire that will not settle
Our flame will always gleam

We are a constant thorn
In the side of the Oppressor
To Deywós we are sworn
We shall be his successors

Verethragna's bravado had served to shake Qorin's confidence. Had he taken sufficient precautions? Should he have double-checked that Dominic was indeed safe? He was now afraid that he might have underestimated his fellow *Tsel's* ability to bring about a serious disaster.

What if Verethragna has actually done it? What if no one has been able to stop his plan? If the launch is successful, and the city is unprotected, and Dominic hasn't gotten to safety, what a terrible loss that would be!

To make small talk as they stood there waiting, Qorin wondered aloud, "I wonder if Ali realizes what he has brought about."

Verethragna turned to face him. "You know, Ali seemed like a smart guy, but I doubt he ever really asked himself how the plan was supposed to work. He thought he was exposing a weakness in the Iron Dome security system. But apparently, he never stopped to consider how much he was depending on the information from the general."

He smiled broadly as he said the word *general*. "The program Ali wrote to deactivate the missile defense system won't set off any alarms by itself. Its presence will only be noticed if the Iron Dome defense is activated. The general had promised him that the simulation would alert the IDF to a problem with their defense software. But what if there is no general? What if this isn't a simulation? What if the attack is . . . . real?"

Qorin wondered. *Would Ali, the Tsel's unwitting accomplice, feel his gut tighten into a knot when he realized that the attack was not a simulation? Has he, even now, begun to mull over the possibility that he has been used? Is he, at this moment, frantically trying to sound the alarm, keenly aware that it's probably too late? Or is he, like the rest of the country, ignorant of the danger, blissfully enjoying a false sense of security?*

Qorin was lost in his thoughts when Verethragna spoke again, "During this twenty-minute window, you see, the Israeli military will still think the anti-missile system is functioning correctly. If there were a simulation, they would discover the weakness Ali found. The simulation would reveal the vulnerability and the software could be patched. However, it is a different situation when there is an actual incoming missile. Radar operators will detect the missile, but at the same moment, discover that the Iron Dome has failed to engage."

"During my Internet chats with Ali, I told him we wanted to prove to a friend that there was a vulnerability in the system." Verethragna laughed and slapped Qorin on the arm. "We convinced him this project would result in a more secure situation once the weakness was identified and the software patch was in place."

Verethragna continued, "I convinced him this would make the world a safer place." He wore an evil smile as he looked over the horizon, "No, Ali hasn't made the world a safer place. We could, I suppose, call it all off; but, since he worked so hard on writing this software, I think it would be unkind to not, at least, reward everyone with some fireworks."

Verethragna turned to scan the Jerusalem skyline, "Something is going to appear on their radar any moment now. At that point, the technicians will notice that the Iron Dome isn't engaging. But there will only be minutes until impact and absolutely nothing they can do."

Ch 58. Up to Zion

(Jerusalem, 20 minutes before the Fire)

> *For there shall be a day when the watchmen will cry on Mount Ephraim,*
> *'Arise, and let us go up to Zion, to the Lord our God.'*
>
> Jeremiah 31:6

2:40 AM

It was early morning—hours before dawn—and the group was sitting on the ground unsure of what to do next. They had emerged from the darkness of the underground room to find themselves still in darkness as the power was clearly out in their immediate vicinity. Dominic looked at his cell phone; no service. He rose to his feet and could see candles flickering in a few of the windows of the houses around them. On the street nearby, some people were standing outside their homes looking around like they were trying to make sense of what had just happened.

Dominic looked around at buildings farther up on the surrounding hills and saw city lights. He said, "I don't think it was an earthquake. There must have been some kind of underground explosion near here. I can see lights in the distance."

Khaled, ignoring Dominic's comment, asked, "What do we do now?"

Joseph was the first to respond. "How about if Khaled and I go get the car while you guys wait here with her?"

Dominic objected, "No. Whoever put her in that hellhole might be nearby. We need to get her away from this place as fast as possible."

Benjamin agreed, "And, we're not supposed to split up. We need to stay together and go up to the holy place in order to live."

Joseph looked at his brother, "Benni, what do you mean? Did someone tell you that?"

"Yes. The angel."

"What angel?"

"The one from my dream. It's like he's communicating with me. Come on. We need to go."

"Okay. That works for me," Khaled said as he stood up. "Which way?"

Benjamin said simply, "Up."

Dominic looked around again. "Across the field is too open. If someone is keeping an eye out, they might see us taking her away."

Joseph offered, pointing, "Right over there is the street that goes up to the City of David and on to the Temple Mount. If that's where we need to go, let's just cut over and go up that way."

Dominic and Joseph lifted the woman gently to her feet. She still wasn't talking, but they found she could move her legs if they supported her. The group stepped around holes and over cracks in the ground, looking side to side as they walked. They could see some people looking out of windows, others walking around in the streets and adjacent fields. They were relieved that no one seemed to be following them or even paying attention to them at all. Maybe given everything that was happening, there was nothing odd about an injured woman being taken to safety.

They eventually made it to the street. Sensing that they needed to move faster, Dominic simply picked the woman up in his arms and began carrying her up the hill. Struggling to catch his breath as he walked, he said to Joseph in a hushed, labored voice, "See, look! Just up the street. The lights are still on up there. And there's no earthquake damage there. The streets, the houses . . . everything's perfectly fine."

"Maybe it was one of those extremely localized superquakes."

Dominic doubted that such a thing even existed but decided not to argue the point. Between breaths, he said, "You know, the darkness and that crack in the ground back there were kind of scary. But I think the streetlights and the people walking around up ahead might be worse. I prefer not to be so exposed right now."

"I hear you. We do look a little suspicious, carrying an unconscious woman up the street. Do you want me to take her for a while?"

Dominic tried to set her down on her own feet, but she collapsed to her knees. "Sure. You can take a turn."

They continued slowly up the inclined road, taking turns carrying the woman. When the street forked fifty meters further up, they veered to the left, into the dark, choosing the way with no streetlights.

Less than a minute later, a car came slowly driving down the well-lit, right-hand fork. They pressed against the wall in the shadows and waited as the car, passing less than twenty meters from them, continued down the hill.

After another three minutes of struggling up the hill, stopping every few steps to listen for any clues of approaching trouble, they paused to rest just opposite the Pool of Siloam.

Just then, they heard an engine rev and saw lights coming up the hill toward them. They couldn't take a chance. They had to get off the street. But where?

To their left, Dominic saw a set of stairs climbing up. It was their only chance to escape being seen.

They raced as fast as they could up the stone stairway, old houses of stone and brick rising on either side of them. When the stairs leveled off into a narrow lane, the houses all around them made them feel more secure and less exposed—except, that is, from the people inside the houses that might be observing them.

Dominic felt like they were being watched. *Is this a dead-end path? Are we headed into a trap?*

They continued up the narrow path. All at once, the faint moonlight revealed what appeared to be a grassy field sloping up toward the Old City. They crossed a dirt track running parallel to the slope, then turned and continued up a street. On their left, a short distance ahead, they could see a run-down house with several old cars parked in front.

Khaled stopped for a second and said between breaths, "Wait, can we rest here for a minute?"

Dominic who was again carrying the woman, panted, "I'd love to . . . but there's no time . . . we have to keep going."

Khaled responded, "But I recognize this neighborhood. That abandoned house up ahead . . . that's where my grandfather used to live."

2:50 AM

Just then they heard a sound and saw the lights of a car turning a corner down below them. As it slowly approached, they realized it was the same car that had passed them below. Hoping they had not yet been seen on the dark road, they stepped onto the sidewalk and hurried up the street looking for a place to hide. Finding no place of concealment, they pressed themselves against the wall of a house, immobile, and hoped the car would pass by.

But they had already been seen. The car drove straight to where they were and out stepped Omar with an evil smile. He stood on the other side of the car from them and took out his phone, saying, "I found her. She's with some others, and I'll need your help. I've sent you a pin with the location so you can meet me here."

He ended the call, then looked at the four boys. Seeming to read their minds, he shook his head to indicate they shouldn't try anything. Then, pulling out a gun, he motioned for them to sit down.

Khaled, recognizing his friend and recovering from the shock of seeing him alive, started toward him, saying, "Omar! I thought you were dead. What happened? Where have you been?"

Omar pointed the gun right at him, and the boy took a step back, terrified. "Omar? It's me, Khaled! What's going on?"

"Shut up!" Omar spat out angrily. "All of you just sit down and be quiet. This will be over soon."

Khaled and Joseph quickly sat down on the ground. Benjamin remained standing, but as he was younger and smaller, Omar ignored him.

Dominic, who had laid the woman's head carefully on the ground, crouched rather than sat beside her. It might be the middle of the night, but his mind was fully engaged, his muscles taut, ready for action.

Omar, feeling in control, relaxed and continued, "Let me tell you all something. The day I heard Nehemyah teach about how God works all things together for good, suddenly everything made sense. At that time, I was lonelier than I ever thought possible; rejected by friends and family, because I associated with infidels, while also rejected by Jews and Christians because I wasn't really one of them.

"Then it struck me—I was where I was because God had ordained it! But why had God put me among you? Think about it. If

God can work His will through any situation, I might as well remain a Muslim and stay faithful to Allah. If Christianity is true, the will of the Christian God can still be accomplished because 'He works all things for good.'

"That night, I stopped despairing about my loneliness. I made up my mind to return to Islam and the next day I met with the sheikh. Greeting him with a smile, I said, '*As-salamu 'alaykum.*'[197] I knew he had heard about my conversion and baptism, so when he warmly responded, '*Wa-'alaykumu s-salam*'[198] it was as if the heavens had opened up. I knew at that moment that, if he really thought I'd abandoned the faith, he would not have wished me peace.

"I was bursting with enthusiasm, but I was also afraid. I told him that I wanted to return to the faith, but that I wanted it to be more than just words. I was ready to prove my loyalty. I explained how I'd become depressed, how I had no good options, and that my family wouldn't even look at me.

"I. Got. Baptized. So what? It was a moment of weakness. It meant nothing. I got a little bit of water on me. One innocent mistake and suddenly all the doors to my community were closed in my face. Khaled, you can understand how hard that was for me, right?"

He didn't wait for a response but immediately continued, "Then it dawned on me that my position among you afforded me a very interesting opportunity. I could work undercover, from within the Messianic Jewish community. I still remember the light that filled my heart when the sheikh smiled at me. He reminded me that the Quran says, 'The unbelievers plotted and planned, and Allah too planned, and the best of planners is Allah.'[199]

"Yes, the sheikh understood me. He knew I would have to continue to endure the shunning of my Muslim friends and family for a while longer. And he knew I would pay any price to regain my honor."

---

197. Arabic: "Peace be upon you"
198. Arabic: "And upon you be peace"
199. Quran 3:54 A.Yusuf Ali translation

The young man stopped as if to listen. "What was that?" he asked, looking around suspiciously.

After a moment, he continued, "I gave him a weekly report of all the activities of the kibbutz. I'll admit, at times, it felt like I was betraying Nehemyah. Even so, when the sheikh explained his plan, I knew I couldn't say no to him. You see, I will never again leave the true path!

"When he asked me to fake my own death, I was surprised," Omar continued. "But it was essential if we were to gain access to the software needed to hack into the Iron Dome. I had hoped to also teach Nehemyah a lesson, but I guess it turns out he wasn't home when I left that surprise for him at his house."

As Omar talked, Dominic's keen eyes noticed a slight movement across the street. The front door of the run-down house slowly opened. Omar, with his back to the house, his attention on his captives, and his ears tuned to listen for the arrival of the sheikh's car, didn't hear the stealthy approach of the dark-robed figure. Then the sound of a sandal scuffing on a cobblestone caused Omar to turn his head in surprise.

At that moment, Dominic sprang up from the ground. As Omar was swinging his pistol toward the figure approaching him from the house, Dominic grabbed Omar from behind in a vicelike grip. Omar struggled to free himself, desperately trying to stomp on Dominic's feet while at the same time attempting to point his gun at the stranger standing in the shadows.

Omar pulled the trigger, sending a bullet into the wall as the stranger advanced swiftly, bringing his walking stick down onto Omar's extended hand. Screaming in pain, Omar dropped the weapon. The stranger quickly picked it up and pointed it back at him. Taking a few steps back, the stranger told Dominic, "Let him go, son. He won't be bothering you anymore."

Dominic squeezed even tighter. “No way! We can’t let him go. He wants to kill us. We need to knock him out or at least tie him up.”

Benjamin spoke up, interrupting his thoughts. “Dominic, the angel says you can let him go now.”

“Right, the angel,” Dominic exploded. “Benjamin, where is the angel? Is *he* going to make sure this character doesn’t kill us?”

“I won’t hurt you,” said Omar. “I swear it. Just let me go.”

“Not a chance!” Dominic said, squeezing harder. “You just shut up!”

After a moment, Benjamin spoke again. “Listen, Dominic, he won’t hurt us. The angel says that you have to trust in God.”

All was silent except for Omar’s continued groaning as he tried in vain to free himself from Dominic’s grip.

At last, Dominic gave him a final squeeze, then pushed him away, as he told them all, “You know this is crazy, right?”

Omar grabbed his injured wrist and looked over at the stranger, who seemed to read his thoughts. “I’ll keep the gun. You get in your car and get out of here.” Then, turning his attention to the boys, he said, “You too. Out of here. I don’t want any more trouble on my street.”

Dominic turned to see Benjamin cradling the woman’s head in his hands. Joseph noticed this too and knelt down beside her. “Are you feeling better? Can you walk?”

She nodded her head but said nothing.

Dominic came over and, along with Joseph, helped the woman to her feet, saying, “We’d better get going.” As the group began walking up the tiny street again, Khaled hesitated, glancing back at the stranger and at Omar, before hurrying to join his friends.

Omar watched his prey escaping and wondered if he might make a move to regain his pistol. But the stranger, brandishing his stick in his left hand and the gun in his right, said, “Don’t try it. Get in your car and get out of here.”

He walked slowly to his car and, as he opened the door, he glanced up at the kids now nearly out of sight, then back at the stranger whose face was hidden in the shadows.

Dominic looked back as the car sped away and said to his friends, "I don't think we've seen the last of him." As they continued up the stone path, Benjamin seemed more and more agitated. Finally, he reached out and took the woman's hand, saying, "We've wasted a lot of time. We have to reach the Holy Place. He's expecting us soon." None of them questioned him about where they were going or who was expecting them; they simply quickened their pace.

Soon, the path began to resemble an actual street—wider now and paved with asphalt. They passed a few more scattered houses, including one that appeared to have only a few sheep as residents.

They climbed as fast as they could up a few more flights of stairs, then struggled up a steep street past a cemetery that housed the remains of Oskar Schindler.

As they approached the main road around the Old City, even at this late hour, there was quite a bit of traffic. Dominic said, "Now, what? We can't stay out of sight here!"

"No, but Omar wouldn't dare attack us here; there are too many witnesses," Joseph said as he led the group to the right, toward the Temple Mount.

Benjamin stopped in his tracks. "Not that way, Joe. We need to go to the left." Joseph turned to face his brother. "Benni, the Temple Mount is right over there," he said, pointing. Benjamin was already walking the other way. "We're not going to the Temple Mount. We need to go further up."

The traffic cleared, and the group followed Benjamin, crossing the street and heading west. As they walked uphill along the street called Ma'ale HaShalom, or the "Ascent of Peace," suddenly Benjamin dashed off through the bushes, following a path that hugged the ancient city wall. The group crouched in the shadows to avoid being seen whenever they saw a suspicious-looking car, and twice they hid under the bushes growing next to the wall. These measures slowed their progress, but they didn't want to risk Omar spotting them again.

Finally, as they approached the ascent up to the Zion Gate, Benjamin spoke up, "Yes, this is the way. I remember it from my dream."

"Shh!" Dominic grabbed Benjamin by the shoulder and motioned for the others to get down behind a bush, as he whispered, "There's Omar! I knew we couldn't trust him. And now he's got friends!" Omar was seated in the passenger seat of a car that was cruising slowly past them. They couldn't see the driver, but they could see at least two men in the back seat.

"We need to go through the Zion Gate here," said Benjamin, pointing to the right.

Dominic eased Benjamin's hand back down out of sight and continued in hushed tones, "I'll be glad to get off this main road, but the entrance through the gate is exposed and well lighted. We'll have to move quickly, but no running. We don't want to attract any attention. We have no idea if Omar has others out there as well."

Crouching and moving quickly and quietly, they entered the city walls at the Zion Gate without being noticed. Then, taking a left, they went farther up until they reached the southwest corner of the Old City. At that point, the street turned right, and they headed up through the Armenian Quarter toward the Jaffa Gate.

The farther they walked up the narrow street, the more giddy Benjamin became. The others were puzzled and looked at each other, unsure what to think. Meanwhile, Dominic grew more apprehensive with every step. The narrow street was hemmed in by stone buildings with no side streets. He looked around nervously as he realized the single-lane street had essentially become a tunnel, literally passing right through a building. They were surrounded by stone. Dominic felt trapped.

His thoughts closed in on him too. *Omar is after us. In a car. Why did I let him go? Who knows how many others are after us now. They've probably seen us. Why did I listen to Benjamin? He's only a child! A strange child at that, supposedly being guided by invisible angels! Why did I come here tonight? Why did I even come to Israel? If I survive this night, I'll . . . .*

Before he could finish his thought, they reached the end of the tunnel, where he saw on his right a sign that announced "*St. James Street*" in Hebrew, Arabic, and English. It was a street, but not wide enough for vehicles. *Good! If necessary, we can escape into the maze of the Old City through there.*

Benjamin was still leading the group; the others followed close behind. As Dominic passed the arched entrance to St. James Street, he slowed to give a quick glance for future reference. What he saw made him instantly freeze. In the dimly lit passageway, he saw a group of young men walking toward them, about five meters away. In the center of the pack was the unmistakable face of his LA stalker.

"We gotta run!" Dominic yelled, as he tried to get them to move faster.

They ran up the narrow street lined with stone walls. There was an opening to the right. A small shop. *Should they duck into the corner shop?*

No. Then they'd really be trapped. Keep running.

Dominic knew that just up ahead the street started to descend a little and grew wider. There was a small police station ahead on the left and after that the Tower of David. Farther up on the right was the Mount Zion Center. *Surely there would be some other people around there. Friendly people. Can we make it? We have to!*

Just then, a car appeared in front of them and, the next moment, they were blinded by its headlights. Friend or foe? There was no way to tell. The car pulled to a stop and Dominic, who had stationed himself at the back of the procession in an attempt to protect his friends from Abdowan and his gang could only watch helplessly as someone grabbed the woman. Another pointed a flashlight and pistol at Dominic and his friends.

Dominic froze. He heard what sounded like a gunshot, and he ducked. Then another shot, and another. Six total. He hadn't been shot but he couldn't tell if any of his friends had. It was all happening so fast, and Dominic felt totally powerless to act. He was out of strength. He closed his eyes and, for a moment, the night became eerily quiet. Then suddenly a voice rang out, "There he is!"

Part 5

This is my Father's world:
Oh, let me ne'er forget
That though the wrong seems oft so strong,
God is the ruler yet.

This is my Father's world,
The battle is not done:
Jesus who died shall be satisfied,
And earth and Heav'n be one.[200]

200. From the hymn "This is my Father's World" by Maltbie D. Babcock

Ch 59. The Fire

(Jerusalem, 22 July, 3AM)

It's the End of the World as We Know It
(And I Feel Fine).
R.E.M. from their album, *Document*

Qorin, deciding to let Verethragna enjoy his moment of glory alone, flew off to watch the missile attack from a short distance away, and was soon joined by Nabu, who cursed as he landed, "I've been crisscrossing back and forth through the Shadowlands for hours looking for Deywós. Where is our fearless leader when we really need him? At this point, the only hope is to talk some sense into that annoying, long-haired Persian Prince, attempting to rearrange the map of the Middle East without asking permission or even consulting other *Tselim* in the region."

Ptah and Hubal arrived as well, both eager to give Verethragna a piece of their mind. Qorin stayed put and watched as the three princes headed off to confront Verethragna. Still several hundred meters away, they stopped, realizing it was too late; they could see a missile streaking across the sky directly toward Jerusalem. No one had been able to stop Verethragna's madness.

Watching the light cross the sky, they were transfixed: Verethragna relishing the climax of years of preparation, Qorin hoping the Israeli military had a backup plan, and Nabu forcing himself to watch while cursing the Persian prince. After a few seconds had passed, they all realized no Israeli counterattack was coming; it was clearly too late to stop the quickly approaching missile from striking Jerusalem.

Then, suddenly, the streaking missile was gone! It simply disappeared! No defensive strike, no explosion! They waited, knowing that light travels faster than sound even when viewed from the Shadowlands. A few seconds later, they heard a small "pop" like the opening of a soda can. The Persian prince, his back to the rest and unaware of their presence, looked up and down in confusion.

Then, a second missile caught their attention as it streaked across the sky toward Jerusalem, but it met the same fate as the first one. This was followed by a third. As they looked down on Jerusalem, they counted six pops. The missiles from Syria seemed to have simply disintegrated on their own. Not only was there no damage to the city, clearly no counterattack had been launched.

As if frozen in place, Verethragna stood breathlessly waiting as the seventh and final missile crossed the horizon. He reasoned, *Surely, whatever new countermeasure had taken out the six conventional missiles would be too little or too late to stop the grand finale: the nuke*. Then, when it was almost directly above Jerusalem and no defensive strike nor explosion had appeared, it inexplicably stopped in midair. Turning into a simple point of light, it began to get brighter as it gently descended down to Jerusalem's Old City!

Dominic, still hunched over on the Armenian Patriarchate Street, opened his eyes and slowly straightened himself up. Looking around, he saw that he and his friends were surrounded by armed thugs, one of whom was still pointing a flashlight directly at them. Its light, however, was no longer visible because a light many times brighter now illuminated the entire scene, a light so bright it left no place for shadows of any kind.

He looked around confused. The last thing he had heard was a voice that shattered the silence with the words, "There he is!" He was wondering to himself, *Who* was *where?*, when his eyes landed on Benjamin who was looking up, smiling, pointing, and saying again, "There he is!" At that, everyone looked up to see the light shining down on them from above. Dominic thought, *What in the . . . ?*

His thoughts were interrupted by a blinding flash immediately followed by a thundering roar, and then . . . nothing.

The three *Tselim* approached Verethragna in the ensuing silence and witnessed his confusion turn to rage. As he screamed, pounding his fist and stomping his feet, he turned and saw the other *Tselim* advancing toward him, a hundred meters away and approaching quickly. His anger turned to embarrassment and fear, but he stood his ground. They encircled him without a word, staring at him accusingly. Then Nabu spat, "We know what you tried to do. It's lucky for you we were able to deactivate those bombs. Don't you realize how much trouble you would have caused if you had succeeded in damaging that city? From now on, stay out of matters that are above your pay grade."

Verethragna opened his mouth to defend himself. He would tell them he had every right to take steps to ensure the success of the Rebellion. Then, it occurred to him that he was dying to know how they had stopped his missiles. *Should I ask them? No,* he decided, *Nabu would merely laugh at me.* Looking up at their angry faces, he closed his mouth, staring daggers back at them. After a long while, he eventually broke, averting his eyes and accepting his defeat. Nabu and his company then turned their backs on Verethragna and flew off in a huff. The Prince of Persia slumped away in the other direction, his shoulders drooping, knowing he had failed, knowing he would never be part of their group, and knowing that, if he were to become too weakened by the unrest in his territory, he could even lose his principality.

Qorin, surprised as the rest when the first few missiles simply vanished, decided to hide out of sight and watch Verethragna. He saw as Nabu and his cohort approached the Persian after the seventh and final missile and thought, at that moment, they looked less like fearsome gods and more like the plebeians he had seen running from the fiery lava of Mt. Vesuvius many years before. He had been about to step out of hiding, but he thought better of it when Verethragna turned and spotted Nabu. He decided to wait and listen.

After Nabu and company had words with Verethragna and left, Qorin set off quietly to join the Persian prince. He coughed when he got within four or five meters to announce his presence, as he didn't want to startle the dispirited *Tsel*. Verethragna turned, dejected, and when he saw it was Qorin, he slumped to the ground. "Come to gloat over me, have you?"

"No, not at all. I've come to see if you'd like to join forces with me. Look, this was a setback, but we still have options. For one thing, I'd like to try to reach out to the Prince of Palestine, and I believe you have connections in this part of the *Olam* that might help. In addition, I have important information about the young man I've been keeping my eye on for almost twenty years. I believe if we work together, you and I can create a formidable alliance."

Verethragna didn't look convinced, so Qorin added, "And as for those three idiots you were just talking with? Don't worry about them. By the time we are finished with our plan, they'll be begging to be allowed to work with us."

Part 6

The Gate of Heaven

Ch 60. Where Angels Tread

(Jerusalem, 3 hours after the Fire)

When Christ ascended Triumphantly from star to star,
He left the gates of Heaven ajar.

Henry Wadsworth Longfellow,
The Golden Legend

6:00 AM

Dominic awoke lying flat on his back. Opening his eyes slowly, he saw a single cloud floating in a beautiful blue sky. He felt wonderful and thought, *This must be heaven.*

As his mind cleared, he felt the hard surface below him. *I'm not lying on a cloud, that's for sure.* He turned his head to the right. He saw a tree. He turned to the left. He saw a church. *Wait, I know that church. That's the Mount Zion Church!*

He sat up slowly, expecting to feel either ethereal bliss or searing pain. He felt neither. Then he heard voices behind him. "Look! Dominic's awake now, too."

He turned to see Benjamin, glowing with excitement, stand up and walk toward him. He was barefoot and holding hands with a young woman, also barefoot. "Dominic, we're so glad you're awake. Joseph and Khaled are awake too." Then, he added, "Oh, this is Devorah."

Joseph and Khaled were rising from the stone courtyard. Dominic got to his feet and then they all sat down at a nearby table. It was early in the morning, but the sun was shining brightly.

Dominic shook his head, trying to make sense of what had happened. "How did we get in here? The last thing I remember, we were out on the street, surrounded by people who wanted us dead. Then there was that light. What was that?"

"That was the angel," said Benjamin. "He came down and talked with us. But you missed him. Now he's gone back up."

"I see," said Dominic. "Did Joseph and Khaled see the angel?"

They shook their heads, and Benjamin answered. "No. They only saw his brightness, just like you. They woke up about five minutes before you. But Devorah saw him and even talked with him."

Dominic was still confused. "Who's Devorah?"

"Nehemyah's granddaughter. The woman we rescued!"

"Nehemyah's granddaughter Devorah?" He turned to her, "But . . . you died in a terrorist attack!"

Devorah said, "Apparently not. I'm pretty sure I'm alive." She smiled and extended her hand. "Hi, Dominic, it's nice to meet you. I suppose technically we met last night, but I don't remember much about that. Although Benni here has filled me in on how you helped break me out of that horrible cell."

As she shook Dominic's hand, she paused and said, "You seem very familiar. But I can't tell now if I'm remembering you from a dream or real life."

"About that . . ." replied Dominic, looking around from Devorah to Joseph to Khaled and then to Benjamin. "Did you tell her about our dreams?"

"No. Not yet. Do you want to tell her about them?"

Dominic shook his head slowly. "No. Maybe later. I want to hear about the angel. You said that an angel saved us. Are you saying an *angel* literally came down and rescued us?"

Dominic looked around at each of them as they silently nodded. "You know how crazy that sounds, right? They all just kept nodding. "And that this is really Devorah, the one who was killed months ago in a bus bombing?" Dominic asked incredulously.

Joseph spoke up. "The three of us know Devorah pretty well and I can say without a doubt that this is definitely her. And I can promise you this: She is the last person I would expect to make up a story about talking with an angel. She's a hardcore scientist. To be honest, the last I knew, she didn't even believe in angels."

Devorah was pensive. "Yes, there are a great many things I've doubted over the years. Not that I ever doubted *God himself*; It's just that I struggled at times to believe some things people *said* about Him." Then she smiled, "But to be fair, I never communicated I didn't believe in angels. I believe my exact words were that I didn't *know* if angels existed."

Joseph smiled as Khaled joined in, "Dominic, look. Devorah and Benjamin are both convinced they saw and talked with an angel. I know it sounds crazy, but I'm leaning toward believing them. We were surrounded. You saw Omar taking Devorah away to the car. You heard the shots. How do you explain the fact that we're not all dead?"

Dominic looked at his hands, turning them over. "Maybe we are dead. Although, it's not quite what I expected the afterlife to be like . . . ."

"To be honest," replied Devorah, "this *is* what I thought heaven might be like. I feel wonderful, and more alive now than I ever did before."

She noticed that Dominic remained silent, so she continued, looking right at him. "Okay, if you think we are, in fact, dead, then test that hypothesis. Evaluate what you are experiencing right now.

Is it significantly different from what you remember of your life on earth?

"If the answer is no, then accept the possibility that we're not dead, that we escaped the people trying to kill or kidnap us. But how? Benni says it was an angel who saved us. As strange as it sounds, when I opened my eyes, I also saw and talked with an angel. Now you have our accounts of what just occurred.

"Can you accept the possibility that Benjamin is correct when he says that he spoke with an angel? I assure you, he and I did not collude or conspire about this in any way. And yet I am also convinced I spoke with an angel. Can you propose some other explanation that covers the facts at hand? You are, you must admit, at a distinct disadvantage here. You have already stated that you have no recollection of the period of time in question. So, I feel compelled to remind you that your explanation will have to be regarded as hearsay over against our firsthand accounts."

Joseph smiled and looked at Dominic. "I told you she was a hardcore scientist! What do you think of that?"

Dominic turned back toward Devorah. "I concede. As unlikely as it seems, you could have seen an angel."

"And do you still think we are dead?"

He smiled. "I guess not. But to be fair, I merely offered the possibility that we *might* be dead. I never said I believed we actually *were* dead."

"I think," she said, "I'm going to enjoy getting to know you, Dominic."

At that moment, a door opened at the other end of the courtyard and an elderly man stepped out.

6:30 AM

Devorah jumped up and started running toward him. "Saba!" she cried. "You're here!"

The boys turned their heads to see Nehemyah shuffling along as his granddaughter ran toward him. They embraced for the longest time without a word. He continued to hold onto Devorah as if to never let her escape again, while managing to say between sobs, "I was sure that you had perished in the bus explosion! I thought I'd lost you forever. Now look at you after all this time. You look wonderful!"

The boys rose and then, one by one, joyfully embraced the beloved patriarch. Eventually, he led them inside the church, and they sat down together. The boys all joined in telling him about the adventures of the previous night and about Devorah's rescue.

Joseph did most of the talking until he came to the part about the bright light. Then he said, "At this point, Benni better take over. The rest of us don't remember anything. We were knocked unconscious or something."

Benjamin explained, "It was the angel. Everybody was looking up when they saw the brightness of his coming. Then he greeted us and came down to the ground."

"That was a greeting?!" Dominic exclaimed. "It sounded like thunder. What did he say?"

"He said, '*Shalom*.' Then, when he touched the ground, the light got brighter. I think that's when everybody fell down. He touched me on the shoulder and told me to rise, so I did. Next, he went over and touched Devorah. Of course, none of us knew at the time that it was Devorah. But after he touched her, she woke up and she was all cleaned up and beautiful again, like the normal Devorah."

Everyone smiled and looked at Devorah, who turned an attractive shade of pink.

Nehemyah laughed. "Congratulations, Benjamin, I don't think anyone has gotten my Devorah to blush since the fourth grade." Then, wishing to give his granddaughter a distraction and also to hear more of the story, he asked Benjamin, "Did you talk with the angel?"

"Yes. When Devorah first woke up, she asked where we were. You see, she hadn't been fully conscious during the whole night. And then I was going to answer, but when I looked around, we weren't on the street anymore, and the people who had been chasing us were all gone, so I was confused too. Then I realized it wasn't night anymore. We went from the middle of the night straight to bright morning."

Then Devorah added, "The angel simply said, 'This is a holy place.' I honestly thought that we had died and gone to heaven."

Benjamin continued, "But then I looked around and saw that we were at the Mount Zion Church. I think the angel read my mind because he looked at me and said that this place, Mount Zion, is the new Gate of Heaven, and angels will descend and ascend at this location. He said this is also where Jesus will one day stand with the 144,000 sealed ones."[201]

Nehemyah was shaking his head. "This is incredible! Simply amazing! I want to hear more, but I really should make a call first. Don't say anything important until I get back, okay?"

While the others kept chatting, Nehemyah called Agent Peretz. "Hello, Levy? Can you come to the Mount Zion Center as soon as possible?"

They heard on the speakerphone: "What is it, Uncle?"

"We can talk about it when you get here. But believe me, you should drop whatever you are doing and come as quickly as you can."

"I'll be there in twenty minutes."

---

201. Revelation 14:1–5

Ch 61. Questions and Answers

(Jerusalem, 4 hours after the Fire)

When you have excluded the impossible,
whatever remains, however improbable, must be the truth.
Sir Arthur Conan Doyle,
The Adventure of the Beryl Coronet

7:00 AM

When Agent Peretz arrived, he found Nehemyah waiting for him outside the church and asked him, "Uncle, what's so urgent? You are aware we are in a state of alert, right?"

"Yes, I know. Trust me, I have news you will be very happy to hear. But I wanted to talk with you in private first and ask you a few questions, if I may."

"Go ahead."

"First of all, what happened last night? There are all sorts of rumors. There were reports of a missile attack, an earthquake, even a nuclear bomb near the Temple Mount! The news said these were all false alarms and that there is no danger, but . . . ."

"I can't tell you very much. I will say that it appears there were two attacks, possibly coordinated. One was a conventional bomb set off near the Western Wall that caused minimal damage. About the same time, our radar detected incoming missiles heading directly for the center of Jerusalem. We have multiple radar operators whose accounts all agree about that. But for some reason, the Iron Dome did not engage. In any case, the radar screens eventually all cleared up, and no missile strikes were observed."

"I've also heard reports of a strange bright light near here last night."

"I've heard that too, but we have no solid evidence corroborating that, nor linking it with any missile attack. Also, we have confirmed that some debris was found near Temple Mount, but again, there is no evidence that this has anything to do with any missiles. At the moment, the official word is that the radar scare was merely a computer error.

"However," Agent Peretz added, lowering his voice, "just between us, we have confirmed that some debris scattered around the Temple Mount area has tested positive for radiation. We don't know yet what that means and we're still investigating. But, Uncle, I didn't come to give *you* information, but to *get* information from *you*. What have you called me here for?"

"There's someone here you will be very relieved to see. Let's step inside," offered Nehemyah.

As the entered the room, Agent Peretz saw Devorah and his mouth dropped open in surprise. Before he could say anything, Nehemyah addressed the assembled group, saying, "Since I am the oldest one here, I guess I should start things off. This is merely an informal meeting to try and understand what in the world has just happened. We will, of course, need to make official statements to the authorities regarding what we know about Devorah's abduction. But I've asked Agent Peretz for a small indulgence, and he has agreed that we may take up to an hour to attempt to make sense of some of the events of the last several hours. He will be recording this meeting and is in charge."

Nehemyah continued, "Okay, where to start? As you can see, here is my beloved Devorah, safe and sound. How is this possible? Khaled, you were on the same bus with her. You stepped off and then, moments later, while she was still on the bus, it exploded."

Khaled was shaking his head and had no explanation, so Devorah spoke up, "I can explain at least that much. It was Omar's doing. He escorted Khaled off the bus and then got back on himself."

"Okay, but the bus was completely destroyed. How did you survive?"

"After the bus took off, we turned the corner out of sight. Then, we stopped again, and Omar pulled me off the bus and pushed me into a waiting car. As we sped away, I heard the bus explode. I think the whole event was designed to make you think I'd been killed."

"And equally important," added Agent Peretz, "to make us think that the briefcase you were carrying had been destroyed."

They all looked at Agent Peretz, and Devorah asked in surprise, "What do you know of that briefcase?"

"*That* we will discuss in another setting. Suffice it to say that Mossad contacted us and we know about the contents. We've been almost as concerned about that information getting out as we were about your own safety."

"You mean you thought I might be still alive?"

"We hoped as much. No DNA from either you or Omar was recovered from the remnants of the burned-out bus. That in itself wasn't conclusive, seeing the bomb had reduced the bus to ashes. But Khaled confirmed that you had been on the bus, and the fact that you left no trace at all did give us hope. We began to piece together enough information to guess that, instead of the random bombing of a Jerusalem bus, this might actually have been part of a bigger plan."

Nehemyah asked, "Okay, my love, what happened next? Where were you taken?"

"I can't really say. It was underground, dark, and musty, and I couldn't hear any traffic noise."

Dominic spoke up, "We found her half-buried in what looked like a secret tunnel not far from here."

"How, may I ask, did you know where she was?"

"An angel told me." All eyes looked at Benjamin.

"An angel?" Agent Peretz asked.

"Yes," Devorah offered. "I saw the angel myself, with my own eyes."

"Actually," Joseph added, "Benjamin had a dream last night at the kibbutz. He saw a woman begging him to come rescue her. She said she was in hell."

"In hell?"

"Yes," continued Joseph. "I tried to tell Benjamin that it could wait until the morning, but he wouldn't listen. He would have gone out the door to search alone if I hadn't stopped him."

"I might be to blame there as well," added Dominic. "I felt sure Benjamin's dream needed to be acted on immediately, because I had a dream too, and my dream confirmed his dream."

"So, the four of you drove off in the middle of the night, guided by Benjamin's dream and found Devorah?" Nehemyah asked slowly, not expecting a reply. "I call that foolhardy. And yet, you have my deepest appreciation."

Agent Peretz asked, "Did the angel tell you where to go?"

Dominic answered, "Not really. It was a group effort, requiring a measure of deduction. We came to see that the Hinnom Valley might be what the person in the dream was referring to as 'hell.' So, we went there but didn't know exactly where to look. Then there was an earthquake, and afterward we started looking again, guided by Benjamin. Using my phone as a flashlight, we found a place where the ground had recently caved in. When we looked, we saw what seemed to be an underground room with its roof partially fallen in. Climbing down into the room, we found Devorah more dead than alive."

"That is what is remarkable to me," said Nehemyah. "My granddaughter looks as strong and healthy as she did ten months ago. They must have treated you very well in your captivity."

"No, Saba, do not misunderstand. When Dominic said that I was 'more dead than alive,' he wasn't referring to injuries caused by the cave-in. When the boys found me, I'd been starved and tortured to the point where I could neither stand nor talk. Before they arrived, I expected to die at any moment, and I'd given up all hope. I remember Omar standing over me, telling me that no one would come for me, that no one knew where I was. I heard him leave and knew that was the end. But then I thought of you. I remembered your faith in the darkest days of your imprisonment, and I cried out in my heart one more time to the God I thought had abandoned me."

"And then what happened?"

"The room shook, and parts of the roof began to fall in. I looked up and I thought I could see a little moonlight coming in through a hole in the roof. I tried to call for help, but it felt useless."

"Boys, you didn't see anyone around when you arrived?"

"No, sir."

"Okay, but Devorah, I still don't understand how you have recovered so fully after such a terrible experience."

"Well, sir," said Joseph, "none of us can really understand that. I believe that God simply healed her, although it seems that it happened in stages. What we do know is that while we were fleeing to safety, just as we were arriving outside the walls of the Mount Zion Center here, Omar caught back up with us and grabbed Devorah. It seemed like there was some kind of a gunfight, then we looked up to see a sudden flash, and we felt an explosion. The explosion knocked us to the ground, and when we woke up, there he was."

"There *who* was?"

"The angel," Benjamin said. "As his feet touched the ground, suddenly the people chasing us were gone, we were all safely inside this courtyard, and it was daytime. I don't know exactly what happened, but I saw him touch Devorah, and she woke up."

"When he touched me, I felt the pain and sickness leaving my body," said Devorah. "My mind was clearer than it has been in years. The verse from the Psalms that I had prayed when I cried out to God was, 'Be still, and know that I *am* God.'[202] That is what I did. I gave up trying to understand God in my own strength and asked Him to reveal Himself to me so that I could know Him. And He did. I don't have the answers to all my questions, but I no longer doubt the supernatural power of God."

After Devorah finished telling her story, Agent Peretz took his recorder and notes and told the group that he would be calling them to come down to the station and make formal statements. Then he approached Nehemyah and put his arm around him, but instead of addressing him, leaned in and said to Devorah, "You cannot know how grateful I am to see you safely returned to us." With that he turned to leave.

Nehemyah spoke again, "Perhaps before you go, there is another matter of significance that should be mentioned. You see, it's not a mere coincidence that I am here at the Mount Zion Center so early this morning. I was brought here by God."

They all looked at one another, and Nehemyah continued, "Not directly by God, but God used Bill to get me here in the middle of the night. Moshe drove Bill and me here at about two in the morning. We prayed for a while, and then Bill said he was going to step out for a bit. The thing is, he hasn't come back, and I have no idea where he is."

Agent Peretz asked, "When did you see him last?"

"Sometime around two in the morning."

"And what is your best guess as to where he went?"

---

202. Psalm 46:10

"What I consider my best guess I will keep to myself for now. All I know is that he told me that the Lord was calling him into His presence. Then he stepped out of the office where we had been praying, and I haven't seen or heard anything from him since."

Nehemyah added, "Moshe is out looking for him even as we speak. But if what I am calling my 'best guess' is, in fact, true, I expect that Bill is perfectly fine."

Ch 62. The Daily Sacrifice

(Jerusalem, 7 hours after the Fire)

And Enoch walked with God; and he was not, for God took him.

Genesis 5:24

10:00 AM

After the police had left, Benjamin and Joseph's parents arrived and stayed on to talk with Nehemyah, Devorah, Khaled, and Dominic.

"What does all this mean? What is happening?" asked Dominic.

Nehemyah answered, "For all of my life I've heard about the great miracles God did for His people in the past, but my question has always been, 'Why not now?' Through the years, I've heard reports of modern-day miracles performed by televangelists, faith healers, and others. But it has always seemed that so many of these events were shrouded in suspicion of deception and fraud. And I wondered, will God ever work wonders again that are clear and undeniable, as He did in the past?

"What I heard God saying several months ago was, 'Yes! That day is coming soon!' The report today about how God miraculously intervened to rescue my Devorah, and how an angel appeared and proclaimed that this area right here in the courtyard of the Mount Zion Center is literally the Gate of Heaven . . . well, I think that this is beginning of the very end of this age, and that God is beginning to show Himself with power."

Dominic said, "You might remember a young man named Chad who visited here last year. He told me that he went back to LA specifically looking to rescue someone. When he saw me, he said he knew I was the one and he told me I needed to come here to see the power of God. Chad had been here for what he called the start of the Jerusalem Revival, and he felt that God had told him that the end would come within one year."

"Yes," Nehemyah said, "Chad was there that first day when we all witnessed the multiplication of bread and wine. Since then, we have had worship services at the Mount Zion Center twice a day, every day, meetings that last for hours. This has been going on for months now and, reminiscent of the priestly offerings in the Old Testament, people have begun calling these worship services the '*daily sacrifice.*'"

"Okay," said Dominic, "but when I listened to Shimon and Menachem, the evidence seemed to clearly point to the fact that the Lord will return *after* the Tribulation. That seems to mean that the end is still many years away."

"That debate about the timing of the Rapture was all well and good. And I agree with Shimon that the Scriptures teach God's people to prepare to go through the coming Tribulation. But in the case of Chad, I think there is something else at work. God has at times given His people special promises made just for them.

"Consider when Jesus was talking to Mary and Martha about the Resurrection. They thought He was speaking of the end-times when He told them their brother would rise again. A few moments later, the promise of resurrection was fulfilled right before their eyes when Lazarus came walking out of his tomb.

"God's promises about future events can at times be mysterious, Dominic. We search for answers and try to put God in a box; but not everything comes to everyone at the same time and in the same way," Nehemyah said enigmatically.

"Well," responded Dominic, more to himself than anyone else, "When I search for truth, I am never satisfied until I've found it."

Benjamin turned to his father and whispered, "He and Kenan would probably get along just fine."

His father replied, "Please, my son, do not mention that insolent, young know-it-all. Mark my words, his excursions into Kabbalah will come to no good."

1:00 PM

Dominic needed some time to himself, so when they all arrived back at the kibbutz he went to his room. Realizing his parents might soon hear about the events in Jerusalem and be worried, he decided to send them a text to reassure them he was fine.

Just wanted to let you know that there has been some excitement here. You might hear on the news about a suspected terrorist attack on Jerusalem. We don't have a lot of news yet, but we are all fine. As a precaution, for the moment we are staying close to the kibbutz. I'm not sure where Bill is at the moment, but Nehemyah was out with him last night and assured us that he is fine. I sent him a text but haven't heard back yet. Dominic

That night Pablo called. "Son, I saw the news. Thanks for texting. I'm relieved you are okay."

"Yes, we are just hanging out at the kibbutz for the time being."

"What about Bill?"

"We still haven't heard from him. But I will let you know as soon as I hear anything."

"Thanks."

"Listen, I need to keep this short. We're only supposed to use our phones for emergency messages."

"Okay, talk with you soon, son."

"Okay, bye."

Ch 63. A Phone Call

(Jerusalem, 3 days after the Fire)

...to deceive, if possible, even the elect.

Matthew 24:24

Three days later, the state of alert was lifted. The news broadcast explained that there had been a terrorist attempt at the Western Wall. A small bomb in the back of a furniture van had been detonated, killing the driver and passenger, destroying the van, and doing minor damage to the surrounding area. There had been talk of a nuclear device, but the police assured everyone that that was a false rumor. The mystery of the bright light reported to have been observed in the Armenian Quarter, however, was still being investigated.

Dominic took advantage of the freedom to move about again and went into Jerusalem to a meeting at the Mount Zion Center. Just as he was arriving, he got a text from Bill. "Hey, Dominic, where are you?"

Dominic was shocked to hear from his friend and responded, "Mount Zion Center. Where are *you*?"

"I'm at the House of Prayer. Can you meet me here?"

"Sure. But, where have you been? We've been looking for you for days. We were really worried about you."

"Just come here. I'll explain everything."

Dominic quickly texted the news to Nehemyah and started walking.

Arriving at the House of Prayer, he looked around. He was just going up the stairs to look inside when a movement to his left caught his eye. He turned to see the man in the hooded sweatshirt and sunglasses who had introduced himself three days before as Eván.

"You!" Dominic let his annoyance show.

Eván held up a phone. "I've been wanting to meet you, but the city has been on high alert. I was hoping you might come by."

"That's Bill's phone. How did *you* get it?"

I went inside the House of Prayer hoping I might find you. Looking around, I saw this phone in the lost and found. No password, so I looked through it, and what should I find but the name *Dominic.* I texted you, and here you are."

"What have you done with Bill?"

"That's what I'm trying to tell you. I'll take you to him now," he lied.

They walked to the car and started driving out of Jerusalem. Dominic was quiet, and his companion said, "You know, Dominic, I've already told you one important thing about me: that I'm a god from another realm. But there's more: I know all about you. In fact, I'm the only person in the world who knows who you really are."

"Yeah, the last time we met, you told me the same thing. If you are hoping I want to know more about you, I can assure you that is not the case. Just being near you creeps me out. I really have no interest in talking with you. I only came because I want to find Bill."

After a few moments of silence, Eván said, "Dominic, I know that you have been searching for your real father. That search has come to an end."

"What are you talking about?"

"Alessandro told you the truth; he wasn't your father. You've been wondering why I look like Alessandro? Well, you and I are linked by more than just destiny. I am the one who brought you into this world; I am your real father."

Dominic's mind started reeling. He thought back to his conversations with Chad, who claimed his father had come from another world and had supernatural powers. As if reading his mind, Abdowan said, "Yes, just like your friend Chad. But here's the thing. I don't want you to turn out like him. He could have had a powerful future, but he joined the wrong team. You, on the other hand, are smart. Together, you and I can change history."

He smiled as he continued. "You know what? Those stories about Hercules, Zeus, and Mars coming to earth and interacting with humans . . . that stuff really happened. And it's happening again."

Ignoring that last comment, Dominic countered, "What do you mean 'You hope I don't turn out like Chad'? Being told I am like him would be a compliment. I hope that someday I'll have the kind of faith and assurance he has."

"*Had*," Eván replied. "You may not know it yet, but Chad's gone. He's been eliminated. Forget about him."

He looked into Abdowan's cold eyes and felt like he had been punched in the gut. *It can't be true,* he thought. *I was just with Chad a few weeks ago, and he was fine. On the other hand, that would explain why he hasn't responded to any of my texts.*

He felt anger rising up inside him. *Not Chad! He's the one person who gets me. He said we were* Gibborim, *mighty men. He helped me make sense of my life. My longing for something more than what I can see here around me.*

Danger. He began to sense he might be in danger at that very moment. As if reading his mind, Eván quickly spoke up in a soothing tone, "Dominic, don't worry. It's okay to miss Chad, but now it's time for you to move on. Because you're not like him."

Evan's words were beginning to make more sense to Dominic. *It's true. I'm not like Chad. I never spoke in tongues. I never had a flame of fire over my head. I'm somehow different.*

Evan's soothing words continued. "That's right, you have a *higher* calling than he did. Mark my words: With my help, one day you could rule the world."

Dominic's heart suddenly began to race, and thoughts came to his mind. *That would explain how easy it is for me to learn and remember things. That's why I have nearly superhuman strength sometimes. That's the reason for my keen sense of justice. YES! Ruling the world; I believe I could do that and do it well.*

He could feel himself being pulled, almost against his will, toward a life of power greater than he could have ever imagined. As he looked over at Eván, he began to imagine himself speaking a word and changing the destiny of every person on Earth.

Carried away by these thoughts, he hardly noticed as the car pulled over at a gas station. Kenan opened the door and hopped in the back seat. Dominic found himself, as if in a dream, turning to face the boy and extending his right hand to greet him. Then, releasing Kenan's hand, he turned and reached out to clasp hands with Eván.

Suddenly, a car screeched to a halt a few meters away and a man with graying hair and an athlete's build jumped out. Hurrying over to Dominic's side of the car, he pulled open the door. Dominic turned and his mouth opened in surprise, but no words came out. Time seemed to stop. For a moment, he held Eván's hand with his right hand while looking the other direction into the face of Pablo Sánchez.

Pablo touched Dominic's shoulder and, all at once, the spell was broken. Dominic released Eván's hand and jumped out of the car. He felt himself being wrapped in his father's arms as he saw Moshe getting out of the driver's seat of the car behind them.

Dominic turned to look at the two people in the car and said, "Eván, Kenan, I won't be going with you. I'd like you to meet my *father,* Pablo Sánchez." Eván looked at Pablo, who was still holding onto Dominic, and saw Moshe's powerful form walking toward the car. Realizing he had lost for now, without a word, he started the engine and he and Kenan drove off.

Ch 64. The Bearded Stranger

(Jerusalem, 4 days after the Fire)

> *There are simply too many barriers for Muslim immigrants to understand Christians and the West by sheer circumstance. Only the exceptional blend of love, humility, hospitality, and persistence can overcome these barriers, and not enough people make the effort.*
>
> Nabeel Qureshi,
> *Seeking Allah, Finding Jesus*

The next morning, back at the kibbutz, Joseph, Benjamin, Khaled, Devorah, Dominic, and Pablo were together in the meeting room at the kibbutz along with Nehemyah. Pablo had his arm around Dominic, his heart still warmed as he remembered Dominic's words from the night before, "*My father.*"

Nehemyah was saying, "I don't know how you did it, Pablo. When you arrived at the kibbutz and said you wanted to see your son, we had just gotten a message that Dominic had gone to the House of Prayer to meet Bill. But as we headed there, you insisted we change course and make our way out of Jerusalem. How did you know Dominic would be there at the edge of the city?"

Pablo held up his phone and said, "Bill is always losing his phone, so he and I use a tracking app that allows me to locate it."

Dominic added, "And since that fellow had Bill's phone, my dad could track our location. Which led you to me. But now the question is, 'Where's Bill?' Our only lead was that phone, and they took off with it."

Nehemyah answered, "The police tracked the phone to Tel Aviv and found it in a garbage can. They told me they'll keep searching for Bill, now with the added help of the information from his phone. But I think it's entirely possible they'll never find him."

Devorah turned to her grandfather. "What are you saying?"

"Do you remember when Agent Peretz asked me about my best guess about what happened to Bill?"

"Yes."

"Here is what I didn't feel at liberty to tell anyone at the time. Based on what Bill had told me on that last night we were together, my best guess is that God took him."

Joseph said, "*Took* him?"

Nehemyah nodded, "Yes, like Enoch."

"But Bill seemed like just a normal guy." said Joseph. "Were we really around someone so special that God literally took him up to heaven without dying?"

Nehemyah answered, "The Book of Genesis says that Enoch 'walked with God'[203] and in the Book of Hebrews, that he 'pleased God.'[204] I'm sure the same could be said of Bill. It doesn't say that Enoch was perfect. God is God. He can do as He pleases and, as even a pagan king in the Book of Daniel observed, no one can restrain God or say to Him, 'What have You done?'"[205]

---

203. Genesis 5:24
204. Hebrews 11:5
205. Daniel 4:35

Just then, there was a knock on the door. Joseph went to answer it, and the others could hear him saying, "Just a minute, please." He came back to the group and said, "There is someone out at the gate waiting to be invited in."

Dominic said, "Bill?"

"No. The guard doesn't know who it is, but it's someone who says he knows Khaled."

Khaled asked apprehensively, "Omar?"

"Why don't you go and see?"

Khaled got up and went out the door. Dominic, Joseph, and Benjamin walked over to the doorway where they could watch Khaled making his way to the gate. Suddenly, they heard him scream. Without a thought for their own safety, they raced over to help him. They found him weeping, wrapped in the arms of a bearded man wearing the typical red-and-white kaffiyeh head covering.

"Khaled, what's happening? Who is this?"

He turned, and with tears in his eyes, said, "This is my *baba*, my father."

Back in the meeting room in the kibbutz, Nehemyah was on his feet, and Khaled said, "Nehemyah, this is Mohammed, my father." After a warm embrace, Nehemyah motioned for Mohammed to take a seat, adding, "You are welcome here, my friend."

Then, turning to his granddaughter, Nehemyah said, "Devorah, would you be so kind as to bring our guest some refreshments?"

Nehemyah and Mohammed were still exchanging pleasantries when she came back a few minutes later, bringing coffee, fruit juice, dates, and cookies. After taking a sip of coffee, Mohammed said, "With your permission, Nehemyah, I would like to tell you my story."

"Certainly. We are gathered here to try and make sense of the surprises we have had in the last few days and weeks. We are all friends of your son, and, I might say, love him like family."

"You can't imagine how that makes my heart happy. Ten years ago, I went to Europe looking for work and have not seen my son since.

"I found work in Amsterdam, but the rain, cold, and long hours that first winter nearly broke me. I became so weak I couldn't work. I was sharing a place with several other undocumented workers, but when I couldn't pay my share of the rent month after month, they finally threatened to put me out on the street. Gathering all my strength, I went out and wandered around the city, looking for a new place to stay. I saw a Christian church, and such was my desperation that I went in and told them I was homeless. I was surprised by their kindness and generosity. They gave me a room while I recovered, and when I was well enough, they found me a job working in a factory for someone from the church.

"My boss did not try to convert me to the Christian faith, but he did share with me how Jesus had changed his own life. Grateful for their help, I decided the least I could do was to investigate their faith. Since I was learning Dutch, I got a Dutch New Testament and began to read."

As he bent over to pull his New Testament from his jacket pocket, his walking stick clanked to the floor and Khaled bent down to pick it up. He noticed dried blood on the heavy metal handle and looked up at his *baba* in surprise, but Mohammed was focused on his story.

Holding the book reverently, he said, "I could give you a lot of details, but the fact is I came to understand God's love for me as I read this book, which we call the *Injil*. For example, I read the words of Isa ibn Maryam,[206] peace be upon Him, who told of a shepherd leaving his entire flock to search for one lonely sheep that had gotten lost.

---

206. Isa ibn Maryam is an Arabic title for Jesus in the Quran, meaning "Jesus, son of Mary"

That story spoke to my heart because I myself was a shepherd as a young boy. I know a shepherd's love and concern for the sheep under his care."

Mohammed caught Khaled's eye and said, "You know a shepherd's staff serves not only to guide the sheep but also to punish those who try to hurt his little ones.

"Well, as God would have it, a few weeks ago, my brother wrote to me with the alarming news that Khaled had left the faith. My brother said he had no choice but to kick Khaled out of the house so he would learn his lesson."

Khaled started to speak, but his father continued, "I feared the worst and immediately decided to come home for a visit. I arrived yesterday, but I didn't want to see my brother yet. First, I wanted to see my son and hear it from his lips. In order to be alone last night, I stayed at my family's now-abandoned house near the Old City."

Dominic exclaimed, "Right before Omar caught up to us, Khaled mentioned that that old, abandoned house had been his grandfather's. Are you saying you were the man in the dark robe last night who rescued us?"

He nodded. "As I told you, I was once a shepherd. I am used to rough accommodation, and the thought of staying in that old house didn't bother me. I was sound asleep when, suddenly, in the middle of the night, I was awakened by a commotion outside. As I stood up and peered out of the window, the scene before me reminded me of innocent sheep being harassed by a stray dog. I saw the danger the boys were in, and my instinct was to protect the ones being threatened with harm.

"But I waited. You see, I've been away a long time. I wasn't sure I should get involved. Then, I heard my son's frightened voice cry out, saw the gun pointed at him, and nothing was going to keep me in that house.

"I didn't really have much of a plan, but I knew I had to act quickly. My only advantage would be the element of surprise. I opened the door and approached cautiously, intending to clobber the villain with my stick. But just then I stepped on a loose stone. He heard me and turned, gun in his hand, and I thought I had no chance."

Turning to Dominic, Mohammed said, "At that moment, this young man pounced like a tiger and grabbed the guy from behind. It was amazing. I've never seen anyone move so fast before. All I had to do then was hit the gun out of his hand and pick it up."

Nehemyah looked at Dominic. "Yes, he is a remarkable young man." Then, turning to the other boys, he said, "I'm just a little surprised. You didn't mention anything about this attack to Agent Peretz."

"No," Joseph said. "To be honest, we weren't quite sure what had happened. It was dark and once Omar dropped the gun all we could think of was getting out of there."

Mohammed continued, "I told them all to leave—this Omar too—I told them I didn't want any more trouble. Maybe I should have detained Omar and called the police. Frankly, I was afraid. I believe Omar has close connections with the sheikh, and he is a powerful man who has connections to important men in our community. Like I said, I've been away a long time and I'm not sure who I can trust here."

Khaled had been waiting to ask, "Baba, do I understand that you have become a Christian like I have?"

"No, my son, I am a Muslim, and though I don't want to offend any of you here, I assure you I have no intention of becoming a Christian . . . or a Jew. I was born a Muslim, and I will die a Muslim."

Nehemyah spoke up, "I am a Jew, but I am a Jew who follows Jesus, *Yeshua Ha Mashiach*."

"*Isa ibn Miryam*," Mohammed said, "is how we call the prophet Jesus, peace be upon Him. Yes, I follow the words of the Messiah, and

I think of myself as a Muslim who has come to love and follow Jesus, peace be upon Him, as a prophet of God."

Nehemyah mused, "A Muslim who follows Jesus . . . well you have certainly given me some things to think about."

Mohammed responded, "I am still learning. But I've come to see that applying Jesus' words to my life brings me great peace. When I first heard my son had left the faith, I was worried. After meeting you, Nehemyah, and hearing that you also follow the Messiah, I am convinced that my boy is in good company, surrounded by devout people, and I intend to talk to my brother and tell him so."

"Thank you, Mohammed. For my part, I want to make sure that we communicate to you that in no way are we trying to isolate Khaled from his family and his community. We are grateful for this chance to be friends with him and now, meeting you, we hope that we can grow together in friendship and mutual understanding."

As that intense conversation concluded, it seemed like a good moment to take a break. Joseph, Benjamin, and their parents excused themselves, and Mohammed rose to leave as well. Khaled asked if he could go with him, and so after shaking hands with Nehemyah, they also took their leave.

Ch 65. The Final Act

(Jerusalem, 4 days after the Fire)

If you and I could stand above Wales,
looking at it, you would see fire breaking out
here, and there, and yonder, and somewhere else,
without any collusion or prearrangement,
it is a Divine visitation in which God—let me say this reverently—
in which God is saying to us:
See what I can do without the things you are depending on;
see what I can do in answer to a praying people;
see what I can do through the simplest,
who are ready to fall in line,
and depend wholly and absolutely upon Me.

G. Campbell Morgan
Lessons of the Welsh Revival

After Devorah also excused herself to take a little rest, Dominic sat on the couch, quietly thinking.

Nehemyah asked, "Dominic, what's on your mind?"

The young man paused for a second, gathering his thoughts. "Well, for one thing, I'm thinking about Khaled's father. He seems as godly as any Christian I've ever met. And he seems like a good person. When I first saw him, I found myself immediately judging him because of other Muslims I've known. It's hard for me to get my head around the idea of a 'Muslim follower of Jesus.'"

"Yes, I can see that. In my years on this earth, I've come to understand two incontrovertible truths: One, there is a God, and two, I am not Him. God's ways continue to surprise me more often than I would like to admit."

Dominic said, "True. And thinking about how I initially misjudged Mohammed reminded me of how I initially misjudged another person."

"Oh?"

"Yes, when I first met Bill, I didn't recognize what a godly person he was or, in fact, what a good person he was. At first, I didn't really understand him or feel like I could relate to him, but during our time together, I grew to appreciate him. And thinking about that makes me wonder about your idea that he was taken up to be with God."

"I see."

"And I want to say, 'If he is now with God, good for him, he was ready to go.' But it's also kind of scary."

"Why do you say that?"

"I don't know. I guess because it seems sudden and unexpected. And because I feel like I've lost someone. I've moved around a lot in my life. Often it seems that just about the time I begin to connect with someone, they move on, or my family moves away, and we lose touch. Now, to think that God is literally moving people around and taking them to heaven, it seems too much.

"And it's not just Bill. Another person I feel I connected with was Chad, the one I told you about. I received news today that I still find hard to believe. I've been trying to get in touch with him ever since I got here to Jerusalem but couldn't. Finally, last night when I called his phone, his mother answered. She said there had been an accident; that he had been killed by a hit-and-run driver."

Nehemyah got up and came over to sit by Dominic. "Oh, I am so sorry. That is so hard to hear over the phone."

"Yeah, I'm finding it hard to think clearly right now. At the same time, as I think back on conversations I had with both of them, it's beginning to make more sense to me."

"Really? For example?"

"Well, like talking with Bill. He believed he would be taken up to be with the Lord at any moment. He was so convinced of it. He expected the rapture of the Church. But it seems the Lord was preparing him for his own homecoming."

"Yes, Dominic, I think you may be right. I was thinking the same thing."

"And it was the same with Chad: He told me he'd heard from the Lord that the time was short. He was sure we had less than a year before the end. And now he's gone too."

Nehemyah said, "The apostle Paul wrote that our life now is like we are looking at things through a mirror, dimly.[207] Things here on earth are often blurry and confusing. I believe Chad did hear from the Lord that there was less than a year on earth left. But perhaps it wasn't exactly how he had pictured it. The Lord told him that *the end was near;* not that it was the end for all mankind, but that *his own* time was coming to an end."

"There's another reason why it's especially hard for me to lose Chad." Here Dominic hesitated.

"Yes? What is it, Dominic?"

"How do I start? The other day in a Bible study, the topic came up about the Nephilim and their children. You know, Genesis six, the sons of God and all that."

"Okay."

"Well, the Bible study leader said that the Nephilim and their descendants all drowned in the Flood and since they came from a

207. 1 Corinthians 13:12

sinful, unnatural origin, their spirits remained in the world and they became the demons that possess people, because they are trying to get back into a body."

"Well, I've never heard that before."

"Then somebody asked about Nephilim after the Flood and what happened to their children and if there were any around today. The teacher said yes to both. He said the Bible talks about Nephilim after the Flood, and he thought there were still Nephilim and their descendants today."

"Okay."

"Then they started talking about what Nephilim and their descendants look like and if they could be saved. Someone said that neither the Nephilim nor their descendants could be saved because they have a demonic origin and that they are a corruption of God's creation. He said that's why God had to bring a global flood, because the human bloodline was being tainted, and if God didn't stop the corruption, then all humans would have tainted blood, and then the promised Messiah wouldn't be able to be the pure and spotless Lamb to redeem the world."

"Hmm. Interesting."

"Everyone at the study seemed to agree with the idea that neither Nephilim nor anyone born from them could be saved. Do you agree with that?"

"I don't know. I think I would need to look into this a little bit. But, Dominic, why do you ask?"

"Well, that's the connection with Chad. I didn't speak up at the study, but I don't agree with what they were saying. That's why I wanted to talk with Chad again. He believed all people have a choice. He thought even the children of Nephilim could be saved. In fact, he told me that he himself was the son of a Nephilim."

"I see. Didn't you say that he played a major role in helping you to come to an understanding of the truth and leading you back to following Christ?"

"Yeah. And he told me about the revival and encouraged me to come here. Without him, I'd probably still be back in LA, without Christ, still alienated from my parents, and having never met you."

"Then I am grateful to Chad as well. And I think his visit here to the Mount Zion Church was felicitous because it led to my getting to know you, Dominic."

Dominic sat, quiet and serious, and Nehemyah asked, "My son, is there anything else you'd like to talk about?"

He hesitated for a moment, then said, "I want to be a part of God's drama, I want to be an active participant in the world's final act. But I have doubts."

"We all have doubts; that's part of being human."

"But I have serious doubts—doubts about me."

"Well, I'm here if you ever want to talk about anything."

He hesitated again. "For example, I came to Israel mainly because of Chad and what he said about the revival here. At his church in California, there were people who had been with you. They spoke in tongues, and I saw flames of fire over their heads. I wanted to experience that . . . ."

"And yet you haven't."

"No. I've been to your church services here. People have prayed over me. I hear others speaking in tongues. I see the flames over them. But it hasn't happened to me, has it? Have you ever seen a flame of fire over me?"

"No, I haven't."

"See, that's what I mean. I think there's something wrong with me. I think there's a reason why I don't have the flame."

"Yes, I believe there is a reason why you haven't received that gift or received that sign. But that doesn't necessarily mean that there is a problem with you. You see, the fact that it's a gift implies that there is a *Giver*. That Giver is God. And we don't always know the reasons behind God's plans."

Dominic nodded in agreement, then added, "I've seen the flame over you. Do you speak in tongues?"

"Yes, I do. But the truth is, for many years—for most of my life, in fact—I did not. I was a believer; I loved God. But God didn't give me that gift. I went to some churches that taught that I wasn't completely saved or that I was spiritually deficient because I had neither spoken in tongues nor had any other supernatural signs in my life.

"I even had people try to teach me how to receive the gift. They taught me to '*prime the pump*,' that is, to start vocalizing something, anything, to help the gift of tongues come. They were good-hearted people, I'm sure, but it didn't feel right to me. So I waited. And I doubted. I kept waiting, and when the time was right—when God decided it was the time—He gave me the gift."

"How long did you wait?"

"About forty years."

"That's a long time."

"Yes. But very early in those forty years, God revealed something to me. He gave me a choice—a three-way choice. One, I could reject this supernatural gift, choosing to believe it isn't for us today, building doctrines to reinforce that belief, and allowing myself to feel a sense of relief. Or two, I could embrace the gift, actively seeking it, confident that as I'd seen in other people's lives, I too would receive the gift without much delay."

"But you chose a third option."

"Yes. Rather than reject or embrace the gift, I choose to seek the Giver himself and to let Him be God."

"I like that: Let God be God. But it seems that's easier said than done."

"It's a full-time job; God continues to surprise me." Nehemyah continued with a smile, "For example, Dominic, do you remember our conversation that first day you came here to the kibbutz? You recognized a photo of a man, Martin Niemöller, and you said you had seen him before in a dream. You remembered a conversation that took place, a conversation that has never been written about anywhere. When I said the words *'Nein! Er bleibt da!—No. He stays there!'* You immediately replied, in German, the next words of that conversation, *'We all stay here.'* How could you have known about that unless you had been there?"

"It was a dream," Dominic replied. "I wasn't really there. That was during World War II. How could I have been there?"

"I don't know, but I do know that 'With God all things are possible.' I also know that in that concentration camp so many years ago, a German guard that looked just like you defended a young, defenseless, Jewish prisoner, allowing him to stay in a meeting where he heard a message of hope. You see, Dominic, I was there in Dachau. I was that prisoner seventy years ago whose life was forever changed by that act of kindness. So, as unlikely as it seems, I'm convinced that you and I have met before.

"I'm also convinced that God has placed a special calling on your life, and I believe that your calling intersects with this Jerusalem Revival. There is a reason that you are here at this exact moment. You were present when my Devorah was found. It's no coincidence that you were on Mount Zion when the angel appeared to Benjamin and the others.

"My sense is that God is beginning to show His hand again. He's beginning to work openly and beyond reasonable doubt. This is what I've longed for my entire life. I don't know exactly where it will lead or what role you or I may play in this incredible drama that God has authored. But I have a feeling that the curtain is going up on this world's final act."

Just then, Pablo entered the room. He could tell that Nehemyah and Dominic were deep in conversation and was about to leave, but Dominic asked him to stay. Pablo sat down across from them. Dominic was quiet, and Nehemyah asked, "What are you thinking about, Dominic?"

He turned and said, "That man who has been following me, I can sense that he is evil. He seems intent on taking me away from here, away from you. He says he is my real father."

Without a word, Pablo came over and put his arm around his boy. Nehemyah, sitting on the other side of him, put his hand on Dominic's other shoulder and recited:

> *Our Father in heaven,*
> *Hallowed be Your name.*

Pablo, with tears in his eyes, joined Nehemyah as they recited together over Dominic:

> *Your kingdom come.*
> *Your will be done*
> *On earth as it is in heaven.*
> *Give us this day our daily bread.*
> *And forgive us our debts,*
> *As we forgive our debtors.*
> *And do not lead us into temptation,*
> *But deliver us from the evil one.*
> *For Yours is the kingdom and the power and the glory forever. Amen.*[208]

Pablo hugged Dominic as Nehemyah continued, "The Lord asks us to pray that we be delivered from evil: from evil situations and from evil people. I am speaking over you this word of protection:

208. Matthew 6:9–13

That man will not be able to approach you, find you, or in any way bother you while you are here with me. You are under the protection of Lord."

About the Authors

John is a career teacher (K-12, university and Sunday school) and a lifelong student of theology, eschatology, and linguistics. He has traveled and lived overseas extensively. He and his wife Lisa have two grown sons, having raised them on three different continents. John and Lisa currently live and teach in Ankara, Turkey.

Mark and his wife Karen have had the joy of raising four children while living and serving on four different continents. They have served in Bible translation and discipleship training, helping make the Gospel understood to those who've never heard. They currently reside in Southern Spain.

All profits from the sale of this book will be given to Christian missions.

www.ingramcontent.com/pod-product-compliance
Lightning Source LLC
LaVergne TN
LVHW050912080826
845145LV00001B/60
* 9 7 8 1 6 3 3 5 7 4 7 2 4 *